GIANNI ARNAUDO

ANTI-DESIGN

GIANNI ARNAUDO

ANTI-DESIGN

SKIRA

Cover
Déjeuner sur l'arbre, table

Back cover
Déjeuner sur l'arbre, painting

Design
Gianni Arnaudo

Copy editor
Maria Conconi

Translations
Clive Foster, Karen Hoare, James Pallas
(for the texts from *l'Arca* no. 69, March 1993)
Martyn Anderson, Sofia J. Teodori
(for the texts from *l'Arca* no. 209, December 2005,
and from *l'Arca* no. 259, June 2010)
Isabelle-Béatrice Marcherat, Julie Munos, Martyn
Anderson, Sofia J. Teodori (for the texts from *l'Arca*
International no. 116, January/February 2014)
Paul Metcalfe for Scriptum, Rome

Photo credits
© Archivio Gianni Arnaudo

First published in Italy in 2020 by
Skira editore S.p.A.
Palazzo Casati Stampa
via Torino 61
20123 Milano
Italy
www.skira.net

Printed and bound in Italy. First edition

ISBN: 978-88-572-4414-3

Distributed in USA, Canada, Central & South
America by ARTBOOK | D.A.P. 75, Broad Street
Suite 630, New York, NY 10004, USA.
Distributed elsewhere in the world by Thames and
Hudson Ltd., 181A High Holborn, London WC1V
7QX, United Kingdom.

Texts
Gianni Arnaudo
Alba Basile
Ennio Bonello
Emanuela Giudice

Articles
Massimo Bignardi
Luisa Bocchietto
Irene Graziotto
Alessandro Gubitosi
Valérie Guillaume

DEDICATED TO ALL THE ARCHITECTS WHO HAVE CREATED SMALL AND BEAUTIFUL POEMS BUT DO NOT HAVE THE STRENGTH TO COMMUNICATE THEM

in memory of Otto Steidle

ANTIMUSEAL

an achronological history of Gianni Arnaudo

Preface

Valérie Guillaume
Conservationist, Head of the Industrial Prospects Department, Centre George Pompidou,
Musée national d'art moderne / Centre de creation industrielle.

Dear Gianni,
it was in Salvador de Bahia where I first realised much of my astonishment – because it was the first time I had noticed it – that you were capable of distancing yourself from architecture. We were visiting São Francisco Church, whose over-abundantly sculpted and guilt baroque ornamentation left no room for empty space, no visual respite. At a certain point I realised you constantly gave precedence to silent breaks in architecture. A structure or surface is left free to allow us to project into the past and future and leave it to the imagination to enjoy contemplating the missing part. In this way the palimpsest of an object or building suggests both previous historical stratification and its source of inspiration or citation. The originality of your approach can be seen in all those works you designed in the early 1970s working for Studio65 and then more recently with Déjeuner sur l'arbre, Milo, Rococò… your creations uncover in depth those transformations which have taken place in the strategies and ascetics of industrial production and design. Your architectural and design work expresses an aesthetics of irony, whose echoes and interpretive developments are always incisive. The irony inherent in a fragment of a capital (Capitello), rod (Attica) or the base of a column (Colonna di piatti), or the ironic force of upheaval and imbalance (Rococò), collage (the desecrating work on a painting by Manet in Déjeuner sur l'arbre) and assembly/bricolage, creating in-between figures, intermediary gaps between the past and the present.
The object is involved in various stories, in architecture and also sculpture, as well as collective protests and memories of the past. Its fragmentation takes us towards the idea of impermanence and the ephemeral.

Recently, in 2007, the staging and setting in space of temporal processes reappeared in the winning project for a competition to build the Capo Verde National Museum on the island of Sal. One side of the façade, clad with wood, features a regular and rythmic pattern of small sqare-shaped apertures calling to mind the side of a galleon sailing the Atlantic as part of the African slave trade. A second set of façades is made of local volcanic stones, as are the five showcases set out in sunburst formation. Designing a museum involves reintroducing part of time and history into a situation of everyday life, to restore the rightful role to an event. Over the last few years your work has not abandoned your radical ideals but rather shifted them from the political to the ethical. I am impatient to visit this new Museum together with you and the people of Capo Verde. Last but not least, tell me, dear Gianni, what is the best way, in your opinion, to support this construction?

l'Arca no. 259, June 2010

Direction de la communication
DOSSIER DE PRESSE
BIG BANG
AU MUSÉE NATIONAL D'ART MODERNE
15 juin 05 – 27 février 06

artists & partecipants

Emile **Aillaud**, Jean-Michel **Alberola**, William **Alsop**, Carl **Andre**, Ant **Farm**, Guillaume **Apollinaire**, Ron **Arad**, Nobuyoshi **Araki**, **Arman**, Gianni **Arnaudo**, Hans **Arp**, **Art & Language**, Antonin **Artaud**, Richard **Artschwager**, Jean **Aubert**, Francis **Bacon**, John **Baldessari**, **Balthus**, Georg **Baselitz**, Jean-Michel **Basquiat**, Hans **Bellmer**, Joseph **Beuys**, Alighiero **Boetti**, Gottfried **Böhm**, Jacques-Andre **Boiffard**, Christian **Boltanski**, Louise **Bourgeois**, Ronan **Bouroullec**, Constantin **Brancusi**, Andrea **Branzi**, Georges **Braque**, Victor **Brauner**, Marcel **Breuer**, Marcel **Broodthaers**, Stanley **Brouwn**, Glenn **Brown**, Günter **Brus**, Andre **Bruyere**, Eric **Bulatov**, Daniel **Buren**, Victor **Burgin**, Alberto **Burri**, Fernando & Humberto **Campana**, Humberto **Campana**, Enrico **Castellani**, Philippe **Cazal**, **César**, **Christo**, Francesco **Clemente**, **Constant**, Peter **Cook**, Coop **Himmelblau**, John **Coplans**, Joseph **Cornell**, Rene **Coulon**, Dennis **Crompton**, Cui **Xiuwen**, John **Currin**, Salvador **Dali**, Giorgio **De Chirico**, Willem **De Kooning**, Christian **de Portzamparc**, Niki **de Saint Phalle**, **Decosterd & Rahm**, Luc **Delahaye**, Sonia **Delaunay**, Robert **Delaunay**, Wim **Delvoye**, Radi **Designers**, Eric **Dietman**, Braco **Dimitrijevic**, Jim **Dine**, Otto **Dix**, Theo **van Doesburg**, Peter **Doig**, Robert **Doisneau**, Cesar **Domela**, Jean **Dubuffet**, Marcel **Duchamp**, Marlene **Dumas**, Charles & Ray **Eames**, Max **Ernst**, **Erro**, Didier **Fiuza Faustino**, Jean **Fautrier**, Lyonel **Feininger**, Robert **Filliou**, Ian Hamilton **Finlay**, Urs **Fischer**, **Fischli / Weiss**, Barry **Flanagan**, Dan **Flavin**, Lucio **Fontana**, Sam **Francis**, Edouard **Francois** / Duncan **Lewis**, Andrea **Fraser**, Yona **Friedman**, Gerard **Fromanger**, Massimiliano **Fuksas**, M. **Fuksas**, **Garouste & Bonetti**, Gerard **Gasiorowski**, Piero **Gatti**, Jochen **Gerz**, Diego **Giacometti**, Alberto **Giacometti**, **Gilbert & George**, Richard **Goldstone**, Natalija **Gontscharowa**, Arshile **Gorky**, Dan **Graham**, Toni **Grand**, George **Grosz**, Marie-Ange **Guilleminot**, Lucy **Gunning**, Philip **Guston**, Raymond **Hains**, Mona **Hatoum**, Raoul **Hausmann**, Jean **Helion**, Ron **Herron**, **Herzog & de Meuron**, Gary **Hill**, Hans **Hollein**, Jenny **Holzer**, Gottfried **Honegger**, Fabrice **Hyber**, Cristina **Iglesias**, Jörg **Immendorff**, Toyo **Ito**, Marcel **Janco**, Jacobus **Johannes Oud**, Jasper **Johns**, Asger **Jorn**, Donald **Judd**, Anne Marie **Jugnet** & Alain **Clairet**, Robert Julius **Jacobsen**, Louis I. **Kahn**, Wassily **Kandinsky**, Yan **Kaplicky**, Ellsworth **Kelly**, André **Kertész**, Anselm **Kiefer**, Kyonori **Kikutake**, Yves **Klein**, Pierre **Klossowski**, Rem **Koolhaas**, Gyulia **Kosice**, Joseph **Kosuth**, Jannis **Kounellis**, Frantisek **Kupka**, Mikhail **Larionov**, **Laurel & Hardy**, Henri **Laurens**, Erwine & Estelle **Laverne**, Bertrand **Lavier**, Louise **Lawler**, **Le Corbusier**, Fernand **Leger**, Eugène **Leroy**, Daniel **Libeskind**, Eli **Lothar**, Dora **Maar**, Rene **Magritte**, Kasimir **Malewitsch**, Piero **Manzoni**, Gordon **Matta-Clark**, Ingo **Maurer**, Paul **McCarthy**, Allan **McCollum**, Alessandro **Mendini**, Mario **Merz**, Henri **Michaux**, Joan **Miro**, Issey **Miyake**, Laszlo **Moholy-Nagy**, Piet **Mondrian**, Francois **Morellet**, Malcolm **Morley**, Robert **Morris**, Sarah **Morris**, Olivier **Mosset**, Studio **Naco**, Bruce **Nauman**, Marc **Newson**, Emil **Nolde**, Jean **Nouvel**, Claes **Oldenburg**, Meret **Oppenheim**, Dennis **Oppenheim**, Gina **Pane**, Cesare **Paolini**, Christos **Papoulias**, Michel **Parmentier**, Ed **Paschke**, Gaetano **Pesce**, Raymond **Pettibon**, Francis **Picabia**, Pablo **Picasso**, Klaus **Pinter**, Sigmar **Polke**, Jackson **Pollock**, Daniel **Pommereulle**, **R&sie**, **R&Sie(n)**, Arnulf **Rainer**, **Man Ray**, Martial **Raysse**, Ad **Reinhardt**, Gerhard **Richter**, Daniel **Richter**, Gerrit **Rietveld**, Sophie **Ristelhueber**, Diego **Rivera**, Larry **Rivers**, Francois **Roche**, Aldo **Rossi**, Mark **Rothko**, Guy **Rottier**, Georges **Rouault**, Ulrich **Rückriem**, Claude **Rutault**, **Saint-Florian**, David **Salle**, Peter **Saul**, Carlo **Scarpa**, Christian **Schad**, Thomas **Schütte**, Rudolf **Schwarzkogler**, Kurt **Schwitters**, Inga **Sempe**, Gino **Severini**, Cindy **Sherman**, Kazuo **Shiraga**, Jack **Smith**, Robert **Smithson**, Alison & Peter **Smithson**, Peter **Smithson**, Pierre **Soulages**, Chaim **Soutine**, Daniel **Spoerri**, Philippe **Starck**, Otto **Steidle**, Frank **Stella**, Jana **Sterbak**, Georges Tony **Stoll**, Kolmac **Studio**, **Superstudio**, Sophie **Taeuber-Arp**, Antoni **Tapies**, Iakov **Tchernikov**, Franco **Teodoro**, **Tetsumi Kudo**, Jean **Tinguely**, Roland **Topor**, Rosemarie **Trockel**, Bernard **Tschumi**, Cy **Twombly**, **UFO**, Zund **Up**, Kees **van Dongen**, Claude **Viallat**, Bill **Viola**, Wilhelm **Wagenfeld**, Andy **Warhol**, Robert **Watts**, Michael **Webb**, Joel-Peter **Witkin**, Gil Joseph **Wolman**, **Wols**, Christopher **Wool**, Jean-Paul **Yungmann**, Remy **Zaugg**

With this exhibition, the Centre Pompidou identifies the fundamental hallmark of Gianni Arnaudo's work.

Big Bang - Destruction and creation in 20th century art

15. Jun 2005 – 06. Mar 2006

press release

The Centre Pompidou will present its collections for the first time, in a thematic, interdisciplinary and non-chronological fashion. Using works from the largest collection of modern and contemporary art in Europe, *Big Bang* will bring together visual arts, video, photography, architecture, design, and literature to confront works and trends from the beginning of the 20th century through today. This exceptional exhibition is based on an original set of themes: the modern "big bang," or the link between creation and destruction in 20th century art. Using an exhibition space of about 45,000 sq. ft., the Centre Pompidou proposes a new way of understanding the cultural phenomena of the XXth century.

Centered on the idea of innovation and revolution, the modern project placed itself from the beginning under the auspices of "positive destruction." In the creative field, artists tried every mode of inversion of established values by putting representation in crisis and placing the art scene at the crucible of radical renewal: destruction of forms by Cubism, disfiguration by Expressionism, subversion of images by Dadaism, etc.

This new exhibition has been conceived around eight major themes: destruction, deconstruction, archaism, sex, war, subversion, melancholy, and re-enchantment.

For this occasion, the Centre Pompidou will exhibit several new acquisitions, in particular, a major work by Bill Viola, *Five Angels For the Millennium*, 2001, shown for the first time in France.

...

(omissis)

VI. SUBVERSION

Pastiche and parody: Victor Brauner, Francis Picabia, Pablo Picasso, Braco Dimitrijevic, Bertrand Lavier, Claes Oldenburg, Paul Mc Carthy, Philippe Starck, UFO, Radi Designers…

Anti-museum: Marcel Broodthaers, Joseph Cornell, Richard Artschwager, Gérard Gasiorowski, Louise Lawler, Bertrand Lavier, Claude Rutault, Andrea Fraser, Roland Topor, Hans Hollein, François Roche, Gianni Arnaudo…

Anti-architecture: Yan Kaplicky, Klaus Pinter, Hans Hollein, Michael Webb,Guy Rottier,Jean Aubert, Zund Up, R&Sie…

Grotesque Ubu: Victor Brauner, Dado, Dora Maar, Rosemarie Trockel, Jean-Paul Yungmann. The grotesque portrait: Gino Severini, Natalia Gontcharova, Georg Grosz, Jacques-Andre Boiffard, Glenn Brown, John Currin, Urs Fischer…

...

From the Centre Pompidou website

The Antimuseal

Irony as a means of demystification and stimulation; paradox and the macroscopic scale as a means of studying phenomena and their significance, which in this way are made more evident. Debunking to underline the contradictions inherent in processes and the blandness of so many "commonplaces" which we take for granted and are so accustomed to.

From my very first works with Studio65, all the most distinctive features of my way of thinking were set in place: a project is not just aesthetic form and technological expression, it must also be a critical tool.
This way of seeing, studying and designing leads to a different way of interpretating the city and objects, as well as the myths and rituals enshrouding them.
It is enough to just change the viewpoint and refuse to accept what is proposed in order to create a different kind of reality. We need only change the optical photographic cone of the pictures taken by the Alinari brothers to rewrite many books of the history of art but, above all, to create a new awareness of the works themselves.
Architecture is now grounded on the fact that an idea can actually be accessible to everybody. Architecture must not just be a technical means of creating forms bereft of cultural meaning and, in some cases, exclusively self-referential; on the contrary it must become the primary means of spreading culture itself.
The readability of a "formula for the structure of a building" must be accessible to everybody, as must its underlying reasons, its nature and history, because great ideas are simples ideas.
The architecture surrounding us is full of commonplaces, the product of undisputed rules which, consequently, generate absolute, predetermined, closed and terribly irreversible forms, leaving absolutely no room for dreaming.
City suburbs are not just places where power has experienced the failure of its town-planning practice, "the waste land" (to quote T.S. Eliot) where nobody recognises each other; they actually represents a mental category for expressing boundless social discomfort.
Most of the architecture designed over recent years is a manifesto for this kind of discomfort, which cancels out the past, hope and even imagination.
The "suburbs" represent cultureless architecture with no DNA, history or even any kind of idea forming its framework, structure or, in other words, beauty.
The truth is that in Italy and elsewhere, from the Second World War onwards and still even today on a massive scale, millions of cubic metres of buildings have been constructed which are completely lacking in DNA or, in other words, without any underlying reason for being, thereby spreading ugliness on a grand scale.
Many of these works are just either partial or total copies of other buildings, senseless transplants and piecemeal replicas desperately striving to "do it strangely" in a hectic and vain attempt to be sensational, self-referential and standardised within the cultural-intellectual-architectural firmament.
Even within the domestic landscape, rationalism to the point of minimalism has not been able to alter the association of ideas dominating the organisation of domestic space and, above all,

the unchanging relationships between the various components of furnishing.

This is a sort of internal manifestation of external blandness, which has resulted, for example, in the houses built by Neutra in California being brutally transferred (with just the odd alteration) all over the world, even today.

Brutal copying, often implemented without understanding what relations hold between the original work and its location and why, motivated solely by the simple need to imitate, has resulted in the land being embellished with "...style" buildings displaying depressing provincialism, compeltely extraneous to the environmental and historical setting in which they are located.

The city designed according to a critical planning method must result in greater freedom and the creation of spaces which peolple can identify with, enabling them to set up harmonious relations with the environment in which they have decided to live.
The social significance of this "revolution" points towards a possible way ahed and method for regaining control of the city, rethinking and redesigning it along emotional lines, identifying "joyful" parts and "sad" parts, highlighting the reasons for the latter and being able to propose radical changes.

This approach is vital for identifying copycat architecture, which is ultimately the source of cultural disorientation and unhappiness.

Every "architectural place", whether it be a building or design object, must first be envisaged through an emotional "vision", as in the case with music or poetry. Many objects which are often labelled as kitsch are actually bursting with astounding joyfulness and notable vitality, in other words they have "a soul", which, despite a certain kind of cultural snobbery, has ensured and is still ensuring they maintain their place in history.
Critical planning, translated into the field of design, draws inspiration from the subversive force of these objects, which refuse to yield to the system of power.
They also escape the kind of stuffiness associated with museums, because they draw their lifeblood from the popular appeal which brought them into being.
Over recent months a major furniture distributor has created an advert showing that a different and free way of envisaging such a small and confined space as a prison cell can trigger off hope for new life.

This is a method which is handed on like a baton to those people who envisage architecture as non-academic and non-museum-like, providing the opportunity to encourage everybody to find in design the desire, joy and revolutionary input required for taking on and destroying the mediocrity (actually raised to the status of a value in certain cases) which has generated so many "suburbs" in our thinking, intellectual work and land.

Gianni Arnaudo
l'Arca n. 259, June 2010

…IN ACTUAL FACT, NO ONE WAS LOOKING FOR US

"SUBVERSIVE WORK"

A HISTORICALLY CULTURAL MOVEMENT is born when it attains awareness of its own ideas and self-consciousness

With this intent I designed the notepaper for Studio65 that has now become a unique example of Pop communication. Featured in the collections of some European museums, including the Centre Georges Pompidou, Musée national d'art moderne in Paris and the Vitra Design Museum in Basel, it has been displayed in the Louisiana Museum in Copenhagen, the Moderna Museet in Stockholm, the Barbican Centre in London, the Henie Onstad Kunstsenter in Oslo, the Emma Museum in Helsinki and the Museum of Contemporary Art in Chicago.
Published in the exhibition catalogues *Asparagus Age*, Galleria TOT, Padua, 1984, and *Pop Art Design*, Vitra Design Museum, Basel, 2012 (p. 53). Arnaudo Archives

ID Card Studio65
Photo taken at the Centre Pompidou exhibition, 2002
Design Gianni Arnaudo
Arnaudo Archives

IT WAS A DECLARATION OF WAR...

...and this is why we had some photos taken in one of those automated booths and I created this work. The notepaper of our firm, designed to present us to clients so that they would be well aware of what we could do... (and what they were getting into.) Now it is an example of an "anti-selfie", not self-celebration but self-denunciation...

...The backdrop of a TOTAL action

Poster, unique work
by Gianni Arnaudo
Artist's proof
Arnaudo Archives

Tr bute to Andy Warhol

Before then, we were just a group of recent graduates and students who set up a firm as a continuation of university and the protest movements born in 1967 at the Polytechnic University in Turin...

Student assembly (Hall 1), 1968
Faculty of Architecture -Turin Polytechnic
Gianni Arnaudo, foreground, Aimaro O. D'Isola, upper right
Photo courtesy of Federico Aprile Arnaudo Archives

Not nostalgia

but an assertion of the need for a different, new, contemporary culture. It was important to get involved in the present with the dream of changing the world.

Led by Arnaudo, Gruppo I was one of the components of Città-Fabbrica in the major investigation of living in Turin.
Some students examined the old city centre and the precarious or inhuman living conditions found there, and others the working-class neighbourhoods of areas like Mirafiori Sud, Nichelino, Falchera and Vallette.

The goal was to formulate an alternative to the form of urban development that had transformed the outskirts and the centre into dormitory zones.
We were fighting for a different culture and a different city but also for a different Faculty, capable of giving space to new ideas.

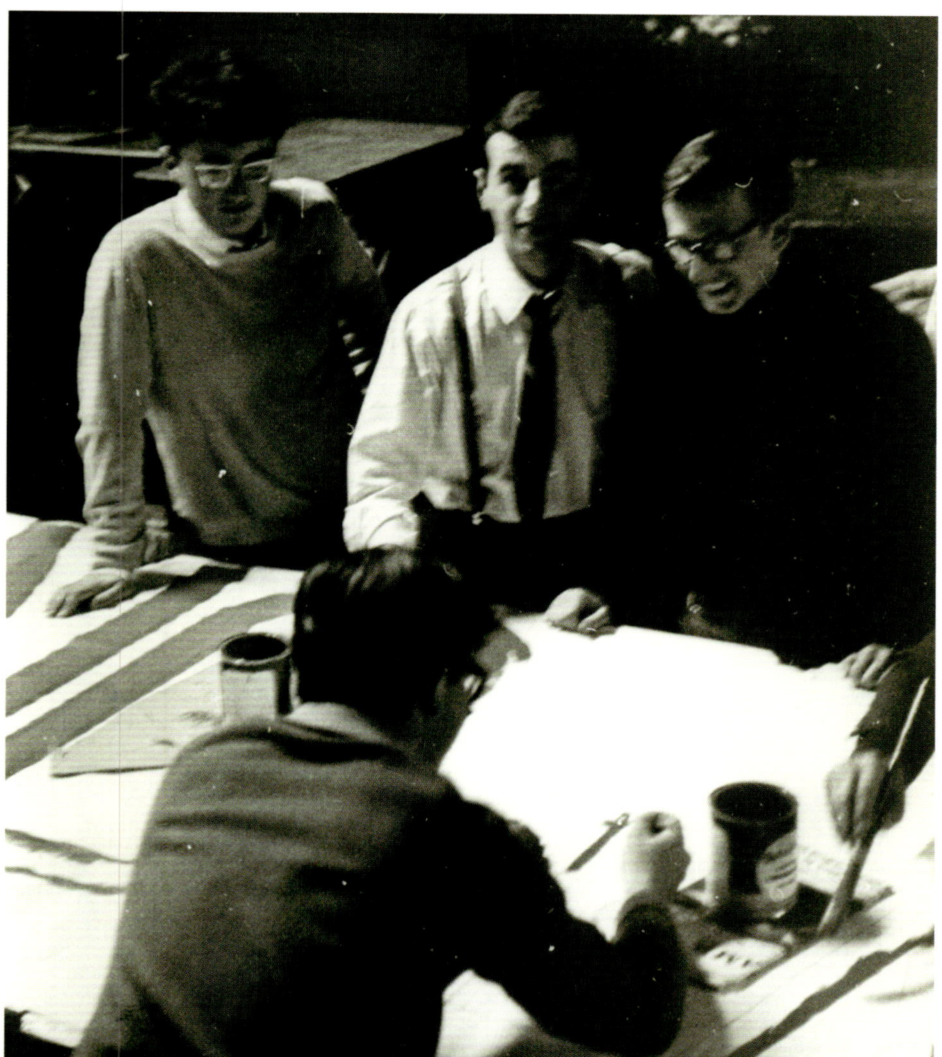

Gianni Arnaudo in the Atelier Popolare workshop of the Faculty of Architecture, 5 May 1967
The revolutionary graphic art for the demonstrations during the occupation of the faculty was produced here.
Arnaudo Archives

All work was conceived as "collective" and undifferentiated, everyone worked for a cause...

The Atelier Popolare workshop in the Faculty of Architecture, May 1968
Photo: Giovanni Isoardi
Arnaudo Archives

In that period, students and workers joined forces in the fight for the right to housing.

Posters designed by the Atelier Popolare workshop during the protests of 1968
Screenprint
designed by Gianni Arnaudo

Posters designed by the Atelier Popolare workshop during the protests of 1968
Screenprint

Forty years on, in 2016, the students of my course in the Faculty of Architecture at the Turin Polytechnic redesigned the old workers' neighbourhood of Mirafiori, laying the foundations for a possible new city.
For them too, the objective is freedom of thought and the reconquest of a city.
Their architectural proposals were displayed in an exhibition at the Mirafiori factory.

Irony in power,

The Turin Faculty
of Architecture during the
occupation in 1968
Arnaudo Archives

the power of irony: graffiti

Graffiti on a wall during the occupation
Arnaudo Archives

Paolo Verzone, professor of History of Architecture, who had previously taught my father, May 196[illegible]
Photo: Giovanni Iscardi
Arnaudo Archives

The hall of the "Vikingi'
Photo: Giovanni Iscardi
Arnaudo Archives

Forty years later...
Presentation of plans for the redevelopment of Mirafiori Sud at the Turin Polytechnic

Mirafiori Sud
Project and research,
course of Architecture,
Construction and City
Turin Polytechnic
Faculty of Architecture -
Lingotto

The method

1968 as a method for the investigation of reality.

Commitment to study in greater depth so that the new culture might become the basis for the evolution of a new architectural language:
the concept of CRITICAL DESIGN was being born.

Architecture as political message. The city had to be closer to our ideals: the relationship between society and university had to be different.
This was one of the reasons why I was to become a professor at the Polytechnic University of Turin.

The Polytechnic University of Turin, Faculty of Architecture - Lingotto
Photo of examinations in the academic year 2015–16 course of Architecture, Construction and City with professors Gianni Arnaudo, Matteo Robiglio, Massimo Crotti and Michele Bonino
Arnaudo Archives

EURODOMUS 4

“LA CASA DELL’IMPERIALISTA”

(creative destruction)

This poster, which I included in the exhibition at the Vitra Design Museum and the catalogue *Pop Art Design*, has since been shown at the Louisiana Museum in Copenhagen, the Moderna Museet in Stockholm, the Barbican Centre in London, the Henie Onstad Kunstsenter in Oslo, the Emma Museum in Helsinki and the Museum of Contemporary Art in Chicago.
Arnaudo Archives

“LA CASA DELL’IMPERIALISTA”

What could be more “IMPERIAL” than living in a column
and bringing all the symbols of power home to flaunt?

EURODOMUS 72

In 1972, Gufram, a small firm owned by the three Gugliermetto brothers in Nole Canavese, was preparing to meet a new challenge and assert its right to a place on the Italian design scene and market. Sponsored by the magazine *Domus* and organized by Giò Ponti together with Cesare Casati and Emanuele Ponzio, Eurodomus left Milan for the Palazzo delle Esposizioni in Turin. An opportunity for the open exchange of ideas through conferences and round-table discussions intended to gather proposals for a new form of living, Eurodomus stood out among collateral events also for its responsiveness to the artistic developments of the period.

Firms producing furniture, many of which were still of an artisanal character, saw the event as a real opportunity to attempt the leap to production on the industrial scale. Alongside Gufram, the major exhibitors included Kartell, Zanotta, FontanaArte, Poltrona Frau, Brionvega, Giovannetti, De Padova e Abet Laminati, B&B (then C&B), Acerbis, Cristal Art, Colli, Boschis and Saportiti. By taking part in Eurodomus, Gufram was able to communicate its company philosophy but also and above all to propose a new and possible model for living, strongly influenced by intemperate but creative young designers, forged in the student protest movements and eager to champion a new culture. The recently concluded uprisings were to lay the foundations for a colourful decade, marked by the optimism of the youth culture, new music and alternative fashion but ending in unexpected, spontaneous, political mobilization. Rather than just looking at things, at historical and political processes, an attempt was made to understand what lay behind them, the whys and wherefores, the DNA, so as to “strike, destroy, debunk and assert new ideas” more easily. Alongside the “good design” of some stands at Eurodomus, it was possible to glimpse the work of those who were to lay the foundations of what was to be known as “radical design”.

Turin was a city in the throes of cultural turmoil. A whole series of groups close to the intellectual world gravitated around the Faculty of Architecture, some of them strongly attracted by trade-union activism and in any case by a political sector in the full swing of change. These included Strum, Studio65, A.ba.co, led by Giuseppe Raimondi, Libidarch, the Vikinghi, "Le rane verdi". Turinese culture drew on the contemporary thinking of a number of groups involved in Eurodomus, including Archizoom, Superstudio, Gruppo 999 and Ufo.

A concept expressed as follows by the Strum group holds for all of them: “Operating in the architectural sphere becomes a way of taking part in the struggles and antagonisms generated by the differences between the need for space and the space actually produced and available”.

The 1972 edition of Eurodomus thus represented an opportunity to put forward precise criticisms regarding society and the discipline of architecture. These operations were given utterance by the members of Studio65, who had this to say about the event:

“*Considering the place – Eurodomus – as a sanctuary of design, our attitude towards this approach takes on challenging overtones to the point of taking kitsch itself as a banner of demystification, whereby the different aspects of ideological communication (both cultural and subcultural) are openly destroyed and kept separate so as to ensure the filtering and debunking of messages. We embrace the subcultural attitude as a challenge laid down by lower culture to higher, by plebeian culture to aristocratic. A tactical and demolishing stance adopted in the sanctuary of Culture…*”

Emanuela Giudice
Research on Gufram
2011

...AFTER THE FACULTY, WE MET

Eurodomus 4: Babilonia '72 stand "La casa dell'imperialista" designed by Studio65 and produced by Zanotta (Aurelio Zanotta was one of our mentors)
Photo: Gianni Arnaudo

HEROES, FAR CRAZIER THAN US

Eurodomus 4

Eurodomus 4: original cover of the circular bed (in cloth), design Studio65
Arnaudo Collection

Eurodomus 4:
Preparatory drawing
Arnaudo Archives

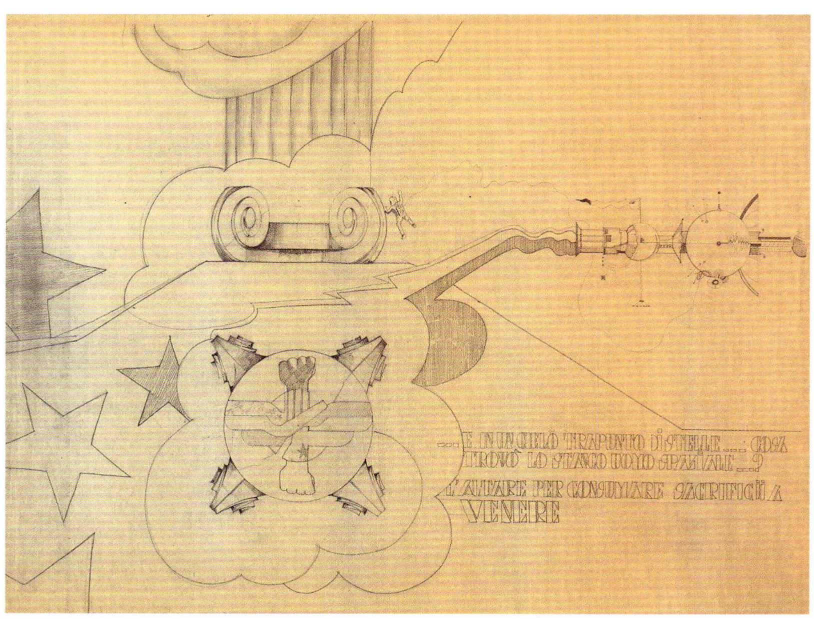

Gufram asked Studio65 to design its stand at Eurodomus 4. Small coloured lamps patiently arranged by hand form an arch to frame the Puffi, Cactus and Fantico models as well as the Bocca sofa, no longer a prototype but substantially modified through collaboration between the company and designers (reworking of the structure and covering with material used for swimming costumes) and finally ready for marketing.

Studio65 had recently joined the group of designers working for Gufram. Graduates of the Turin Faculty of Architecture, mostly between 1970 and 1972, they immediately transformed the firm's production with a massive amount of irony. The deliberate form of irreverence required to subvert a system challenged since the years at university manifested itself in the design of their own stand, Babilonia '72, created (with great courage) by Zanotta and presented at Eurodomus in Turin. This edition saw the participation alongside Gufram of other firms of international importance, including Abet Print with its laminates, Arclinea, which was to create the prototype of the Brazier of Jupiter, and Nonwoven of Milan for floors and fitted carpets.

The task for them all was to seek alternatives and put forward new places for living.

Inside Gufram, together with Strum, Studio65 was the group with most experience of protest and the greatest desire to construct new social models.

As regards the theme of the home, Babilonia '72 saw the introduction into the design of the display space of the same challenging spirit as informed designer articles.

"We thus learned to play the only role that presents itself today for producers of culture, namely that of celebrating imperial capitalism in more or less new forms. And we adopted this role of ours all the way, with no complexes or mystification, to the point where our celebration was interpreted as parody, our humour as sarcasm, to the point of becoming an operation of demystification and contributing to clarification of the meaning of working in architecture at the level of language. Our projects thus became meta-designs and our architecture a discourse on architecture..."

The design presented by Studio65 for Zanotta thus bore the title "Babilonia '72" and took the form of an Ionic column, or rather of its base, housing a continuous space in which the possibility of change can be indicated by four fundamental symbolic places, four objects capable of characterizing the user's social level of life.

The column that contains the domestic space, a kind of macro trinket, thus opens out and becomes the right form both to convey the falsity of the values put forward in order to obtain the effect of selling the home as a good and to mimic the typological values offered by culture to architecture as liberating (space that is open, continuous, multifunctional and equipped, the concentration of facilities in service spaces, modularity).

Emanuela Giudice
Research on Gufram
2011

Eurodomus 4

Eurodomus 4:
the Babilonia '72 stand
"La casa dell'imperialista"
by Studio65
produced by Zanotta
Photo: Paolo Mussat
Sartor
Arnaudo Archives

opposite
Eurodomus 4:
the Babilonia '72 stand
"La casa dell'imperialista"
by Studio65
produced by Zanotta
Photo: Paolo Mussat
Sartor
Arnaudo Archives

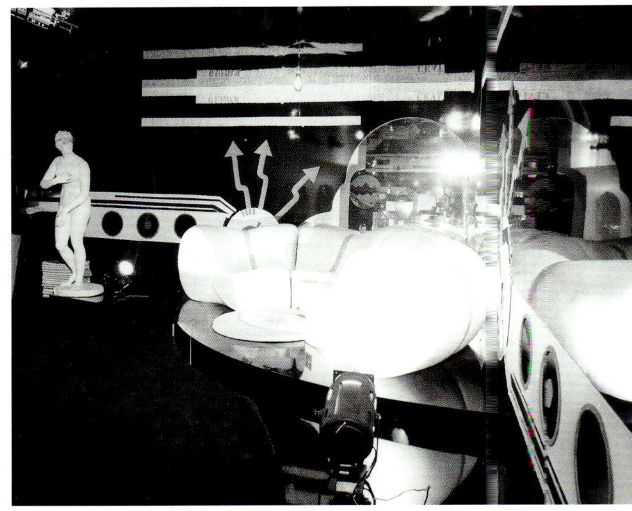

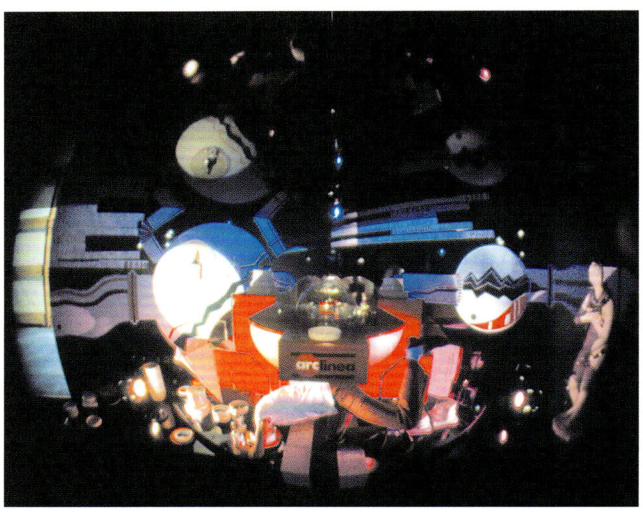

Eurodomus 4

Eurodomus 4:
the Gufram stand
designed by Studio65,
1971
Photo: Paolo Mussat
Sartor
Arnaudo Archives

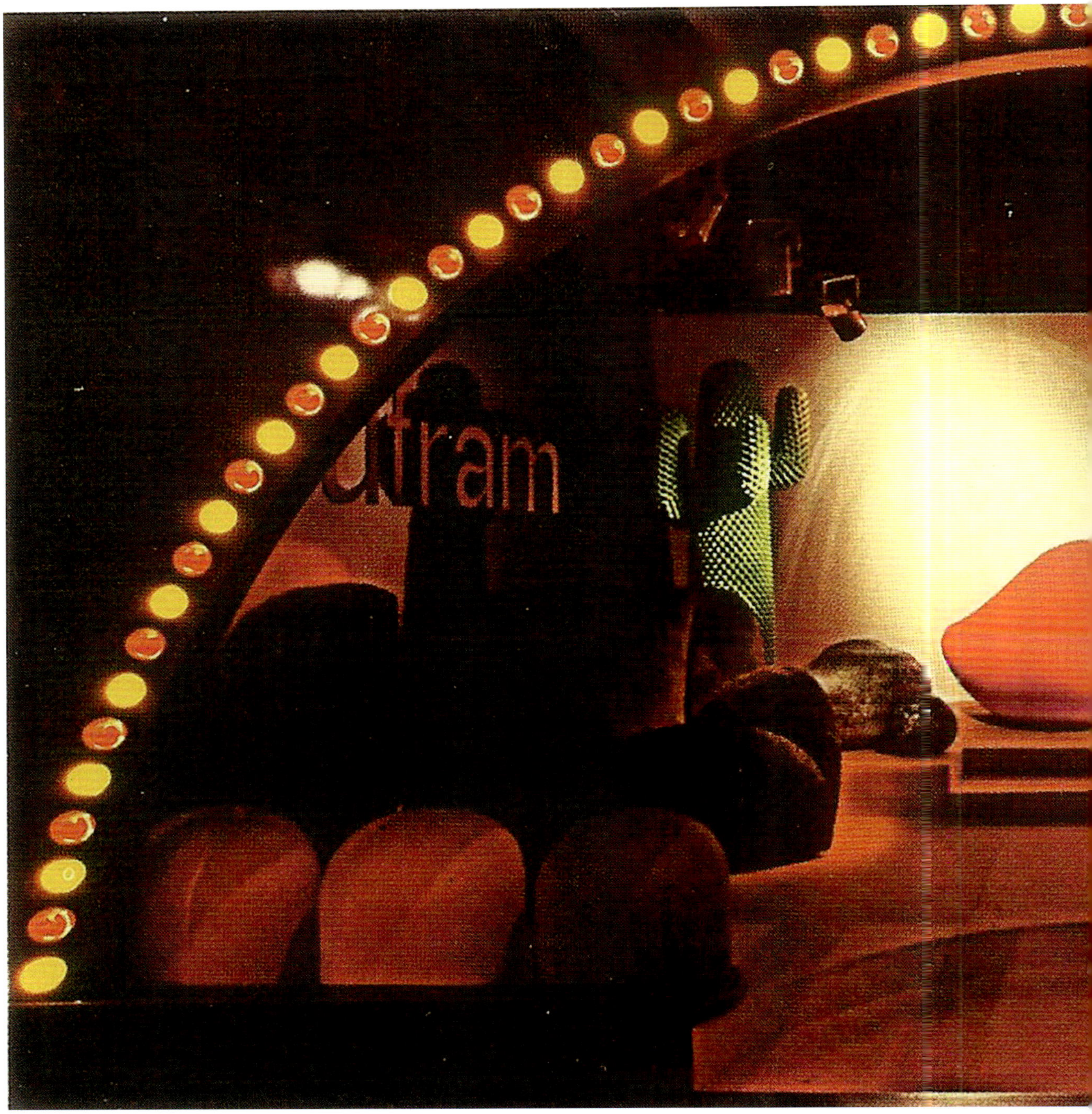

The idea was to reproduce the shooting gallery of a small town fair.

PASSION WAS THERE.
IT COULD HAVE BEEN MUSIC,

IT WAS DESIGN

(Giuseppe Gugliermetto)

Photo of heroes: the Gugliermetto brothers

1

1. Giulia Laverda together with Giuseppe Gugliermetto at the *Multipli Gufram* show held in 1984 at the Galleria TOT in Padua
Courtesy of Ester Gugliermetto
Arnaudo Archives

2. Ennio Chiggio and Giulia Laverda together with Giuseppe Gugliermetto and Ester Gugliermetto at the *Multipli Gufram* show held in 1984 at the Galleria TOT in Padua.
Courtesy of Ester Gugliermetto
Arnaudo Archives

2

The exhibition catalogue *Asparagus Age*
Galleria TOT, Padua, 1984, where the notepaper for Studio65 was published for the first time

1. Giuseppe Gugliermetto
with Gianni Arnaudo
Salone del Mobile, Milan,
2006
Arnaudo Archives

2. The brothers Piero
and Guido Gugliermetto
Arnaudo Archives

1

2

We used polyurethane foam to "debunk" the idea of the piece of furniture completely and made it a manifesto of our form of irreverence, deprived of a supporting structure, a covering and all of its bourgeois connotations.

Gianni Arnaudo

1. Charles and Eleanor Stending were fearless importers of avantgarde Italian design on the American market (from Cara Greenberg, *Op to Pop*, Bulfinch Press, New York 1999, p. 28)

2. Cover of the exhibition catalogue *Italy: The New Domestic Landscape* New York, MoMA, 1972

3. Advertising in the USA organized by Charles Stending New York, 1972 Arnaudo Archives

1

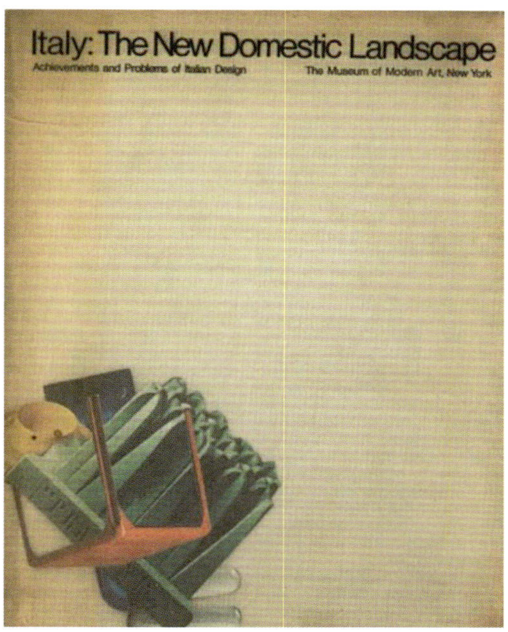

2

3

TO GO FROM THIS...

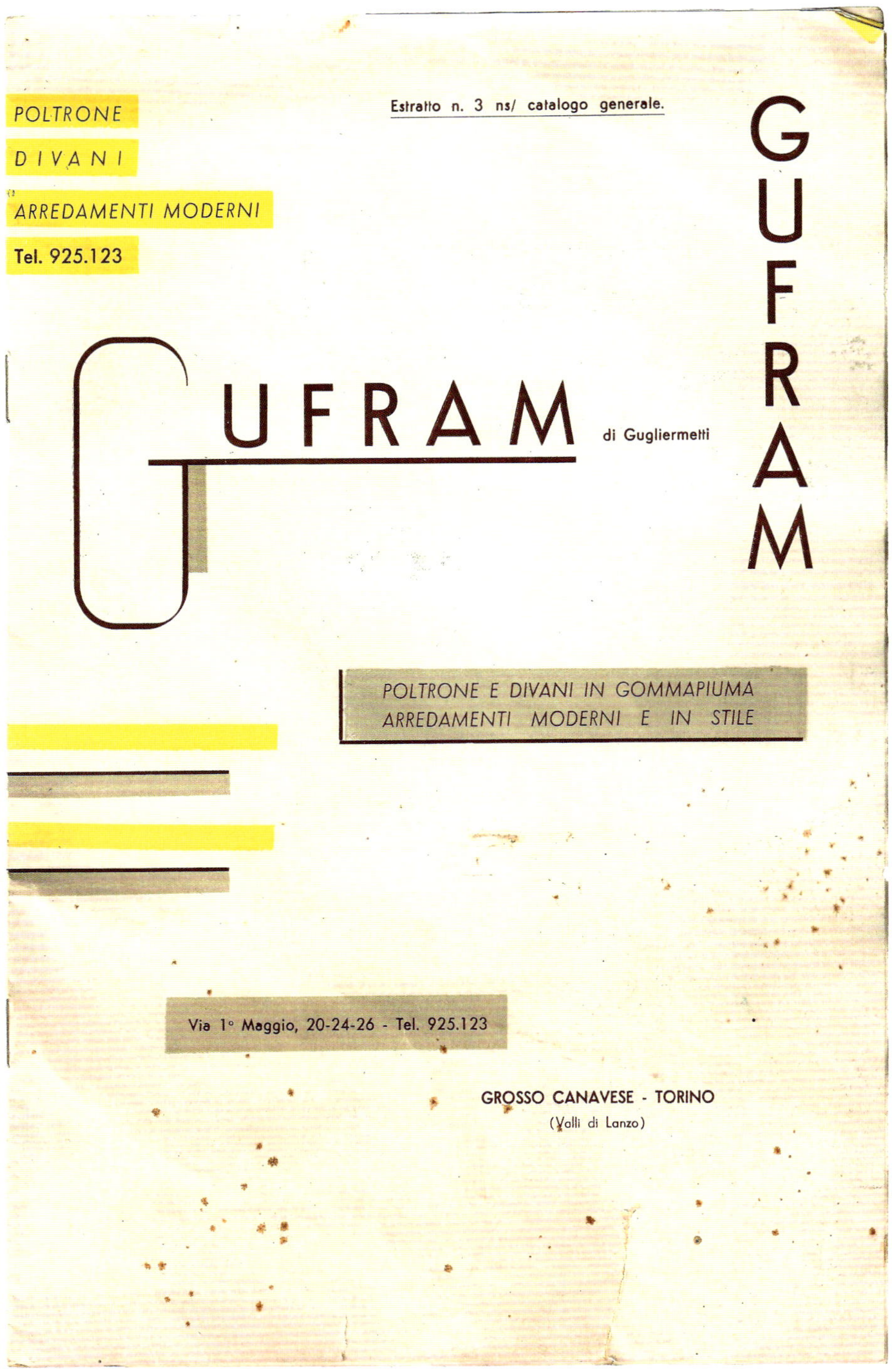

General catalogue of Gufram products, company archives, late 1950s
Courtesy of Ester Gugliermetto Arnaudo Archives

...TO THAT... TOOK SOME COURAGE...

The first Gufram articles
in the world's museums.
Poster for the exhibition
Italy: The New Domestic Landscape
MoMA, New York, 1972
Arnaudo Archives

ORDINATISSIMO / BABY-LONIA

(Studio65 / Gianni Arnaudo)

The Turinese carpenter Quinto was a good person, now old enough to forgive the intemperance of a group of young architects who designed furniture and objects that were a far cry from his tradition of craftsmanship.

He did, however, place his formidable technical expertise at our disposal and thus made it possible to produce many prototypes.

Good relations with the Abet firm ensured the supply at low cost of various sheets of laminate with colours and types – some of which no longer in use – that constituted the basis of our architectural vocabulary.

This led to the birth of the Ordinatissimo, a piece of furniture recalling a set of children's building blocks, with the difference that these multicoloured elements were scaled up and transformed into a cupboard with internal compartments to hold objects of different sizes.

Meaning "very tidy", the name Ordinatissimo was an expression of programmatic intent and a bitterly ironic comment on the bourgeois concept of tidiness (a place for everything and everything in its place).

It was a short step from the source of inspiration of Ordinatissimo to Baby-lonia, offering the intended user the possibility of having a small theatre in their room to set up and dismantle at will as a setting for their stories and a vehicle of the imagination.

"The capitalist's child must always be… ORDINATISSIMO"

In memory of Quinto the carpenter (he was a hero too)

The toy Baby-lonia was derived from the cupboard Ordinatissimo and made of authentic laminated plastic. The capitalist's child's room is thus transformed into Wall Street with all the symbols of power and the dollar sign in the centre of the pediment dedicated to the God Money.
"Order Is" (Louis Kahn): order is the criterion informing the room of the kid that will be president one day.

Studio65 / Gianni Arnaudo, 1971
Photo: Gianni Arnaudo
Arnaudo Archives

Photo with the little Diego Gugliermetto (son of Piero Gugliermetto, founding partner of Gufram)

Baby-lonia
Studio65 / Gianni Arnaudo
- Gufram
Centre Pompidou
permanent collection

KANAL, BRUSSELS
satellite branch of the
CENTRE POMPIDOU
2019

KANAL - Centre Pompidou was born out of the belief that art and culture are essential to bringing people together in an increasingly divided society. The idea is to offer a centre for culture and the exchange of ideas open to everyone, to focus attention on the creative scene in Brussels, and to help enhance the city's cultural appeal.
KANAL - Centre Pompidou is a museum not only of modern and contemporary art but also of architecture and town planning. It is also equipped with numerous public spaces performing a variety of functions.

KANAL - Centre Pompidou,
Brussels

SKIN UP

"The odd leather goods shop Skin Up designed by Studio65 in Turin: a big black box in which giant-sized children's building blocks are laid out and assembled to form the entrance, fitting stage and steps for display.
The sofa is the Gufram 'Chiocciola' and the mirror by Cristal-Art. The white sculpture is a copy of the Medici Venus."

(*Domus* no. 537, 1974
By kind permission of
Editoriale Domus S.p.A.)

Interior design for the shop Skin Up in Turin, 1972.
In the foreground, the Chiocciola sofa produced by Gufram, Gianni Arnaudo / Studio65

Domus no. 537, 1974
By kind permission of
Editoriale Domus S.p.A.
Photo: Paolo Mussat Sartor

I invented the name for the shop,
which sold leather goods
(but the Venus was naked)

THE CAPITELLO SOFA AT THE MUSEO DELLA TRIENNALE, MILAN

for history, it is now radical design,
something strong, unique, heroic and irreverent.

Capitello, Studio65
Gufram 1970
Arnaudo Archives

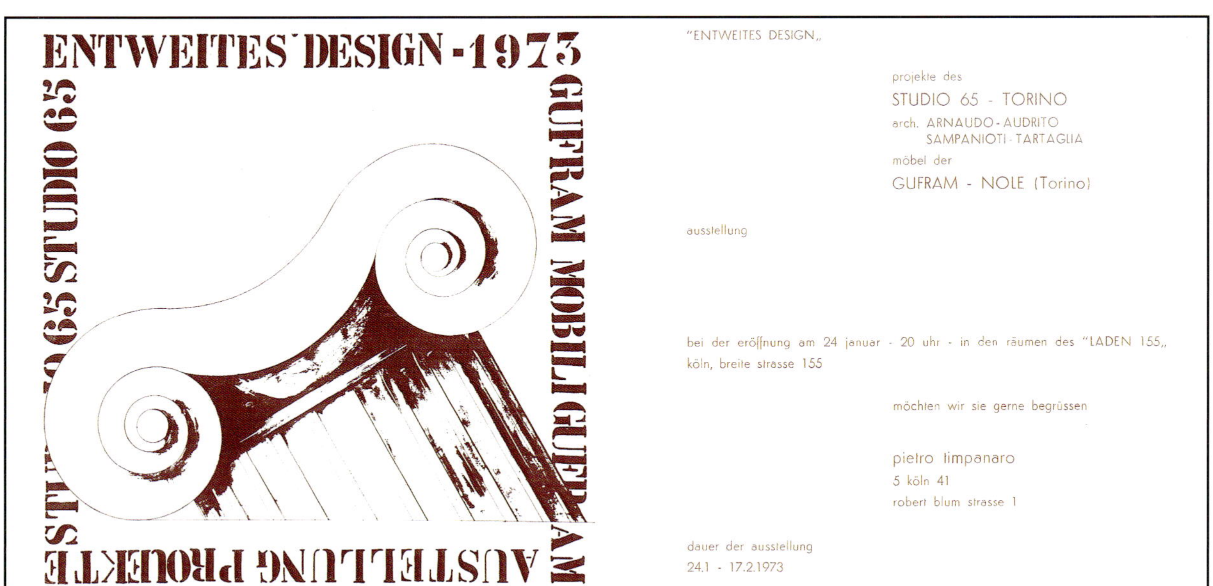

Invitation to the exhibition *Entweites Design* (Irreverent Design), Cologne, 1973

Helmut Newton

didn't want the Bocca sofa and made this very clear to me as we sat on the floor in his home in Monte Carlo examining my interior design for his new apartment. For him, that was only a photogenic copy of Dalí's Surrealist Mae West Lips Sofa, whereas the Capitello was truly original, ironic and subversive, an authentic Pop icon.

Forty years have now gone by and there are many versions of the birth of an icon. What really matters, however, is that the Capitello reflects the irreverent intent of the idea of architecture and design more than any other article produced by Gufram in that period.

The form of the object has no importance in itself and neither does its function. The important thing is that it clearly conveys a message mocking the "repressed desires and frustrated ambitions" of those who still want a word devoid of irony and imagination, i.e. devoid of CRITICAL DESIGN.

This has remained the rationale of my work and my projects.

CRITICAL DESIGN

all of my work is "critical design"

Just as critics express their views through words and Banksy through stencils, architects express themselves through projects made up of signs and symbols, invective and protests.

Design thus becomes a form of analysis and hence a discourse on architecture. It is not a question of inventing new languages, or rather the adoption of new languages is not an end in itself or a way of creating a media circus (…as long as it gets people talking).

Looking at a work of architecture means identifying the DNA that created it and hence the architect's thinking.

"Critical design", i.e. militant architecture in opposition to cliché and conventionality, has always been part of my DNA.

THE TOOLS

Irony
Irreverence
Provocation
Transgression
Paradox
Decontextualization
Deconstruction of language
Assembly of symbols
Subversion

THE MAUSOLEUM

of repressed desires and frustrated ambitions was built near Cuneo as a challenging project, a true example of marked critical decontextualization.

IT IS RADICAL ARCHITECTURE

This architecture is both the forerunner and the antithesis of the post-modern movement that was to be born years later.

The rationality of the absurd

I had a client (a friend of my father, who was also an architect) who sold tiles in Borgo San Dalmazzo near Cuneo.

He came to see me one day about commissioning a new showroom of tiles and sanitary appliances and showed me the sort of thing he had in mind: the image of a huge whale with its mouth wide open on the road from Cuneo to France.

I immediately decided that this would be the right person to tell about the ideas I was developing with Studio65.

The client got what he wanted: all the archetypes of power and culture, irony and provocation.

One strikingly innovative idea was to conceive this new showroom as a meeting place with music for young people, and so it developed from a possible display of tiles into Flash Back.

Having already worked in the disco sector (with the Blue Hill at Lequio Tanaro), I invented a completely new internal layout with the DJ up above the dance floor on a walkway connecting the temple of music to that of tiles.

The Colonna produced by Zanotta for Eurodomus was used to complete the work, making this one of the first major operations of architectural “recycling”.

This “recycling” made it possible to convey more clearly the “nonsensicality” of an absurd design capable of expressing our ideas about architecture better than any piece of writing. Since the birth of a cultural movement corresponds to the definition of a fully formed idea only when it acquires self-awareness, as Gramsci tells us, the Flash Back project provides the basis for an understanding of the ideas of Studio65 in the period when we worked together.

Zanotta’s Colonna was not damaged by fire but all of its wooden structure simply underwent deterioration due to the use of the wrong protective varnish. No other version of the events corresponds to the what really happened.

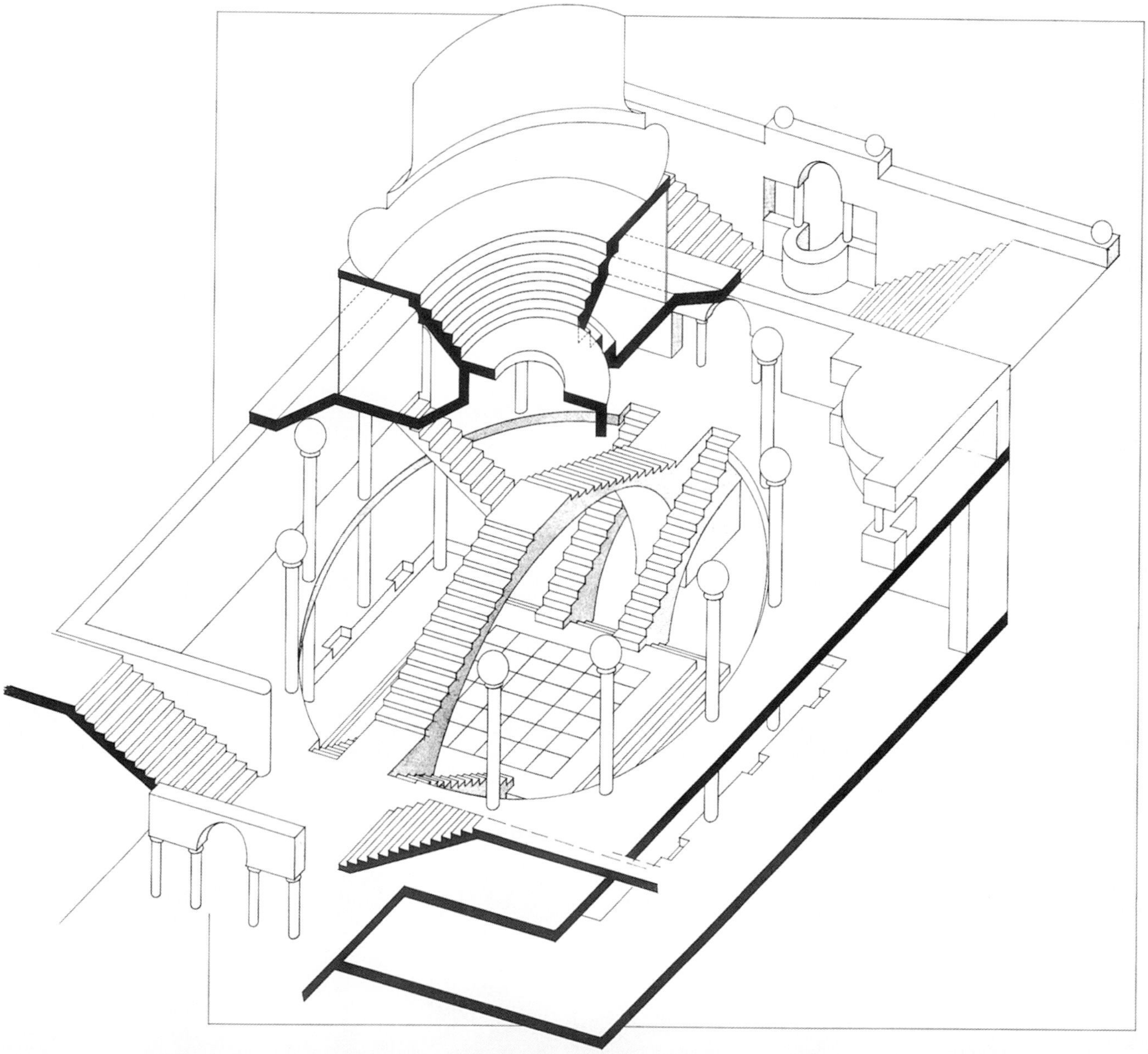

Original design
by Gianni Arnaudo
Axonometric drawing
Arnaudo Archives

Giovanni Battista Piranesi
(1720–1778)
The *Imaginary Prisons*

A critique of post-modernism before post-modernism was even born

Ho seguito le vicende della costruzione del complesso Flash Back- Paolina B.

Questo singolare edificio era stato realizzato grazie alla fantasia innovativa, alla fede ed alla tenacia di mio padre, che pensava di creare sulla statale,che porta da Cuneo alla vicina Francia, un edificio che esprimesse un modo nuovo di esporre le piastrelle, che colpisse il pubblico.

Le sue idee su questo genere di marketing erano notevolmente anticipatrici di quella che sarebbe stata l'evoluzione della pubblicità nel mondo commerciale.

Aveva incontrato il figlio di un amico di famiglia, Gianni Arnaudo, che dal

1970 lavorava a Torino in uno studio formato con alcuni compagni di università.

Dopo aver visto la proposta di mio padre (una grande balena con la bocca aperta verso la strada statale), Gianni Arnaudo gli propose una serie di idee altrettanto spettacolari ed ironiche: un complesso che richiamasse tutti i simboli del "potere e del prestigio" più riconoscibili e storicamente clamorosi.

Ne nacque così un progetto affidato a Gianni Arnaudo, che lo estese al suo gruppo di lavoro, lo Studio 65 di Torino.

Tutti i progetti presentati al Comune di Borgo San Dalmazzo hanno la firma di Gianni Arnaudo.

Gianni seguì tutta la direzione dei lavori della costruzione e dell'arredamento della discoteca Flash-Back e non ho mai conosciuto ne' visto nessun altro professionista dello studio di Torino.

Il rapporto con Gianni era così forte che, dopo qualche hanno, gli si chiese di ampliare la discoteca negli spazi precedentemente dedicati alla vendita di piastrelle e sanitari, diventando il Paolina B.

Tutto il progetto del Paolina B venne ideato ed eseguito unicamente da Gianni e dal suo studio di Cuneo.

Borgo San Dalmazzo,

In fede

Born several years before the post-modern movement, the Flash Back constitutes a stringent critique thereof by virtue of its marked irony.

Interiors of the Flash Back disco
Borgo San Dalmazzo
Studio65
Photos: Paolo Mussat Sartor

opposite
Poster by Gianni Arnaudo
Original: Arnaudo Archives

Also exhibited in *La Boîte de Nuit* at Villa Noailles, Hyeres, in *Night Fever* at the Vitra Design Museum in Basel, together with the entire project, and at the ADAM Design Museum in Brussels, the Centro per l'Arte Contemporanea Luigi Pecci in Prato, the Designmuseum Danmark in Copenhagen and the V&A Dundee in Scotland.

CONDUCTING AN ORCHESTRA

This building toy was a success (the construction kit of imperialist architecture)

Gianni Arnaudo during work on the Flash Back disco in Borgo San Dalmazzo
Studio65
Arnaudo Archives

Photos exhibited in *Night Fever* at the Vitra Design Museum in Basel, the ADAM Design Museum in Brussels, the Centro per l'Arte Contemporanea Luigi Pecci in Prato, the Designmuseum Danmark in Copenhagen and the V&A Dundee in Scotland

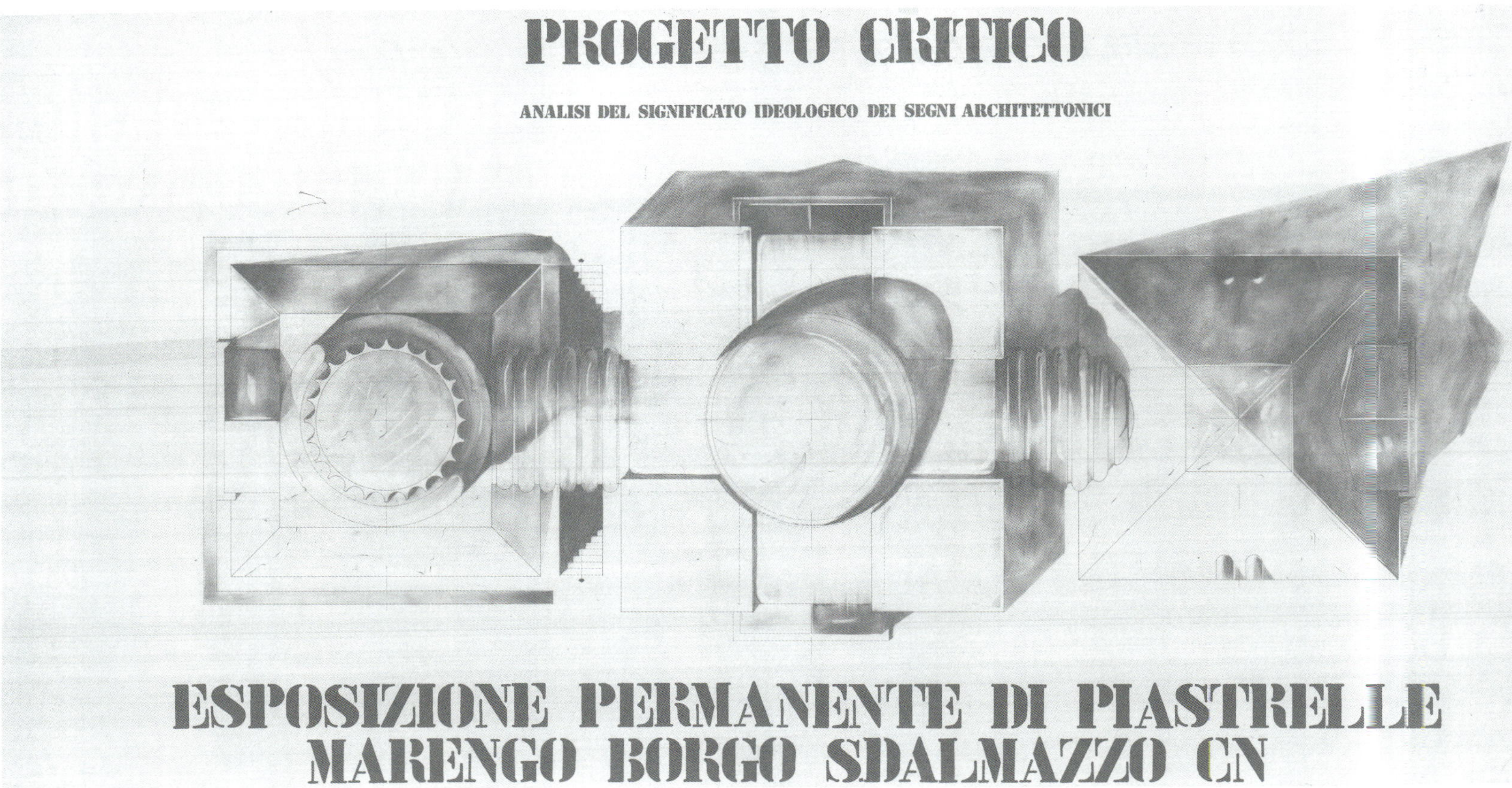

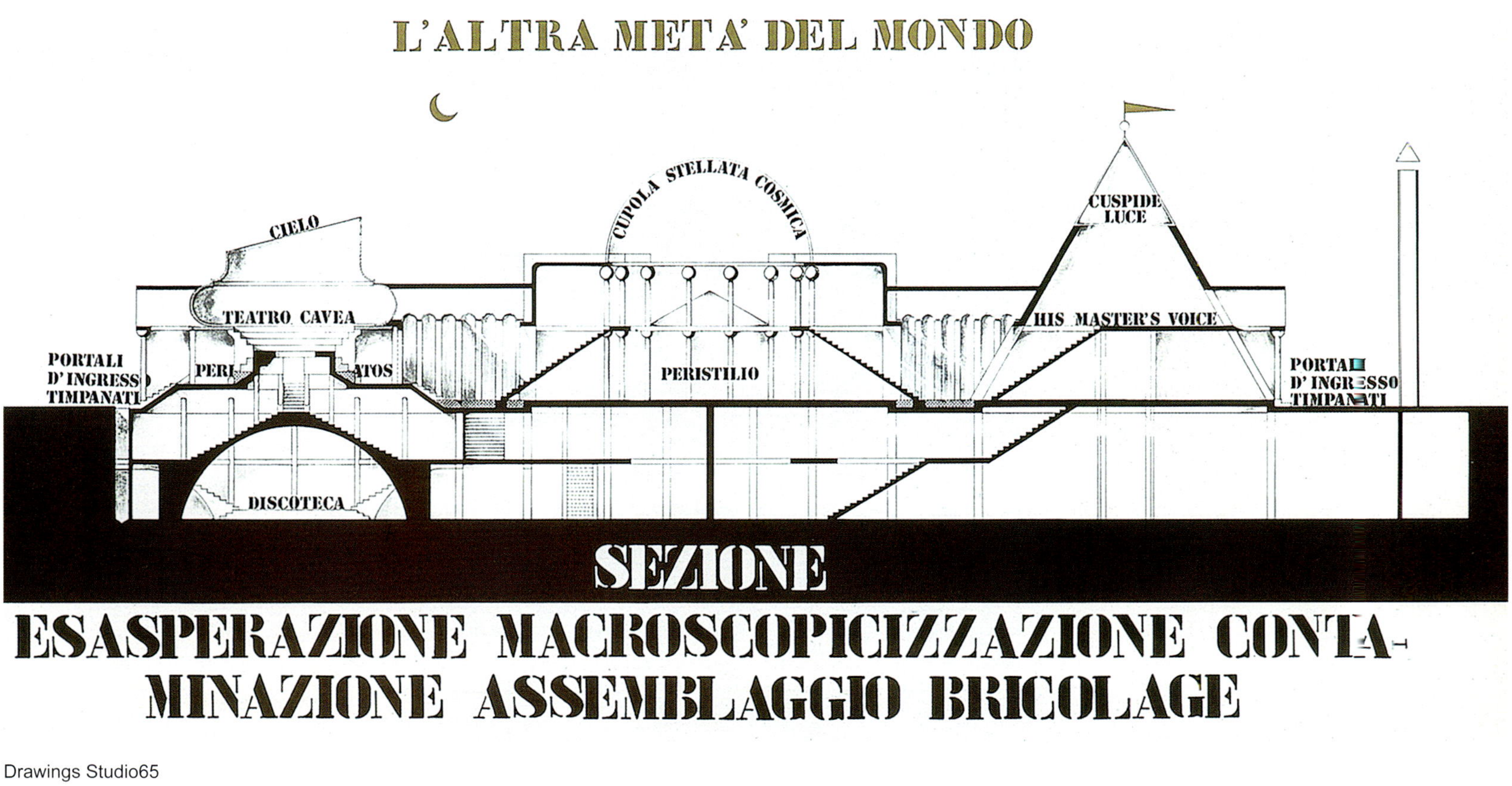

Drawings Studio65

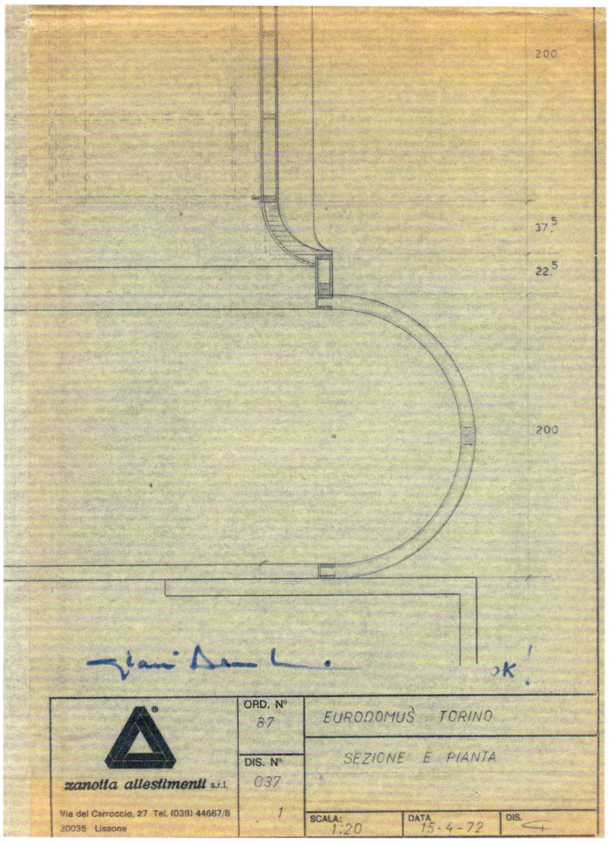

Column design made
by Studio65 for
Eurodomus 4 and reused
for the Flash Back disco
Zanotta Allestimenti
1972
Arnaudo Archives

Municipal archive of
Borgo San Dalmazzo
Initial project, 1973
Arnaudo Archives

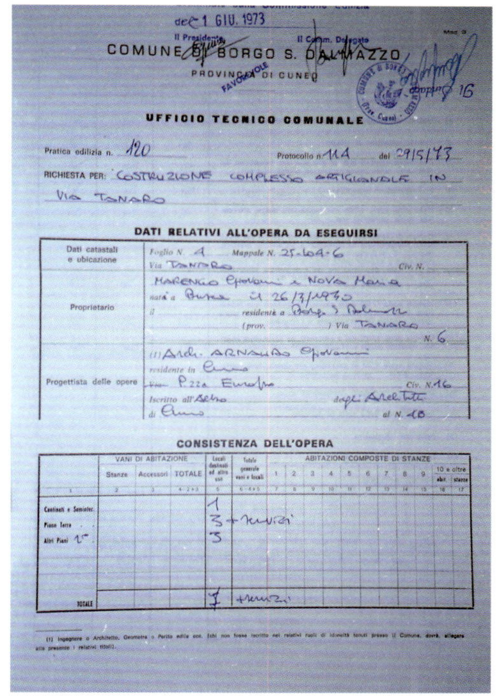

del 1 GIU. 1973
Il Presidente — Il Comm. Delegato
COMUNE DI BORGO S. DALMAZZO
PROVINCIA DI CUNEO
FAVOREVOLE

UFFICIO TECNICO COMUNALE

Pratica edilizia n. 120 — Protocollo n. 114 del 29/5/73

RICHIESTA PER: COSTRUZIONE COMPLESSO ARTIGIANALE IN VIA TANARO

DATI RELATIVI ALL'OPERA DA ESEGUIRSI

Dati catastali e ubicazione	Foglio N. 4 Mappale N. 25-64-6 Via TANARO Civ. N.
Proprietario	MARENGO Giovanni e NOVA Maria nata a ... il 26/7/1930 il ... residente a Borgo S. Dalmazzo (prov.) Via TANARO N. 6
Progettista delle opere	(1) Arch. ARNAUDO Giovanni residente in Cuneo Via P.zza Europa Civ. N. 16 Iscritto all'Albo degli Architetti di Cuneo al N. 48

CONSISTENZA DELL'OPERA

	VANI DI ABITAZIONE			Locali destinati ad altro uso	Totale generale vani e locali	ABITAZIONI COMPOSTE DI STANZE										
	Stanze	Accessori	TOTALE			1	2	3	4	5	6	7	8	9	10 e oltre abit.	stanze
1	2	3	4 = 2+3	5	6 = 4+5	7	8	9	10	11	12	13	14	15	16	17
Cantinati e Seminter.				1												
Piano Terra				3 + servizi												
Altri Piani 1°				3												
TOTALE				7 + servizi												

(1) Ingegnere o Architetto, Geometra o Perito edile ecc. (chi non fosse iscritto nei relativi ruoli di idoneità tenuti presso il Comune, dovrà allegare alla presente i relativi titoli).

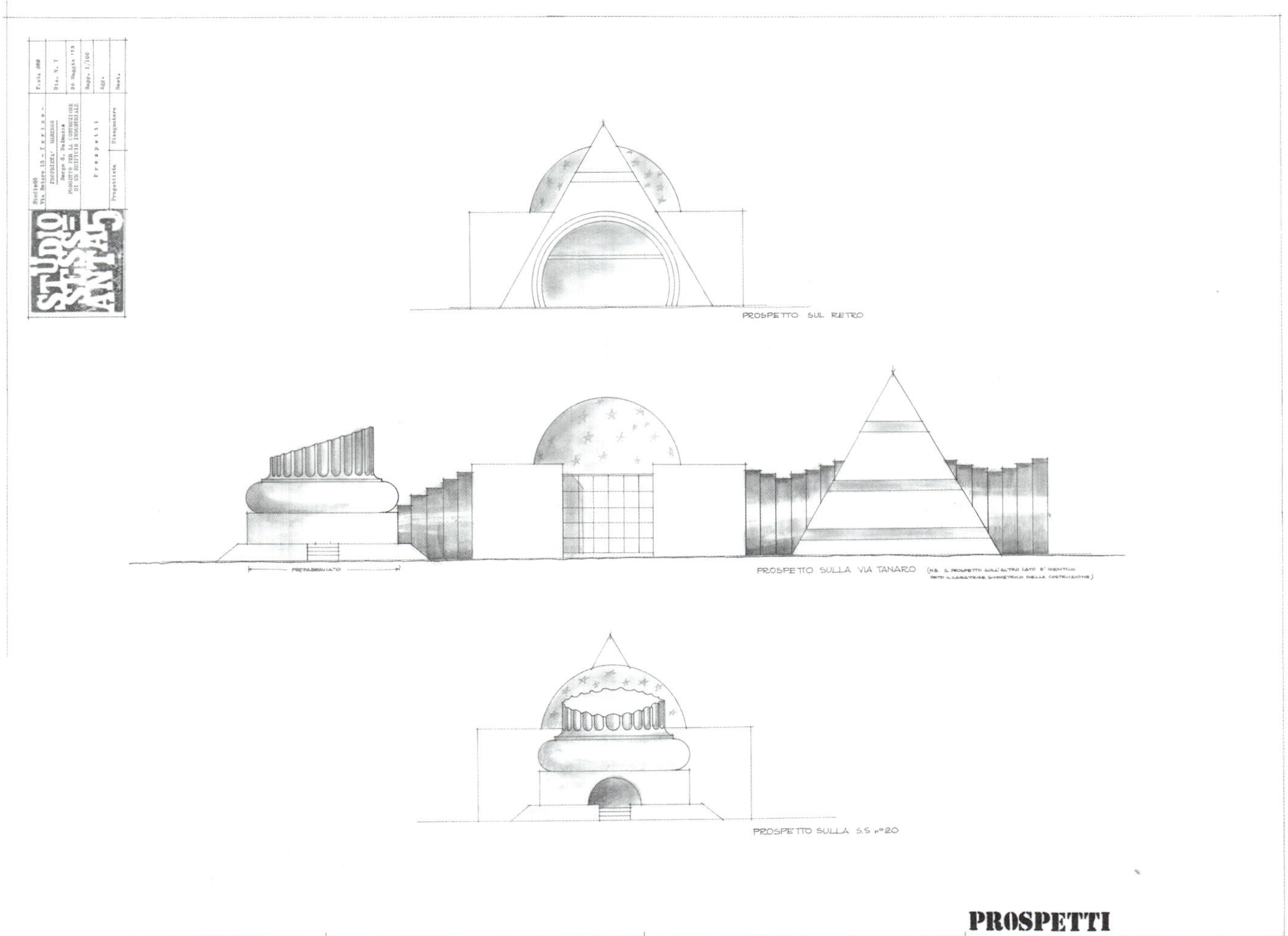

Flash Back

THE SYMBOLS OF

in other words, the three-dimensional translation of the banality of clichés and the

the critical project

Arnaudo Archives

POWER IN HISTORY

contamination of history along a trajectory of thwarted ambitions and repressed desires.

Photos exhibited in *Night Fever* at the Vitra Design Museum in Basel, the ADAM Design Museum in Brussels, the Centro per l'Arte Contemporanea Luigi Pecci in Prato, the Designmuseum Danmark in Copenhagen and the V&A Dundee in Scotland
Original text by Vitra Design Museum

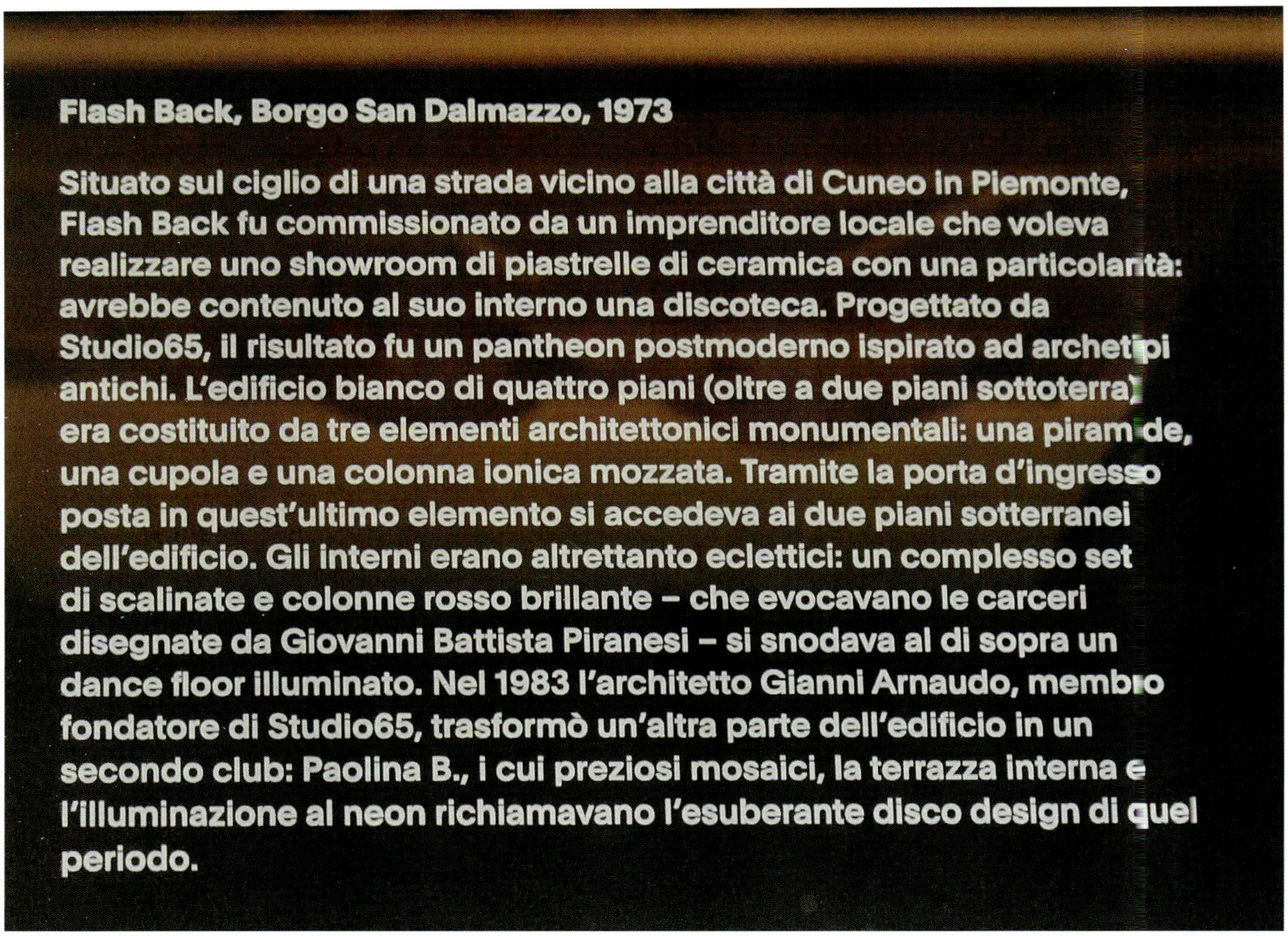

LO STUDIO65

(1970-1976)

NELLA SUA
COMPOSIZIONE STORICA

FINISCE

THE "PAOLINA B"

Gianni Arnaudo 1980–83

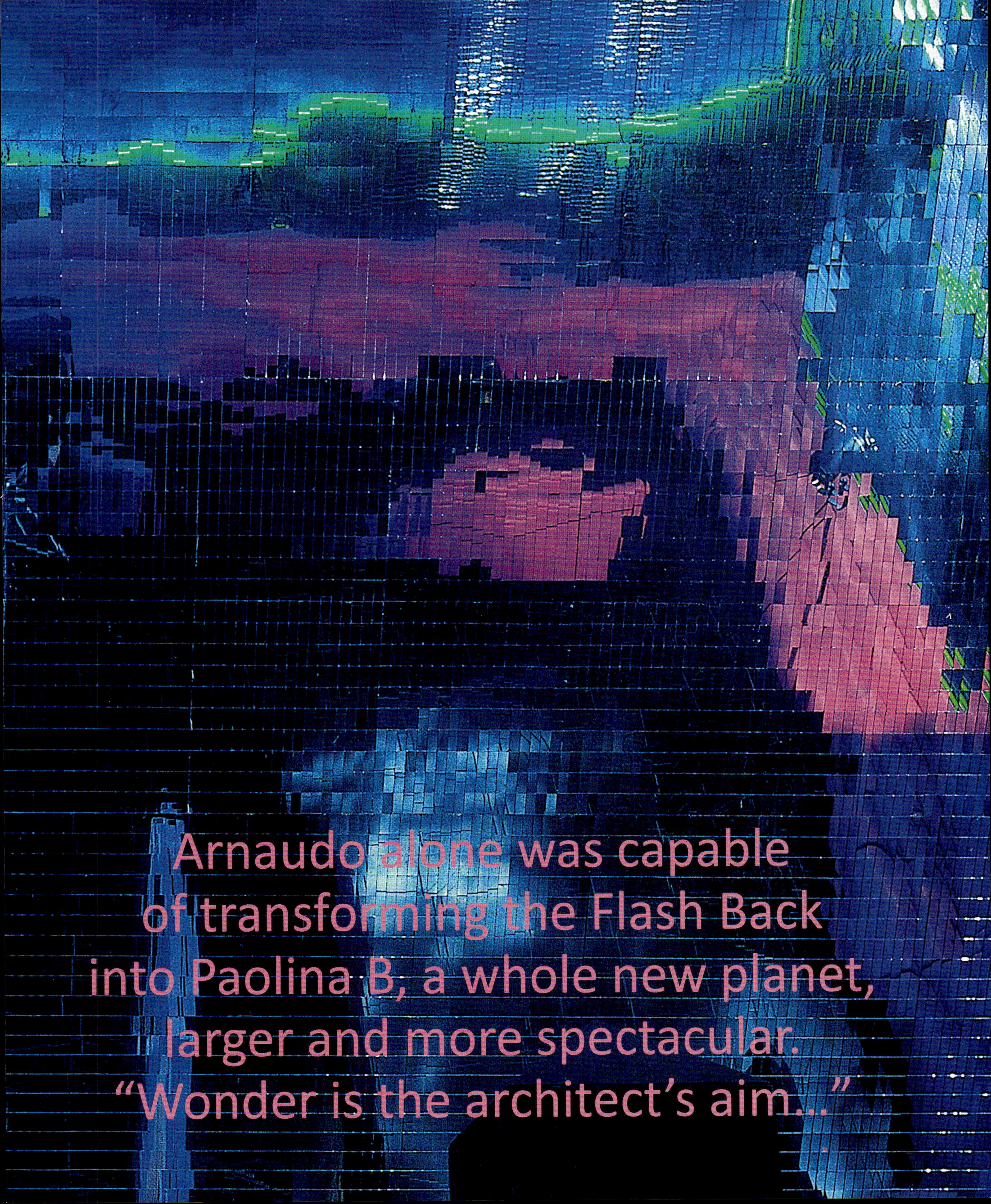

Arnaudo alone was capable of transforming the Flash Back into Paolina B, a whole new planet, larger and more spectacular. "Wonder is the architect's aim..."

The success of the Flash Back prompted the client to commission me a few years later to undertake a large-scale enlargement of the disco. Given the "terribly" classical character of the structure, I renamed it Paolina B as an ironic reference to the famous Jackie O' in Rome.

The new disco had all the elements of the new technology of light and sound. Aficionados could listen to the music on headphones and there were formidable special effects in line with the characteristics of pop music, predominating at the time.

As in the baroque era, architecture, music and ideas rediscovered a moment of interdisciplinary unity.

Poster of the Paolina B disco in Borgo San Dalmazzo
1983
Offset, idea and design Gianni Arnaudo graphic production by Carla Bartolozzi
Exhibited in *Night Fever* at the Vitra Design Museum in Basel, the ADAM Design Museum in Brussels, the Centro per l'Arte Contemporanea Luigi Pecci in Prato, the Designmuseum Danmark in Copenhagen and the V&A Dundee in Scotland

Paolina B: the pyramid and the bridge of crystal
Photo: Paolo Mussat Sartor
Exhibited in *Night Fever* at the Vitra Design Museum in Basel, the ADAM Design Museum in Brussels, the Centro per l'Arte Contemporanea Luigi Pecci in Prato, the Designmuseum Danmark, Copenhagen and the V&A Dundee in Scotland

This period saw the publication of *Il Kitsch. Antologia del cattivo gusto* by Gillo Dorfles.
This project expresses my ideas about kitsch.
While Dorfles utterly condemned this entire world of popular production (or at least aimed at the masses), I was instead fascinated by the irony, magic and contradictions inherent in so many objects disparaged as the embodiment of bad taste.
The glass snow globes with the image of a very popular pope and a gondola sold in Venice are a concentration of absurdities to be viewed as nonsense in all its mocking irony.
In the same way, certain richly spangled cocktail cabinets of the 1950s complete with music box and scantily-clad dancing lady constituted a form of escape into a world of dreams for the owner.
This is what must be grasped in kitsch: the cheerful humour, irony, absurdity, contradiction, transgression and subversion with respect to every "sacral" object produced by cold, sterile rationalism.
Escapism can thus be found inside this pyramid, where people laughed and had fun precisely because of the absurdity of the space and the constant references to the "world" I have described.

Interiors of the Paolina B
disco in Borgo
San Dalmazzo
Design by Gianni Arnaudo
1983
Photo: Paolo Mussat
Sartor

Photos exhibited in *Night Fever* at the
Vitra Design Museum
in Basel, the ADAM
Design Museum in
Brussels, the Centro per
l'Arte Contemporanea
Luigi Pecci in Prato, the
Designmuseum Danmark
in Copenhagen and the
V&A Dundee in Scotland

While the Flash Back was created as a conventional showcase, the Paolina B was a spectacular and markedly innovative container for rock music. Its fame spread as far as Monte Carlo and the Crown Prince Albert decided to pay a visit. It was a sensational event. A beautiful model in a gleaming white body stocking reclining on a Paolina sofa with her hair in the style of Canova's famous sculpture of Pauline Bonaparte greeted the enthusiastic public.

The famous overhead walkway of glass beneath which so many young men waited in ecstasy to admire the legs of the ladies passing above.

The scandal was so great that the disco was closed for nearly a month and reopened with a "chaste" length of carpet, which was soon removed, however, to the delight of all concerned.

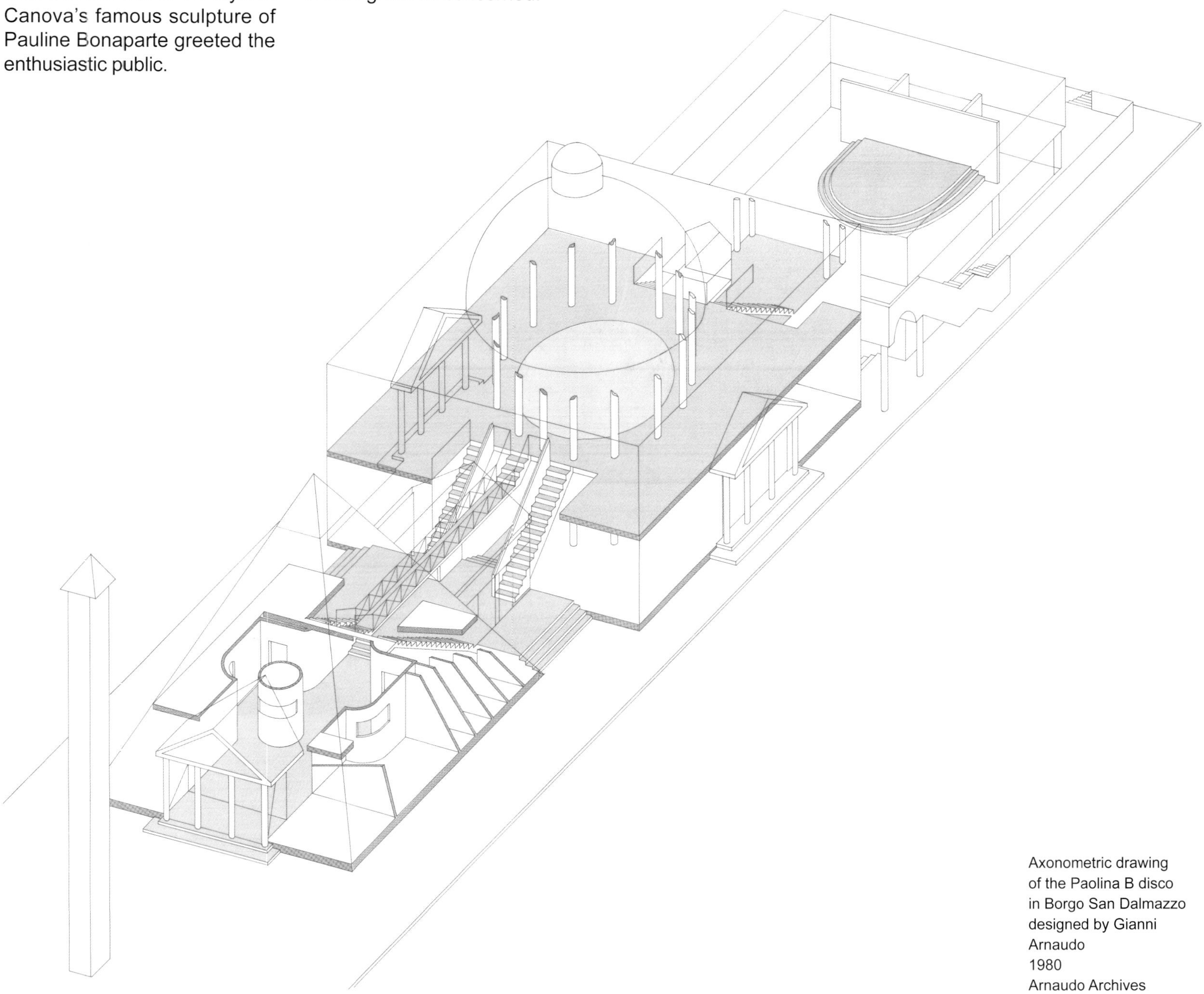

Axonometric drawing of the Paolina B disco in Borgo San Dalmazzo designed by Gianni Arnaudo
1980
Arnaudo Archives

THE WALL STREET JOURNAL.

IDEAS | ICONS

Nightclub at the Museum: Decades of Disco Design

At an exhibition in Germany, furniture, photos, music, art, lights and more

New York's Palladium nightclub in 1985, with a mural by Keith Haring. In lower Manhattan in the 1980s, club culture and the art scene overlapped. **PHOTO:** TIMOTHY HURSLEY, GARVEY|SIMON GALLERY NEW YORK

Gianni Arnaudo's Aliko chair designed for Flash Back, a discotheque in the Italian town of Borgo San Dalmazzo, near the French border. **PHOTO:** ANDREAS SUTTERLIN/GIANNI ARNAUDO

By J.S. Marcus
March 16, 2018 12:38 p.m. ET

The beat goes on from now through September at "Night Fever," a new German exhibit where visitors who may never have made it past the velvet ropes will get to rummage through several decades of nightclub design—complete with vintage fliers, techno-inspired fashion, nightclub furniture and dance-club inspired artworks.

Subtitled "Designing Club Culture 1960–Today," the exhibition at the Vitra Design Museum in Weil am Rhein, just outside the Swiss city of Basel, uses everything from whimsical Italian club decorations of the 1960s to a scale rendering in cork of Berghain, Berlin's longstanding techno temple housed in an old East German power plant.

The French created the discothèque, as its name implies, says Jochen Eisenbrand, the museum's chief curator and co-curator of the new show. The first discos of the postwar years combined live music with records. In the 1960s, a group of iconoclastic Italian architects, collectively known as the Radical Design movement, gave the format a dramatic makeover. Often disdainful of creating ordinary buildings, the architects jumped at the chance to design nightclub spaces.

The show features plenty of photos documenting Italian clubs launched in the 1960s, like Rome's Piper and Florence's Space Electronic, and includes surviving pieces of furniture, like a pink chair with a doughnut-shaped seat from a Bolzano club, Il Grifoncino, by Radical Design architect Cesare Casati.

These Italian clubs had distinctive interiors, marked by bright colors and sleek shapes, and the recovery of their history is "the most exciting part of the exhibition" for Konstantin Grcic, the celebrated German furniture and product designer who also designed the layout of the new Vitra show. The architects "invented the typology of the club," he says, adding that their approaches to overall club design "are still valid today."

Some of Mr. Grcic's designs are produced by Vitra, the Swiss-owned furniture company that specializes in midcentury modern masters like Charles and Ray Eames and Denmark's Verner Panton along with contemporary figures like France's Ronan and Erwan Bouroullec. Over the years, Vitra has moved from furniture into architecture, commissioning Frank Gehry to create a design museum in 1989 on its Weil am Rhein campus. In the 1990s, British architect Zaha Hadid designed the campus fire station, topped by what looks like a giant shard.

The eerie 2013 photo 'In the Waves #1,' by Chinese artist Chen Wei, shows models pretending to be at a club, dancing alone. **PHOTO:** CHEN WEI/LEO XU PROJECTS, SHANGHAI

An opening party at that fire station will be as close as the show comes to a real disco. "I was against re-creating a club experience in the exhibition," says Mr. Grcic. Instead he has equipped a gallery with headphones playing four types of music one might have heard in the clubs evoked by the exhibition. There's pre-disco (Barry White, for example), disco itself (think Donna Summer), house (featuring a track from Frankie Knuckles, the innovative Bronx-born DJ), and techno tracks, from the likes of Germany's Kraftwerk. A light installation created for the exhibition by Matthias Singer, a Munich-based lighting designer with club events to his credit, will surround listeners.

After Italy, the exhibition makes a stopover in lower Manhattan in the 1980s, where club culture and the art scene overlapped. The show features graphic art by Keith Haring, who first attracted attention for his chalk-based graffiti art in the New York subway. The exhibition includes Haring's 1983 drawing of a DJ, possibly at Paradise Garage, whose resident DJ Larry Levan paved the way for "house music," and a 1985 Haring invitation to a party in honor of Mr. Levan. That year, Haring painted a giant canvas mural that presided over the dance floor at the Palladium, one of New York's top clubs during the 1980s. The show has a photo of the Palladium interior, whose signature mural is now part of the collection of the Keith Haring Foundation.

The exhibition then moves back to Europe—in particular to Berlin, where 1990s nightlife took over cavernous spaces in the urban wilderness that still marked the edges of East Berlin. One was Tresor, the go-to techno spot of the early 1990s, created out of the vaults of a former department store on a spot near the former Berlin Wall.

Inside Berlin's Tresor club, 1996-97. **PHOTO:** GUSTAV VOLKER HEUSS

Next comes a pit stop in Antwerp, Belgium, where an ascendant fashion scene held sway in local nightclubs. Techno music is associated with Flemish designer Walter Van Beirendonck, who says his collections in the late 1980s and '90s "fit the atmosphere, look, vibe and energy" of the techno club scene. Three of Mr. Van Beirendonck's designs are on view in "Night Fever," including his thigh-covering "Hardbeat" boots from his 1989-90 fall and winter collection. He went on to design the costumes for U2's 1997-98 "PopMart Tour."

The Wall Street Journal
Night Fever Exhibition
March 2018

Aliko bench
Gianni Arnaudo for Barel
Interni n. 3, July/August 2019

Forty years later, at the Vitra Design Museum in Basel the ADAM Design Museum in Brussels the Centro Luigi Pecci in Prato and then…

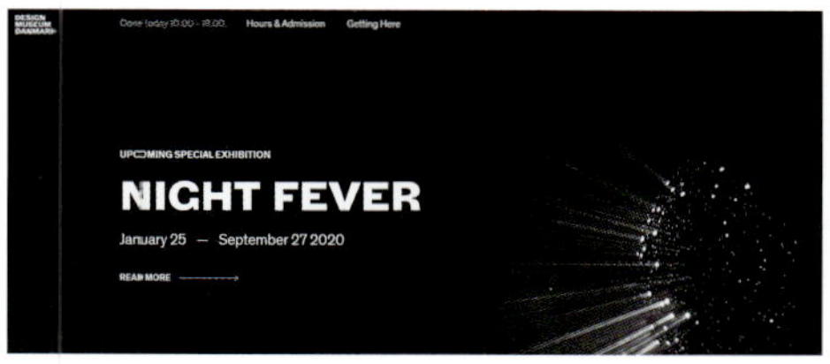

Designmuseum Danmark, Copenaghen

V&A Dundee, Scotland

HOTA HOME OF THE ARTS

Home of the Arts, Gold Coast, Australia

Poster designed by Gianni Arnaudo of the Flash Back disco in Borgo San Dalmazzo (Gianni Arnaudo / Studio65)
Poster of the Paolina B disco, designed by Gianni Arnaudo, Borgo San Dalmazzo

Aliko chair
designed by Gianni Arnaudo for the Paolina B disco in Borgo San Dalmazzo
1982

this is
Rococò ®
SLIDE
Papì ®
Déjeuner sur l'Arbre ®
GUFRAM
Red Carpet ®
Pa[illegible]oro ®
SLI[illegible]E
Youwelcome ®
POLTRONA FRAU
Va' pensiero ®
POLTRONA FRAU
K[illegible]a ®
SL[illegible]E

another story
Lamp Pandoro ®
SLIDE
Colonna di Piatti
CERAMICHE BESIO
Sono stufa ®
Graal ®
FONTANA ARTE
Aliko ®
BAREL
Sua Eminenza ®
POLTRONA FRAU
TEA TIME
Napulì ®
Tea Time ®
SLIDE
Fizzz ®
SLIDE
Milo ®
GUFRAM

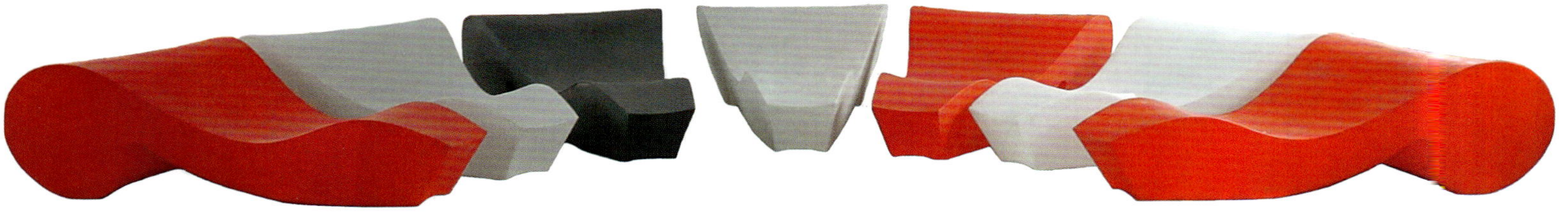

My first encounter with Gianni Arnaudo was Pop: instantaneous, empathic and absorbing. Pop means accepting at first sight, sharing, belonging and identifying with an ironic and detached approach to both form and the world.
Collective affinity but also a common path: my Vas-one was a citation (in terms of its design methods and even its name) of the Pratone brought out by Gufram, where he worked as Gruppo 65 many years earlier, and then there is also the fact that we both came from the suburbs into the Milanese world of design. So we shared the same curious, admiring attitude, but never subservient to the centre of this world around which production, communication and distribution have always gravitated. Coming from outside sometimes allows you to keep your feet on the ground, rooted in the kind of reality which concedes little to attention-seeking and compels us towards a kind of vision and deliberate exaggeration, aimed at overcoming the contingent and bland boundaries of everyday life.

Gianni Arnaudo has always remained faithful to himself, becoming an architect and designer of international renown represented in exhibitions held at MoMA in New York and Beauborg in Paris, but he has never been drawn into the hectic schedule of events in Milan. He designs, travels and studies from afar, making carefully gauged forays aimed at entertaining personal and not just professional relations.
Ha always has a very attentive and enthusiastic eye, ready to cause plenty of consternation, a trait which has always characterised his design work from the very beginning. To those people who are familiar with the places he comes from (the hills of the Cuneo region), which are austere and un-inclined towards open laughter, it is amusing to note the subversive force of his projects. His discoteques, which were postmodern before their time, his desecrating citations of a classical nature created in improbable locations, in "non-places" of faceless modernity, which actually appear to be forcibly claiming the right to the beauty and thoughtfulness of conscientious intrascience.
The contrast between high-flown capitals and transient functional features, linked with escapism and simple obsolescence, creates disorientation. Noble forms are associated with giant dimensions and set out based on almost television-style set design methods, aimed at startling, creating emotion and really capturing our attention.
The system is criticised, but there is also a sincere sense of entertainment in pure Pop style. Pop is, at the same time, both a form of critique and incredulous compliance.
A limit is identified and accepted, in order to describe it ironically, ready to move beyond it. This creative shift plays on surprise, disconcertation and big dimensions.
We will never grow bored of all those fabulous objects created for Gufram in the early 1970s, misunderstood by the public at large but then celebrated at the Italy: *The New Domestic Landscape* exhibition in New York, and which have now become emblematic icons of that period.
How can we fail to mention those disconcerning advertising slogans for the products he designed for Gufram, which add words to design, and how can we fail to be amused by the letter paper designed by Gruppo 65, as Arnaudo and his colleagues became genuine "outlaws" in the field of design.
There is the sheer pleasure of exaggeration, screaming colour and the loud appeal of a manifesto, a legacy of '68, the calling into question of preconceived order, any kind of order, actually achived throught classical order reduced to a desecrating armchair which we sink into Fantozzi-style.
There was the gradual rejection of liturgies and the star system (the new imperious order of communication), so as to constantly get back to genuine, constructed design, partly and especially through architecture.
He always had a disenchanted, ironic but inevitably passionate view of things, which allowed him to take on new projects on any scale without prejudice. Déjeuner sur l'arbre is a recent game, an erudite and istantly desecrating citation taking pleasure in challenging what is widely held to be obvious, in order to turn it on its head. Dear Gianni, may you continue to be so independent and detached. Keep up the good work!

Luisa Bocchietto - President of ADI (Industrial Design Association)
l'Arca no. 259, June 2010

Reinvention of the concept of an icon:

citations of classical art and architecture become subversive symbols by virtue of the ironic use made of them

Colonna di piatti
Ceramiche Vedova Besio e Figlio
Mondovi
Designed by Gianni Arnaudo, 1969
Production 1971
Photo: Paolo Mussat Sartor
Arnaudo Archives

"There was a whole proliferation of underground and 'protest' design. Unlike the films of Warhol and Pascali, however, this was institutionalized, publicized by international organizations and channelled into an elite circuit. Through design of the microenvironment, the explosive contradictions of metropolitan structures were subjected to cathartic irony and sublimation to enter the sphere of private life."

Manfredo Tafuri (*Progetto e Utopia*, Editori Laterza, Bari 1973)

The COLONNA DI PIATTI
or the investigation of everyday expressions
(“pass me that stack of dishes”)

In 1969, while he was still studying architecture, Gianni Arnaudo wanted to experiment with a new material more common than noble porcelain. He therefore applied for a job as a worker at the Ceramica Besio factory, using a false name precisely so as not to exploit the friendship of Marco Levi, the firm’s owner, with his father Albino Arnaudo. As Gianni proved “good at drawing”, he was immediately assigned to the department of decoration responsible for painting the traditional cockerel trademark.
His true identity was obviously unmasked in the space of a few months. On being “paid off”, however, he presented Levi, a banker and patron of the arts, with a proposal for the production of a number of “tête à tête” sets to his own designs, including the “Colonna” of opaque black and white ceramic, the “Rha” with a Pop pattern, as well as a set for smokers called the “Colonna di fumo”.

Marco Levi intelligently realized the innovative value of the proposals, even though they were a far cry from the standard output of his factory, and produced a number of prototypes later exhibited at the historic fourth edition of Eurodomus in Turin.
In 1972, even before the exhibition *Italy: The New Domestic Landscape* at the MoMA in New York, Charles Stending, a great admirer of Italian design, visited the Gufram to negotiate the purchase of exclusive rights to the Multipli of Studio65. Arnaudo then accompanied him to Mondovì to meet Marco Levi and see the Colonna service. Stending was very impressed but his request for an initial consignment of at least 10,000 items came as a shock to Levi, who realized that he could not meet such a large order at such short notice and was obliged to decline.

Colonna di piatti
Gianni Arnaudo
Shown in the exhibition
Renouvellement complet de la Collection Permanente du Centre Pompidou, Paris
2002–2003

The Colonna di piatti is the fruit of collaboration between the long-established Vedova Besio & Figlio firm in Mondovì and Gianni Arnaudo, who came to work there in 1969.
Gianni Arnaudo started off in the department of decoration responsible for painting the traditional cockerel trademark on the plates and dishes produced by the Besio.
As head of company organization at the time, I was informed by the owner Marco Levi during one of our daily planning meetings that I would also be required to work with the young architect, who took a great interest in the art of ceramics and had put forward a proposal for a project so far removed from our normal production as to demand all the technical assistance that my colleagues and I could provide.
I was to ask all the heads of the various processing departments, and especially Arnaldo Bonardo of the moulding shop, to do their utmost to assist in the various phases of production without diverting too much attention from their normal commitments.
The design for the Colonna di piatti service put forward for consideration by Gianni Arnaudo was very different indeed from our normal run of production closely in line with the technical requirements of traditional ceramic crockery, which he practically ignored with his design for a service reflecting the irony of Pop Art.
The major technical difficulties encountered with Arnaudo's Colonna di piatti design lay in the combination of items not only produced by means of two different systems, namely moulding and pouring, but also differing in thickness.
It should be pointed out that the production of a ceramic item with accentuated differences in thickness gives rise to a problem of cracking during the initial drying and then, after the stage of bisque firing, the resulting bisque will absorb the glaze to different degrees because of the differing porosity of the elements produced by means of different techniques.
The end result after the second firing will be differences in colour and finish between the different elements of the service.
Arnaudo obviously did not want such differences to be visible and insisted on all of the items being the same.
The technical solutions we devised together made it possible to obtain what Arnaudo wanted, namely the complete uniformity of the Colonna despite the combination it items produced by different means.
Experiments carried out over a few months made it possible to achieve a satisfactory result with one finish of gleaming white and one of matte black.
We also experimented with cobalt blue and decided to use it for the small smoker's set of ashtray and cigarette case designed by Arnaudo.
Arnaudo suggested publicizing the new product by presentation of the Colonna di piatti at the edition of Eurodomus scheduled in 1972, for which he was already working with his colleagues in Studio65, so as to make his design and the factory known to the public.
For this occasion, the Besio also developed a new trademark with more modern graphic design to be stamped exclusively on the Colonna di piatti items to be displayed on the stand at Eurodomus. This was one way of making the innovative drive of the Vedova Besio & Figlio known also in terms of graphics.

Ennio Bonello
Head of organization, Fabbrica Ceramiche Besio

La colonna di fumo

The Colonna di fumo set
Ceramiche Besio
Design by Gianni Arnaudo
1969
Arnaudo Archives

Inside the Ceramica
Besio factory
Prototyping of the
Colonna di piatti
1970
Photo: Gianni Arnaudo

The Rha service
Ceramiche Besio
Design by Gianni
Arnaudo, 1969
Arnaudo Archives
Permanent collection
of the Centre Pompidou

SO THAT MANET NEED NO LONGER

roll over in his grave on hearing the remarks of all those who forget that his *Déjeuner sur l'herbe* was seen on its presentation to the public in 1863 as so subversive and scandalous as to be relegated immediately to the Salon des Refusés. This was not only due to the female nude of the model Victorine-Louise Meurent, in contrast with the fully clad portraits of the painter and another figure, but also to the unusual juxtaposition of warm and cold colours, the composition and the poses of the figures,

I added to the scene...

a fifth figure

Déjeuner sur l'arbre
painting on canvas, 2005
Gianni Arnaudo
Vitra Design Museum,
Basel and GAM, Turin
Permanent collection

This is what has been written about it:

Citation and shift in scale also characterize a recent item like Gianni Arnaudo's Déjeuner sur l'arbre (2005) for Gufram. In this case, an object of everyday life is stripped of its original function and embedded in an artistic citation (Manet's *Déjeuner sur l'herbe* of 1863) through a bold image that permits a play on words between the title and the name of the product, which becomes *Déjeuner sur l'arbre*. The colour green acts as a unifying element alluding to a natural world that has now been made artificial and reinterpreted in the Pop Art style. In this case, we have citation, change in scale, and an ironic relationship between nature and artifice.
The themes of various sections are interwoven here: *The Spell of Letters*, *Zoom Vision*, *Animalia*. The presence of Pop Art characterizations is transversal in accordance with the interpretive approaches identified for the narrative.

Luisa Bocchietto
Catalogue of the exhibition *Pop design. Fuori scala, fuori luogo, fuori schema*, 2008

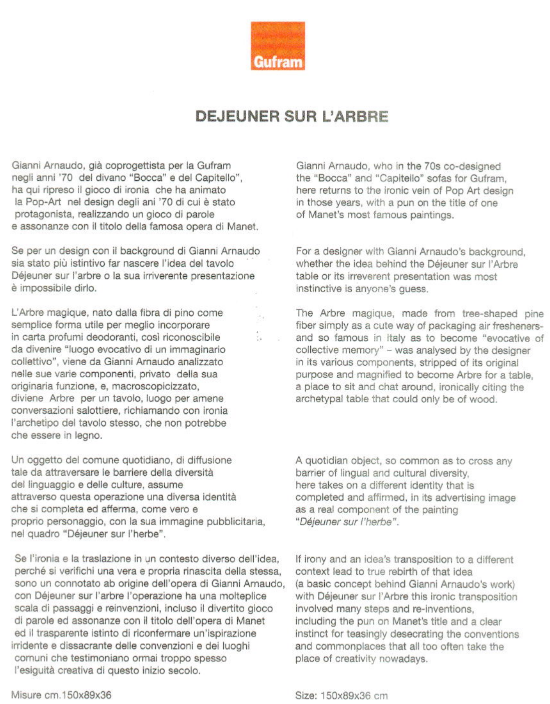

Gufram

DEJEUNER SUR L'ARBRE

Gianni Arnaudo, già coprogettista per la Gufram negli anni '70 del divano "Bocca" e del Capitello", ha qui ripreso il gioco di ironia che ha animato la Pop-Art nel design degli ani '70 di cui è stato protagonista, realizzando un gioco di parole e assonanze con il titolo della famosa opera di Manet.

Se per un design con il background di Gianni Arnaudo sia stato più istintivo far nascere l'idea del tavolo Déjeuner sur l'arbre o la sua irriverente presentazione è impossibile dirlo.

L'Arbre magique, nato dalla fibra di pino come semplice forma utile per meglio incorporare in carta profumi deodoranti, così riconoscibile da divenire "luogo evocativo di un immaginario collettivo", viene da Gianni Arnaudo analizzato nelle sue varie componenti, privato della sua originaria funzione, e, macroscopicizzato, diviene Arbre per un tavolo, luogo per amene conversazioni salottiere, richiamando con ironia l'archetipo del tavolo stesso, che non potrebbe che essere in legno.

Un oggetto del comune quotidiano, di diffusione tale da attraversare le barriere della diversità del linguaggio e delle culture, assume attraverso questa operazione una diversa identità che si completa ed afferma, come vero e proprio personaggio, con la sua immagine pubblicitaria, nel quadro "Déjeuner sur l'herbe".

Se l'ironia e la traslazione in un contesto diverso dell'idea, perché si verifichi una vera e propria rinascita della stessa, sono un connotato ab origine dell'opera di Gianni Arnaudo, con Déjeuner sur l'arbre l'operazione ha una molteplice scala di passaggi e reinvenzioni, incluso il divertito gioco di parole ed assonanze con il titolo dell'opera di Manet ed il trasparente istinto di riconfermare un'ispirazione irridente e dissacrante delle convenzioni e dei luoghi comuni che testimoniano ormai troppo spesso l'esiguità creativa di questo inizio secolo.

Misure cm.150x89x36

Gianni Arnaudo, who in the 70s co-designed the "Bocca" and "Capitello" sofas for Gufram, here returns to the ironic vein of Pop Art design in those years, with a pun on the title of one of Manet's most famous paintings.

For a designer with Gianni Arnaudo's background, whether the idea behind the Déjeuner sur l'Arbre table or its irreverent presentation was most instinctive is anyone's guess.

The Arbre magique, made from tree-shaped pine fiber simply as a cute way of packaging air fresheners- and so famous in Italy as to become "evocative of collective memory" – was analysed by the designer in its various components, stripped of its original purpose and magnified to become Arbre for a table, a place to sit and chat around, ironically citing the archetypal table that could only be of wood.

A quotidian object, so common as to cross any barrier of lingual and cultural diversity, here takes on a different identity that is completed and affirmed, in its advertising image as a real component of the painting "*Déjeuner sur l'herbe*".

If irony and an idea's transposition to a different context lead to true rebirth of that idea (a basic concept behind Gianni Arnaudo's work) with Déjeuner sur l'Arbre this ironic transposition involved many steps and re-inventions, including the pun on Manet's title and a clear instinct for teasingly desecrating the conventions and commonplaces that all too often take the place of creativity nowadays.

Size: 150x89x36 cm

The contact set up between industrial production and designer, deriving from 'subversive' intents, in order to break existing barriers between art and life out on the street, became a way of reinventing the image of these everyday objects.

The product, a symbol of mass consumption, was turned into a "spiritual place" with its own evocative properties, such as to make it a subject capable of interacting with his settings.

Pop Art showed that even a soup tin or a soap powder box could be celebrities like Marilyn Monroe or Mao Tse Tung, as could an air freshner like Arbre Magique. Arbre Magique, originally created out of a pine fibre as a useful way of incorporating deodorant scents in paper, so striking that it became 'a means of evoking a collective image', was broken down by Gianni Arnaudo into its various components, deprived of its original purpose and, after being 'blown up', turned into an 'Arbre' for a table, ironically conjuring up the archetype of a table itself.

An ordinary object, so popular that it crossed the barriers of both linguistic and cultural diversity to take on a different kind of identity, which was completed and enhanced, just like a real celebrity, by its advertising image borrowed from the painting *Déjeuner sur l'erbe*.

If irony and shifting an idea into a different context (so that the idea itself is quite literally regenerared) are a very distinctive feature of Gianni Arnaudo's work, in the case of Déjeuner sur l'arbre this operation has been reinvented on various different scales, including an amusing play on words and sounds referring to Manet's famous painting and the clear-cut intention of poking fun at conventions and most people's most deeply cherished certainties.

l'Arca no. 259, June 2010

Press pack
Déjeuner sur l'arbre
presentation
Salone del Mobile, Milan
2005

"Some say that Gianni Arnaudo has debased Manet's painting and some instead that he has actually improved it…"

Piero Dadone, journalist, *La Stampa*

...through the multiple levels of the operation,

which takes up the subversive intent with a cold colour in contrast to the original hues, now perceived as warm and classical,

which makes a scene that would cause no outcry today challenging once again,

which plays ironically with the evocative power of words,

which embeds an object of real life into the unreal, mocks the bourgeois world, and is itself the macroscopic transformation of an industrial product so common as to have become commonplace in the collective consciousness into a table made not of hard wood but unexpectedly of soft polyurethane,

which is a complete synthesis of Pop Art thinking and makes transversal use of all of its vocabulary and method, i.e. the selection of objects known to the mind and reworking of the same on other planes.

The Déjeuner sur l'arbre reflects the Pop approach to culture and art. As in all works of Pop Art, a consumer good becomes a new myth.

Gianni Arnaudo
with Gian Paolo Re
The Poltrona Frau stand
Palazzo Ex Poste
Salone del Mobile, Milan
2005

Some say that the Déjeuner sur l'arbre was purchased by the Centre Pompidou for its permanent collection as an example not of Pop design but of conceptual art. IN REALITY, IT IS ALWAYS RADICAL ART.

Déjeuner sur l'Arbre ®
table
Gianni Arnaudo
Gufram
2005

This is the last article of design produced by Gufram to have been bought by a museum after the 1970s.

(VICE VERSA) GENETIC MUTATION

Agit Pop was the name of a section of the famous exhibition *Les années Pop*, held by the Centre Pompidou in 2001 and featuring the various creations in the field of the plastic arts, cinema, design and architecture of the period 1956–68, which saw the birth of a popular culture triggered by the wave of economic and social renewal that began to manifest itself in both the old and new worlds, and led up to the protest movements of the 1970s. Those years saw the first works of Coop Himmelblau, Haus Rucker and Co, Zünd Up, Archizoom, Superstudio, 999, UFO and Utopie in France.

In Italy, some artists and young architects and designers evolved with culturally subversive intentions from the influence of Pop Art towards works with a critical and political content.

Described as “critical Pop” within the framework of *Les années Pop* and represented by the figurative works of Celmins, Vostell, Equipo 57, Monory and Pistoletto, this introduced into the world of art an aesthetic characterized by the apparent absence of the artist so as to focus on techniques of expression and the representation of objects drawn from the world of everyday life and commerce. This marked the starting point for the movement of radical design and architecture, which is not tied to a historical period, unlike Pop Art, but represents the continuity of the idea that the design of an object or a building is in any case an opportunity to assert that the author’s intent is to give birth to “critical” messages susceptible of interpretation also on other levels and independently of the function of the product created or the value of the technological research carried out in order to produce it.

The boundaries between art, design and architecture tend to blur or rather to converge on a concept of visual art through the importance attached to the meaning of the work.

The concept of critical design in Gianni Arnaudo’s work undergoes a “genetic mutation” that asserts itself as a “shift in perspective”, as also happens for many artists in other fields of the figurative arts.

Alba Basile

Fizzz®

Fizzz ® table
Gianni Arnaudo
Slide
2007

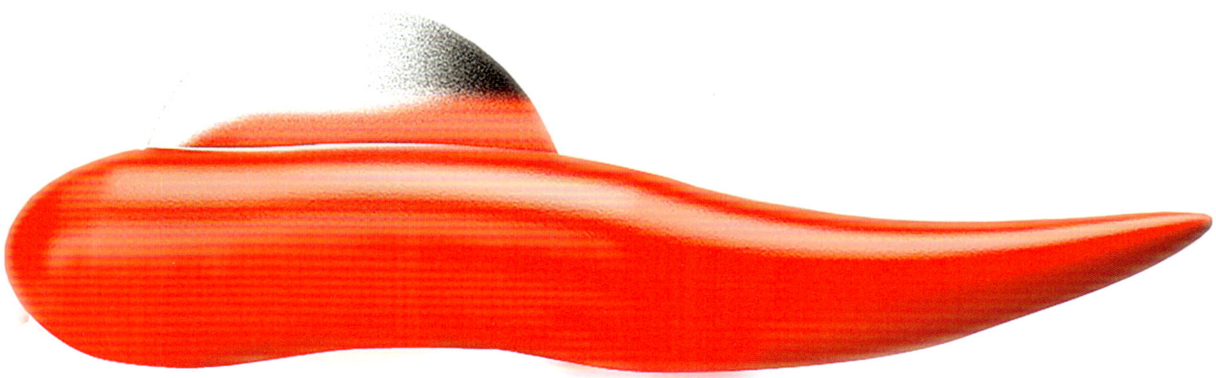

Napulì®
(handle to ward off bad luck)

2018

Italians as the world sees them

Aliko®

1982

Barel poduction
2019

A vision of living capable of arousing emotions: this is Aliko.
Seating created by Gianni Arnaudo for the world of discos, celebrated by the Vitra Design Museum in Basel with the exhibition *Night Fever*, recreating the unique atmospheres of legendary places like Studio 54 in New York, frequented by figures like Andy Warhol, Grace Jones, Rolling Stones, Carole Bouquet, Keith Haring and many others.
Art, cinema and music all together to stimulate creativity, which is always born out of revolutionary ideas developed outside the set canons.
The Paolina B, a disco born in a place on the border between Italy and France, was a world made so fantastic by Gianni Arnaudo that even the young Prince Albert of Monaco wanted to see it…
The design, the photos and Aliko are now on show in the Vitra's touring exhibition, hailed also by the *Wall Street Journal*, because originality is value and is so in everyday life for everyone.
Aliko conjures up the freedom of ludic thinking, the lightness of an original design, and a fragment of contemporary art.

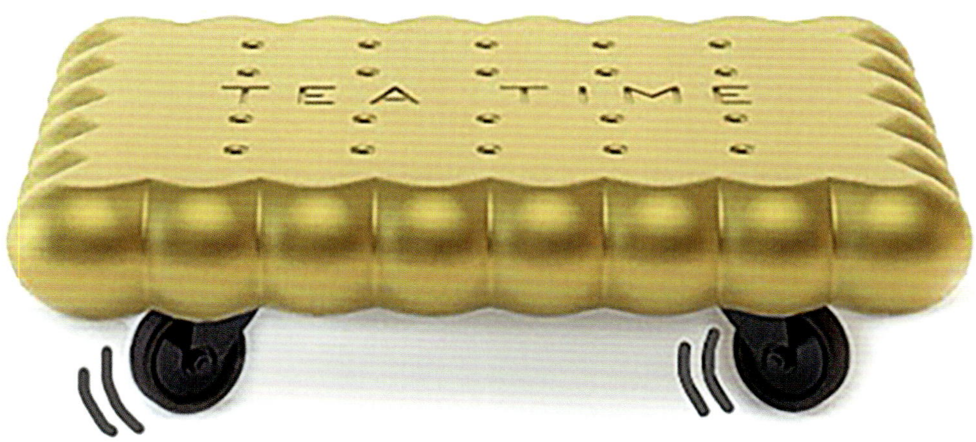

Tea Time®
(roaming table)

Slide
2013

Purchased in the meantime for the permanent collection of the ADAM Museum in Brussels

The real

Pandoro®

Slide
2013

(dedicated to all women)

Sonostufa®

2011

ALTERNATIVE FORM OF COMMUNICATION: Let's patch it up

PAPÌ®

2010

"Laughter can't have been a bad thing if it served to convey truth."
Umberto Eco, *The Name of the Rose*, 1980

Papì represents the archetype, the Platonic idea of the classic Italian armchair (used as a pretext), ironically revitalized with a multicoloured covering to suggest some emblematic aspects of Italian people and their deep desire for fun and vitality.

Faced with an interminable crisis, the colourful "patching up" of an Italy in dire straits expresses the desire for laughter and for self-deflating irony as a way out, a unique stimulus for creativity.

Soft and round like the ducklings of childhood, Papì is a unique article not only because it can be personalized through the combination of colours but also because the patch can be used to write a story, a family emblem, a protest slogan, a line of poetry or a declaration of love.

What matters here is the patch, not the armchair.

A MESSAGE THAT CAN BECOME EVEN MORE EXPLICIT…

DEDICATED TO SOCIAL NETWORK DODGERS

YouWelcome®

Divano Barocco
Reggia di
La Venaria Reale
Turin

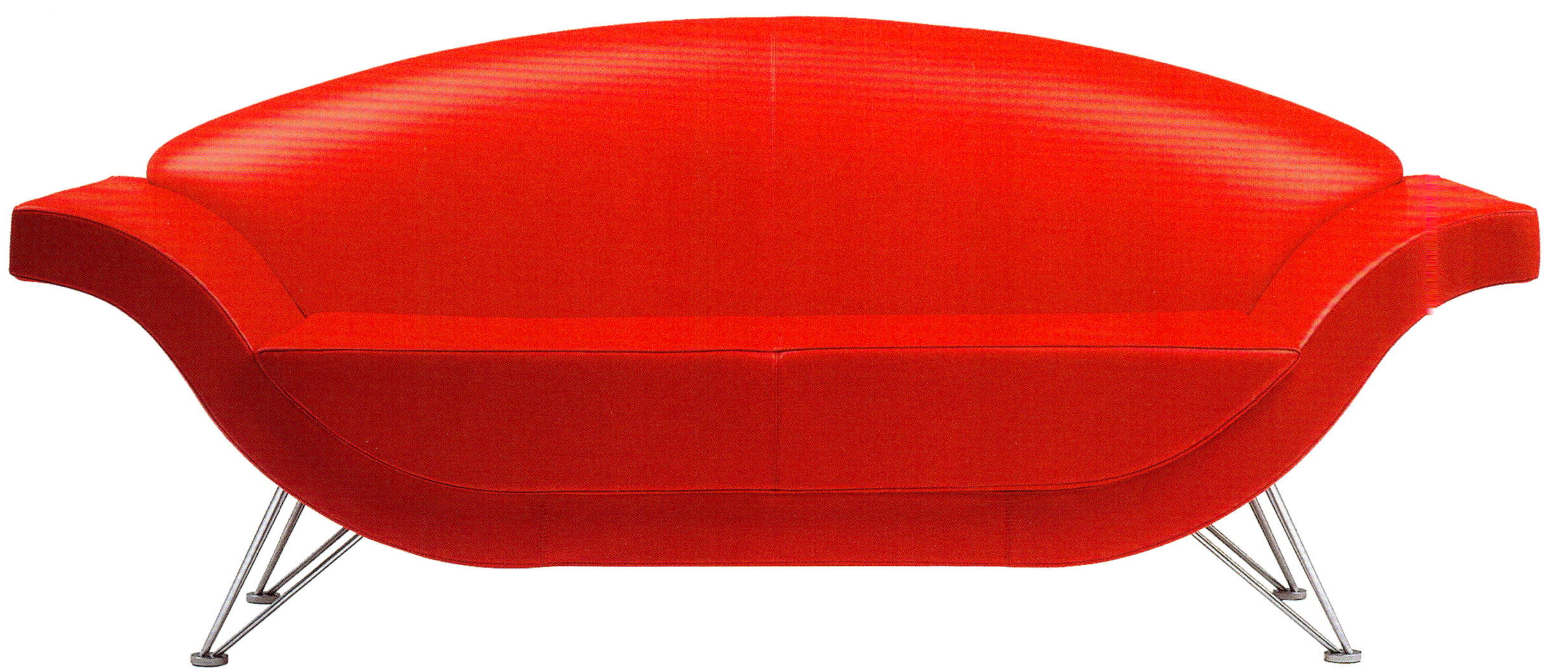

You Welcome ®
2001
Poltrona Frau

YouWelcome was one of the first works designed for Poltrona Frau. My wish was to respect the classic Frau style, with a contemporary reinterpretation.
YouWelcome modernizes the Baroque and the history of Poltrona Frau.

Sua Eminenza®

Sua Eminenza ® armchair
2017
Prototype Poltrona Frau

Mee-Thing®

2019

IN MEMORY OF THE DOG THEO

Cremino and Prendivoglia®

Slide for Venchi
2018

THE DOOR AT ITS HISTORICAL TURNING POINT

THE REVOLUTION IN THE CONCEPT OF A DOOR

1. Elimination of the symmetrical frame

The "Boulevard" door

2. Insertion of a mirror to double the space and introduce a third dimension

The "Sezione Aurea" door

3. Abolition of the frame and magnetic closing

The "MAG" door

1
The illusion of an avenue, the end of a convention

Boulevard ®
Gianni Arnaudo
Bertolotto Porte
2013

The idea of a door as normally and universally defined and its form, give or take minimal variations in decoration, has remained essentially unchanged through time: the door itself with its frame and handle, all in a rigidly symmetrical arrangement.

The value of the object has previously lain and been concentrated in its technology or more frequently its decoration, which constitutes the apparent hallmark of the different models and the different periods of architecture.

The Boulevard is a critical rereading of all this: First and foremost, symmetry is abolished as an emblematic value of elegance. Also abolished is the value of the material through the deliberate use of "authentic" medium-density fibreboard, a recycled and recyclable material, rather than high-quality wood and perfect lacquering.

The asymmetric frame is the debunking of a classical canon and creation of a real space beyond the door, beyond reality.

2
The illusion of a virtual space

Villa Barbaro, Maser
Crociera Room, frescoes
by Paolo Veronese, 1561

Sezione Aurea ®
Gianni Arnaudo
Bertolotto Porte
2014

The Boulevard and Sezione Aurea are biplanar creations. The real function is to suggest to a symbolic correlation between the time and space before and after the opening of the door. In the Boulevard, this aim is achieved by completely altering the ordinary proportions of a door, functionally changed so as to accentuate the perspective reading of the motif of a tree-lined avenue, which is not decoration but the suggestion of an ideally infinite path.
In the Sezione Aurea, starting as always from the name, the message is conveyed through the method of citations that are easily recognizable, not least because of reiteration in a host of different contexts including films, and highly symbolic.
The illusion is that of an open door, created by means of a mirror suggesting an opening onto a metaphysical space. The reflected reality is projected beyond the closed door.
The mirror not only links this door to critical Pop (Pistoletto) and recalls the frescoes of Paolo Veronese in the Villa Barbaro at Maser but also marks a further step because this time its function is essential to any reading of the message. While movement from one place to another can have a cryptic and irrational element, self-critical vision can make the change magical.
The Sezione Aurea goes beyond the traditional door, first and foremost by doing away with symmetry as an emblematic value and with the frame. The result is an object of design and a work of conceptual art at the same time.
The Sezione Aurea is the pursuit of the maximum expression of proportional space, which was invented in Italy and attained its first great manifestation with Piero della Francesca (1415–1492).
The red line of LED lights determines the "golden section" of the space.
In this sense, the theme of the door is more evocative than others in virtue of the host of interpretations documented in the history of art and the immediate metaphysical implications for the interpretation of space.

3

MAG

(a revolution with respect to history)

MAG ®
Gianni Arnaudo
Bertolotto Porte
2017

The MAG marks a revolution in the sector of internal doors by doing away completely with the frame, an element inherent for centuries in the very idea of a door.
The MAG appears to be detached from the wall, standing out like a painting or sculpture.
A new magnetic closing mechanism also makes it possible to dispense with the handle and create the effect of an object of art mounted on the wall, not least through the slashes of light obtained by means of a shiny white material on a completely coplanar surface of matte white.
Lucio Fontana changed the vision of art with his slashes on white canvases. So has Gianni Arnaudo changed the vision of the door.
The MAG is magnetic. The MAG is magical.

XY Door

XY ®
Gianni Arnaudo
Lualdi
2008
Shown in the photo
with a Napuli handle

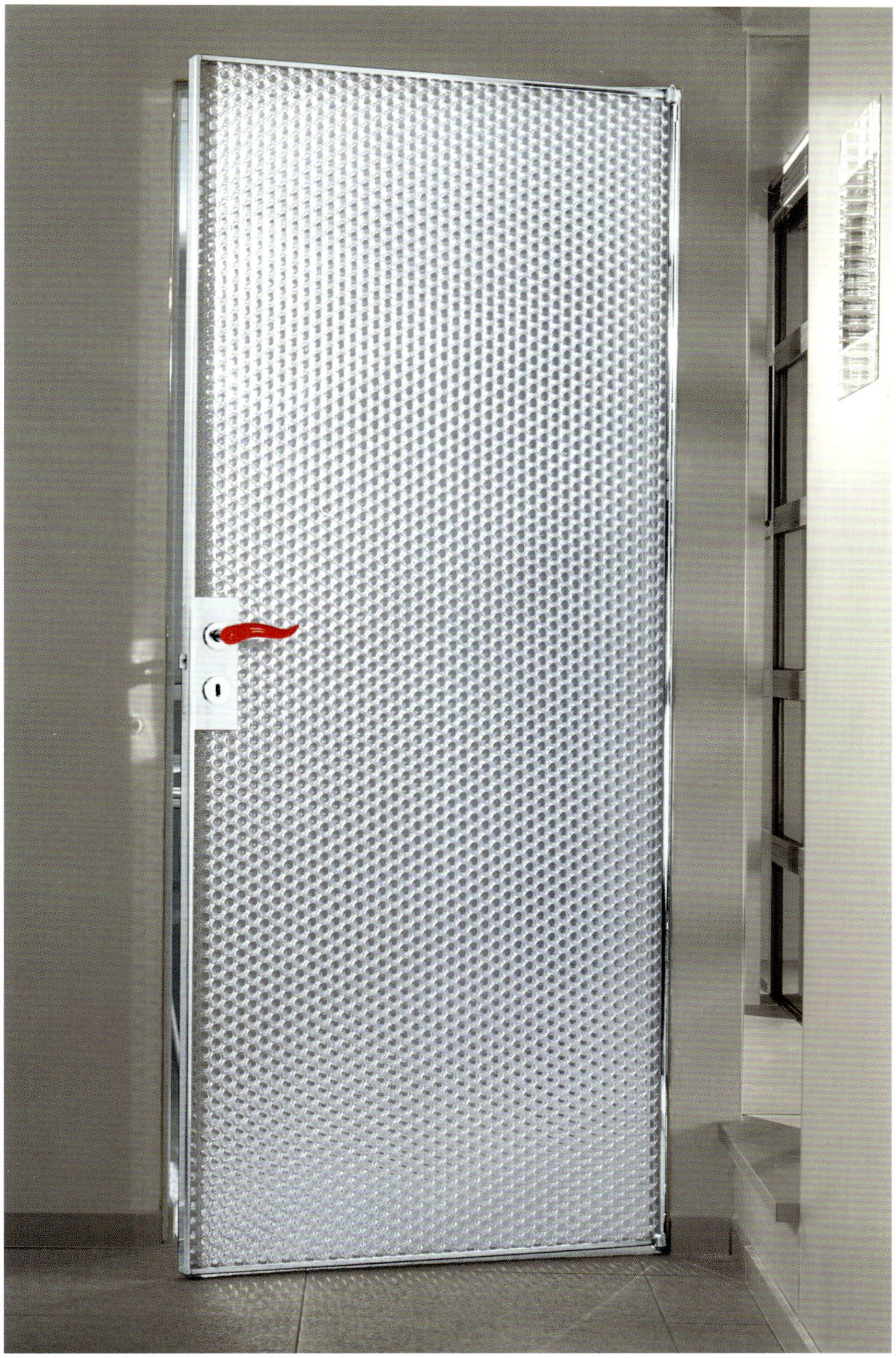

Castello di Montaldo
SPA

2006–2007

One of the Savoy royal residences near Turin has become a design hotel with a spa

Bocca (Studio65), pink version by Gianni Arnaudo, 2007 (subsequently named Pink Lady)
Photo: Dario Fusaro

The colour of Pink Lady was decided upon together with Gufram as a synthesis of the different shades of lipstick used by film stars. The search for a sensational solution is attested and documented by correspondence. And so it was.

Adopted at a later stage, the name Pink Lady was taken from a catalogue of a firm producing two-dimensional elastic fabrics. The colour referred to was, however, a different and much lighter shade of pink.

Graal in the Castle

Detail of the entrance to the spa
A mosaic path winds towards the swimming pool through a forest of five million nylon threads, thus creating a metaphysical landscape
Photo: Dario Fusaro

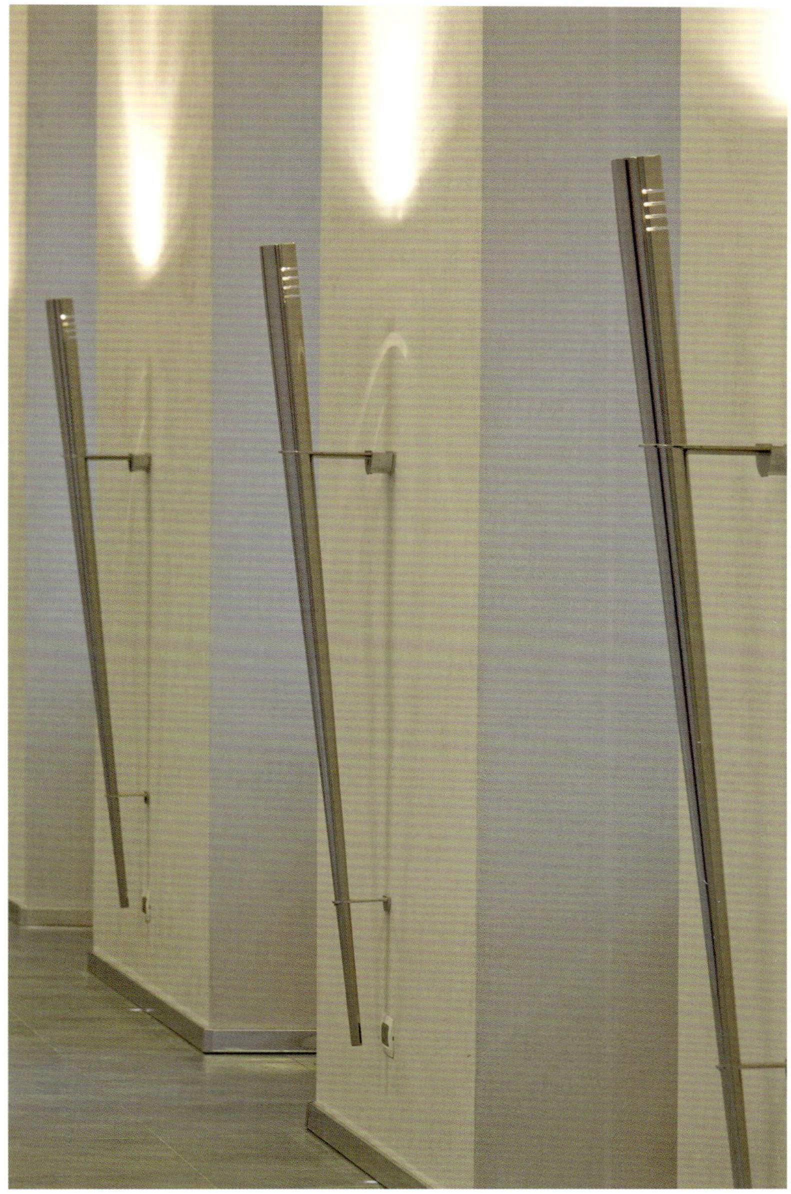

Wall lamp, 2007
Conical tubular body of cold-worked steel with shiny chrome finish
Indirect halogen light at the top and direct white LED in the lower section serving as a guidelight
Graal – FontanaArte

maximum provocation

IF ANDY WARHOL HAD BEEN AN ARCHITECT

this is how he would have designed this winery, **a building like an art installation**, a synthesis of Pop vocabulary ("zoom" vision and change in scale) and radical architecture, of which it has the nature and the function of **critical design**, as manifested with a strong and unique architectural act.

AN AUTHENTIC

CHANGE IN PERSPECTIVE

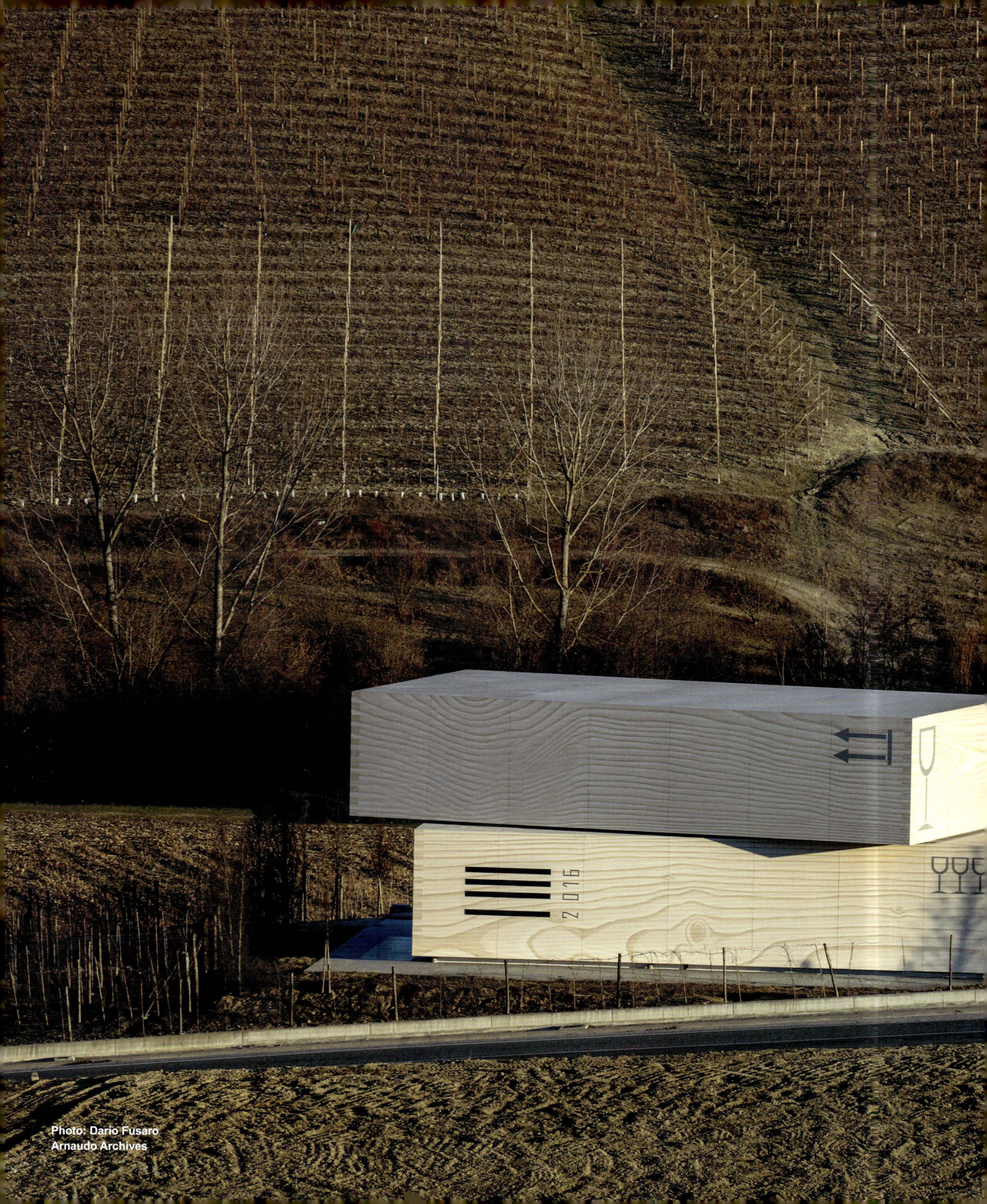

Photo: Dario Fusaro
Arnaudo Archives

"Without risk, courage and subversion there is no creativity, therefore there is no culture, industry, progress."
Oliviero Toscani
(*Dire, fare, baciare*, Rizzoli, Milan 2016)

ANTI-ARCHITECTURE as ANTI-DESIGN,

because my aim is not to provoke or simply shock, as is the fashion nowadays.
The design of L'Astemia Pentita – the idea for which was exclusively mine and no one else's from the very outset (my insistence is due to the fact that someone else has clumsily attempted to take the credit) – was born out of my way of using architecture as a visual tool to write a phrase with a different means. I have never followed fashion and my immediate choice of a particular material to clad the two volumes was not for ecological reasons – even though I am in fact a convinced environmentalist – but simply because wine crates are made of wood. Any other version of the facts – and I have read some hilarious ones – demonstrates a failure to understand the design.
The design of L'Astemia Pentita was presented at the 2012 Venice Biennale of Architecture and awarded the "100 progetti" national prize against competition from a hundred entries submitted by some of Italy's most important firms on 30 May 2018. The building encapsulates all the elements of Pop in formal terms, including the "zoom vision" and references to the advertising of consumer goods, but is radical in the thinking expressed because this is critical thinking. What matters in the design is neither the function nor the form nor the materials but the subversive message conveyed.
The choice of materials was very important. I opted for the Woodn composite of wood particles – recyclable waste from sawmills that would otherwise be thrown away – bound with resin adhesive. I chose it for its greater strength and durability. For the interiors, I decided on what is found in a wine crate and hence a material that reproduces cardboard and a bright red ribbon capable of joining together the different levels of sales and production. This is a far cry from the pursuit of visibility at all costs, as attested by all those who try to pass themselves off as chefs, artists and interior decorators or believe that buying a garage is enough to turn them into Steve Jobs.

Gianni Arnaudo

The original idea was to design the building in the form of two overlapping boxes, drawing inspiration from the wooden containers which used to be used for trading and selling individual bottles of wine, whose distinctive features are mirrored on a macro scale in the project.
It can be traced back to a fragment of the language used in the world of wine; in particular, it refers to the final part of marketing or, in other words, packaging, which has taken on fundamental importance during the present day: the container is becoming more important than its contents.
The design highlights the contradictions in a production system in which marketing and labelling often take precedence over the wine (however legendary it might be, as in the case of Barolo).
The project takes on greater meaning through ethical references by "zooming in" on the object, creating a sense of irony by "blowing up" onto a macroscopic scale the forms often used for appearing rather than the contents of being.

l'Arca no. 259, June 2010

L'Astemia Pentita. Some consider it too modern for a "classic" territory and others maintain that certain barriers should be dismantled. What do you think?

I agree that barriers should be eliminated. Safeguarding the identity of a territory should not be a pretext to consolidate a process of environmental "embalming" at the expense of the community's expectations. In the outcry raised by Maria Teresa Mascarello [a producer of Barolo who objected to the project], we can see all the logic of those who turn to memory so as not to face the present also in terms of vocabulary and creativity. It is like Barolo itself, which finds broad favour among the younger generations and in a whole range of very different international contexts in virtue of its authenticity as the product of a specific territory. What is certain is that the two macro wine crates of wood, the imaginative opening lines of a tradition, **awakened the territory from its slumber**.

What is your reading of the situation?

The debate generated by the work of the architect Gianni Arnaudo with the winery "L'Astemia Pentita" must be considered in the light of the role played by architecture today or rather of its **ethical value**. Where Arnaudo amazes us is in his conception of the **smaller external volumes** – the essential part of the winery being hidden underground, where the organoleptic properties of Barolo are born and shaped – as something placed there temporarily, ready to be picked up, **"in transit"**, on their way from the ground to sumptuously laid tables in homes and restaurants in every continent. He has combined aspects that look to the social impact on the territory, and especially on the young people, who are responsive to the simplicity of this vocabulary because it is so close to their own way of being, with a sense of **present-day relevance**. The **mega inscription** with printed characters also recalls the tags and messages of the graffiti culture, a culture diametrically opposed to the one celebrated by Pop Art. Writing that interprets the keen delight in "transgression", in yielding to Bacchus and the adventure of Dionysian inebriation that accompanies wine.

Extract from an interview with Prof. Massimo Bignardi, lecturer on the history of contemporary art, environmental art and landscape architecture, University of Siena.

Irene Graziotto, "L'Astemia Pentita: perchè ha 'dato fiato al sonno di un territorio', il Barolo", *I grandi Vini*, March 2015.

Photo: Dario Fusaro
Arnaudo Arch ves

Photo: Dario Fusaro
Arnaudo Archives

The hardest thing is to produce a simple design and convey a strong and evocative idea of a product, of a complex situation rife with different meanings.

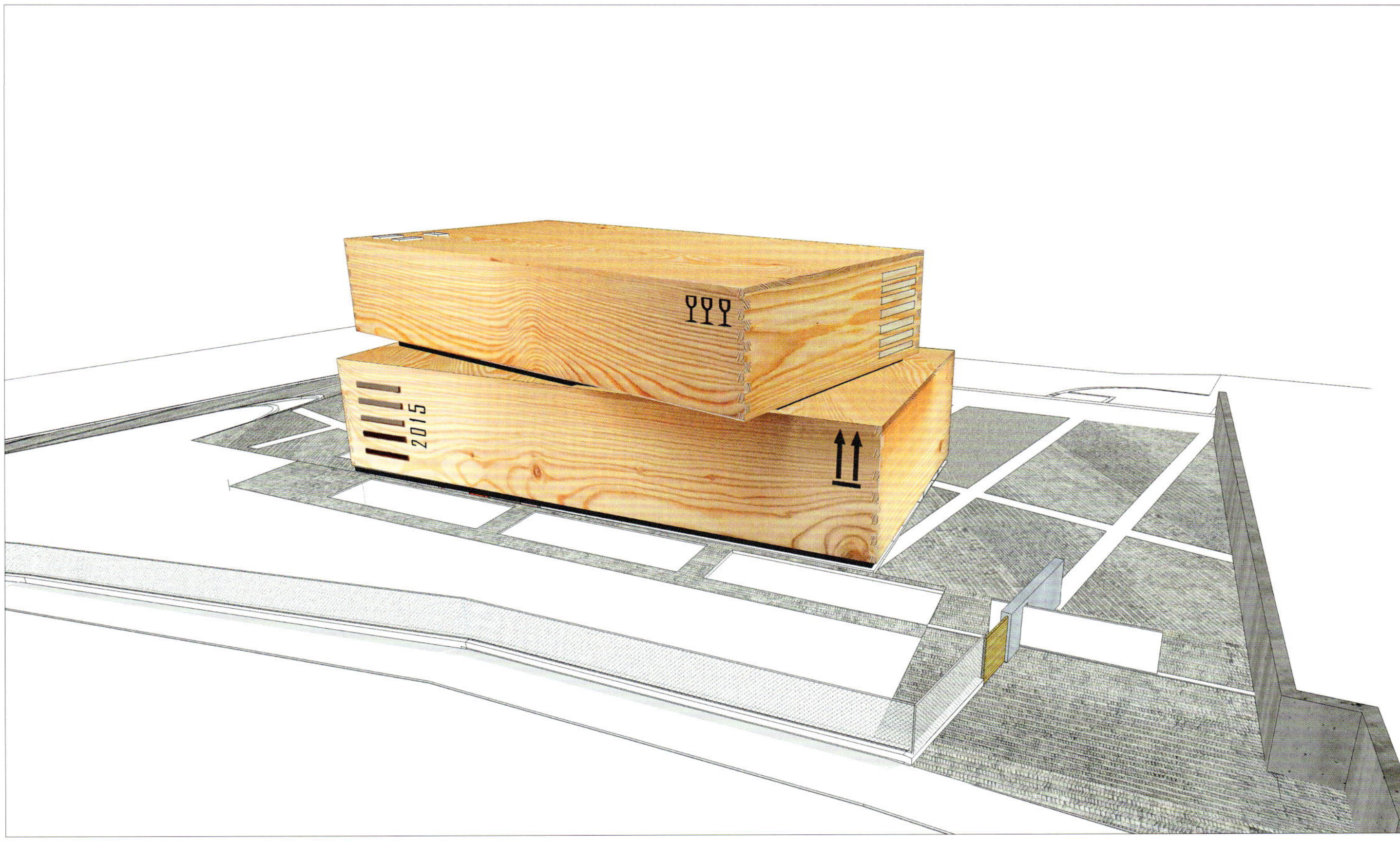

Photo: Dario Fusaro
Arnaudo Archives

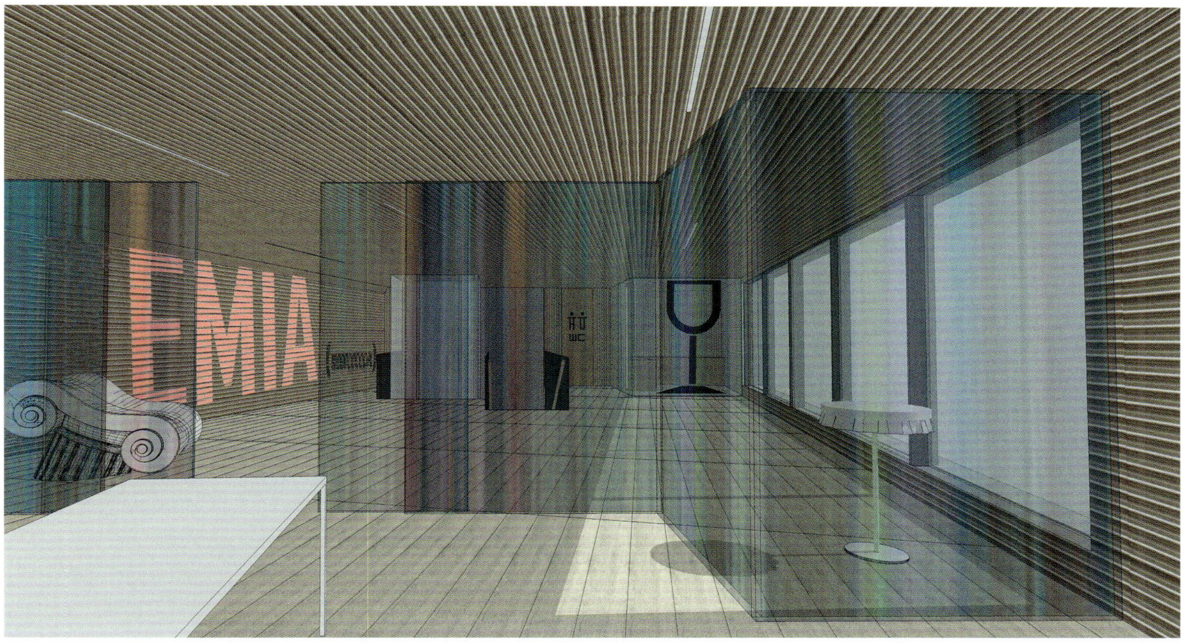
EMIA

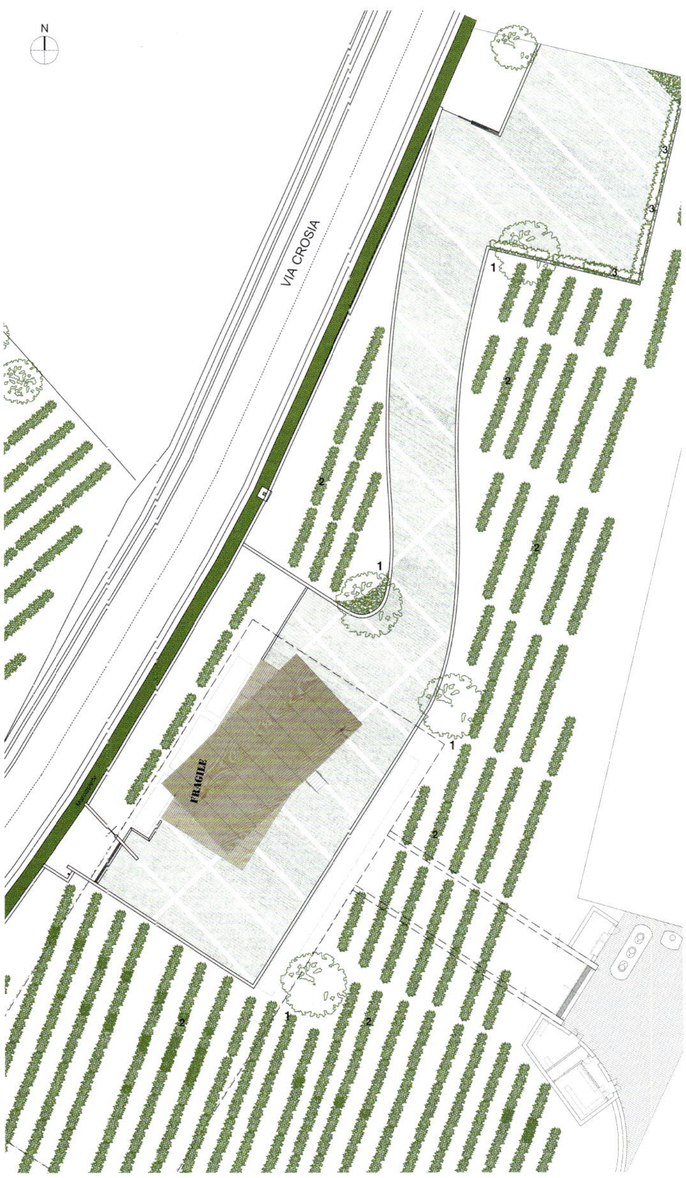
N
VIA CROSIA
FRAGILE

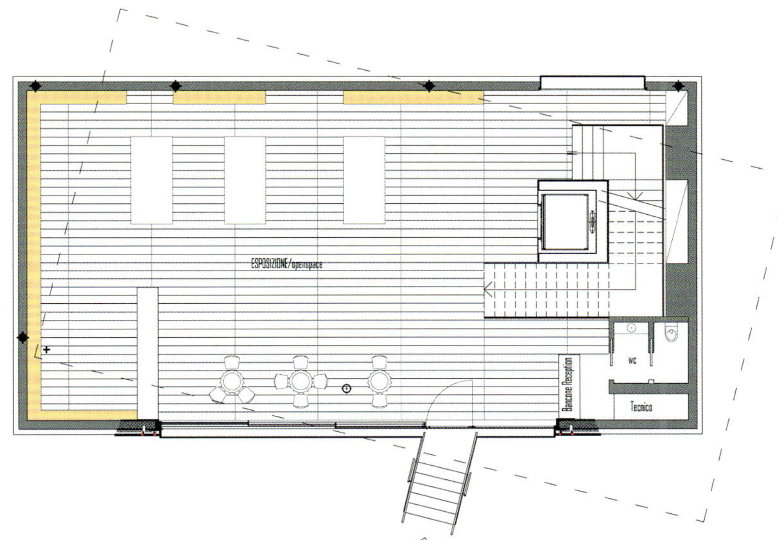
ESPOSIZIONE/openspace
WC
Bancone Reception
Tecnico

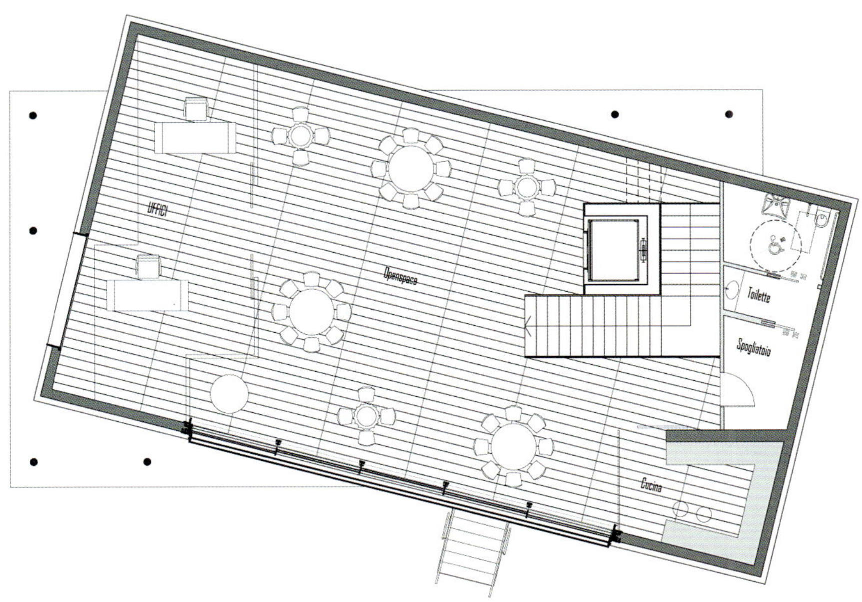
UFFICI
Openspace
Toilette
Spogliatoio
Cucina

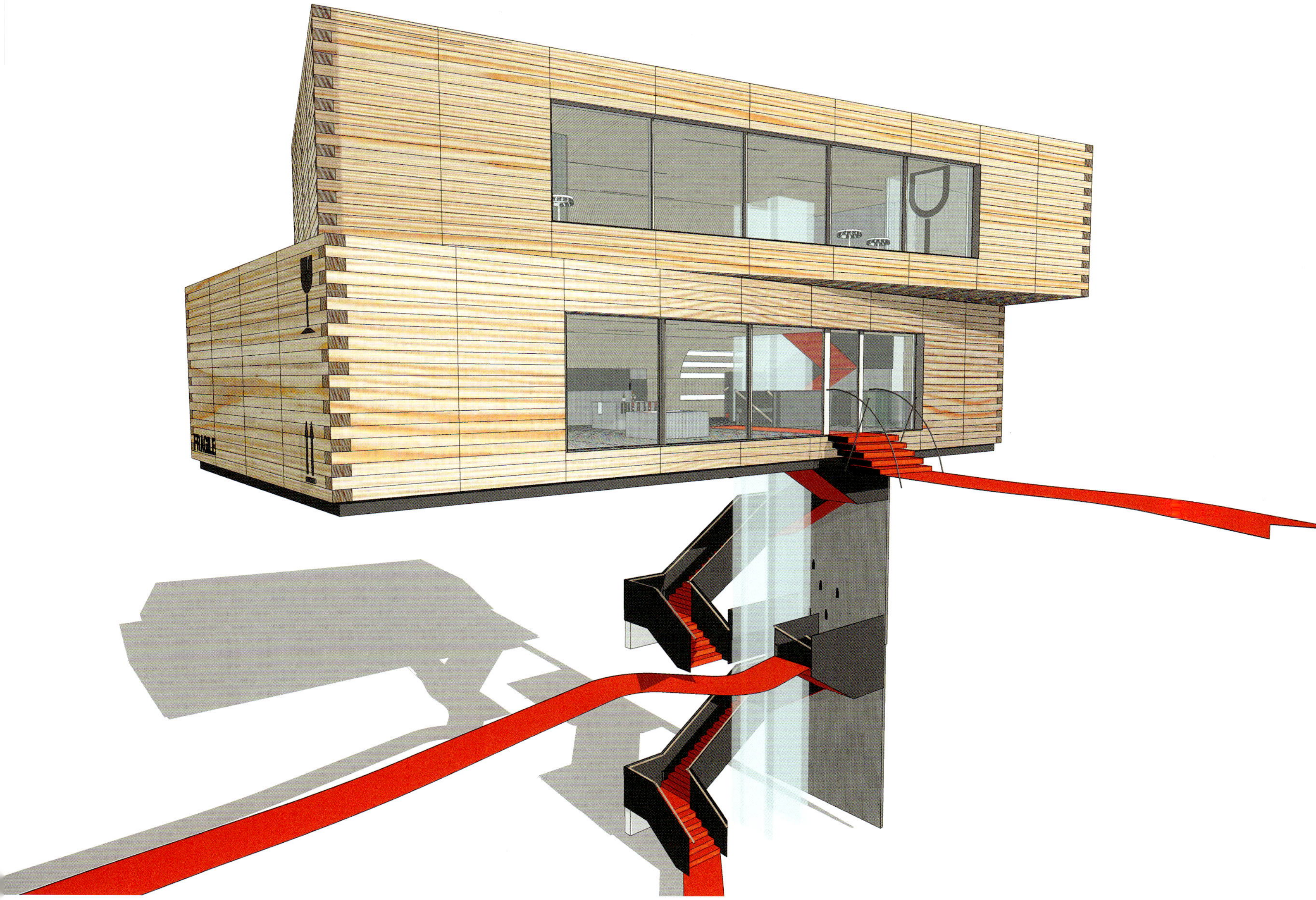

Arnaudo Archives

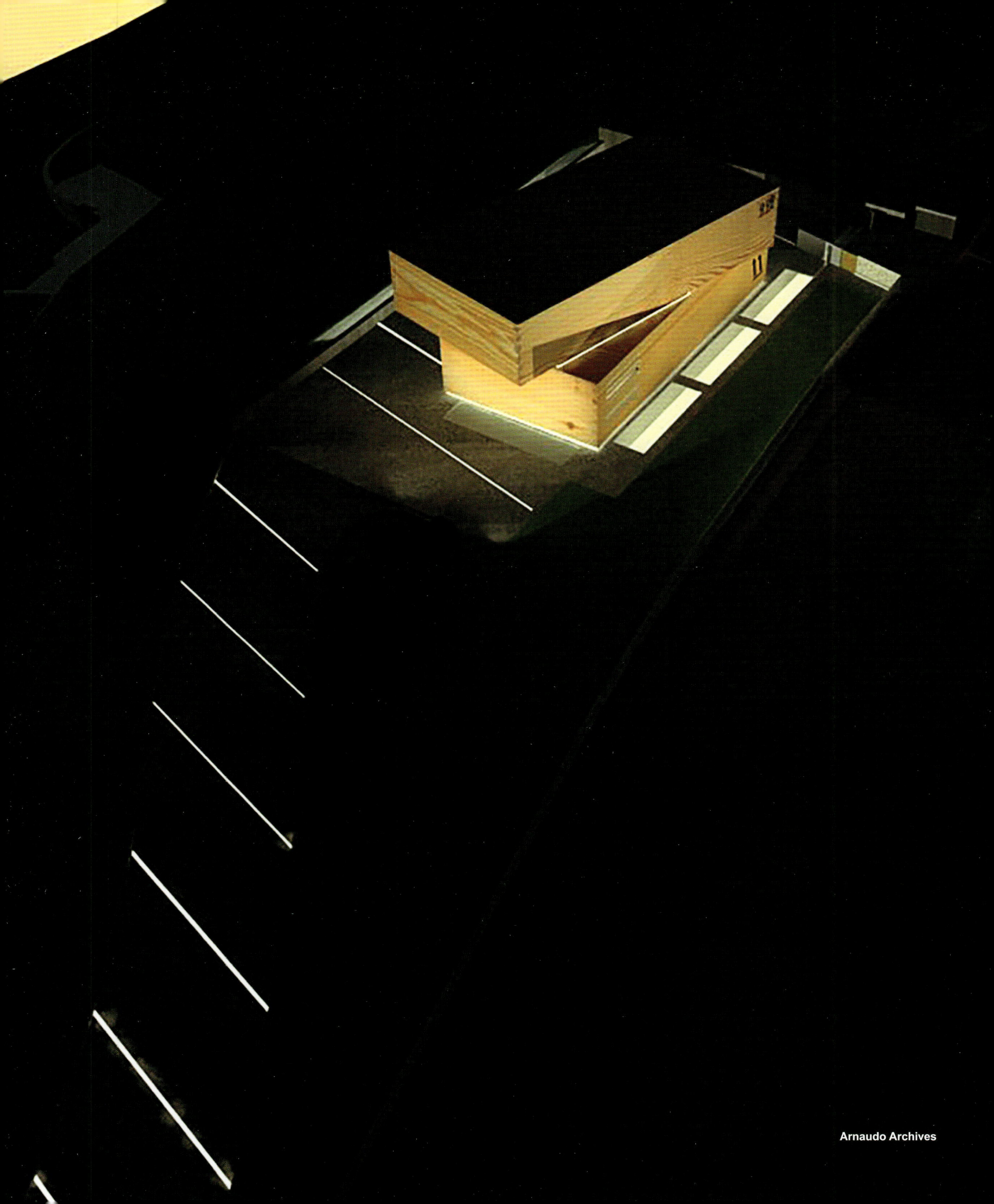

Arnaudo Archives

The ribbon that binds east and west
(the brand building)

Maina factory
Gianni Arnaudo
2015
Photo: Dario Fusaro
Arnaudo Archives

The architectural work must be bold and recognizable because, above and beyond its conceptual values, it strikes the public's imagination and fosters direct experience of an anomalous place.

MY DREAM OF A FACTORY AS A PLACE OF CULTURE

The "zoom" vision is, however, a way of transforming an object into a symbol, of making its evocative qualities immediately recognizable.

A huge red ribbon is wrapped around a panettone factory and the building becomes the first and most spectacular advertisement of the product, conveying all the subliminal messages of the festive occasion with one simple "sign".

The function of the building serves as a pretext for reproduction on the macro scale of the childhood emotion of Christmas, the joy of opening presents and boxes of candy and keeping the ribbon as a souvenir.

It is also a metaphor of what religious festivities have become for the contemporary world, because the playful red ribbon is wrapped around an industrial production centre of excellence.

Photo: Dario Fusaro
Arnaudo Archives

"There are buildings whose imprint is so strong as to rescue the surroundings from anonymity."

Photo: Dario Fusaro
Arnaudo Archives

A single element can recall different worlds and values if it is designed to reflect and to prompt reflection.

Photo: Dario Fusaro
Arnaudo Archives

The red ribbon, which appears to hang in the air (and conceals the staircase) multiplies the messages of the building ideally bringing the western world together with the east, with China and its traditional New Year festivities.

Kalla armchair
Pandoro stool
Design Arnaudo
Photo: Dario Fusaro
Arnaudo Archives

The recovery

recalling old pathways **to create new ones**

Arnaudo Archives

Interiors of the Terre da Vino building, an educational promenade on wine production designed as a walk through a museum with a spectacular view over a sea of barrels.

Arnaudo Archives

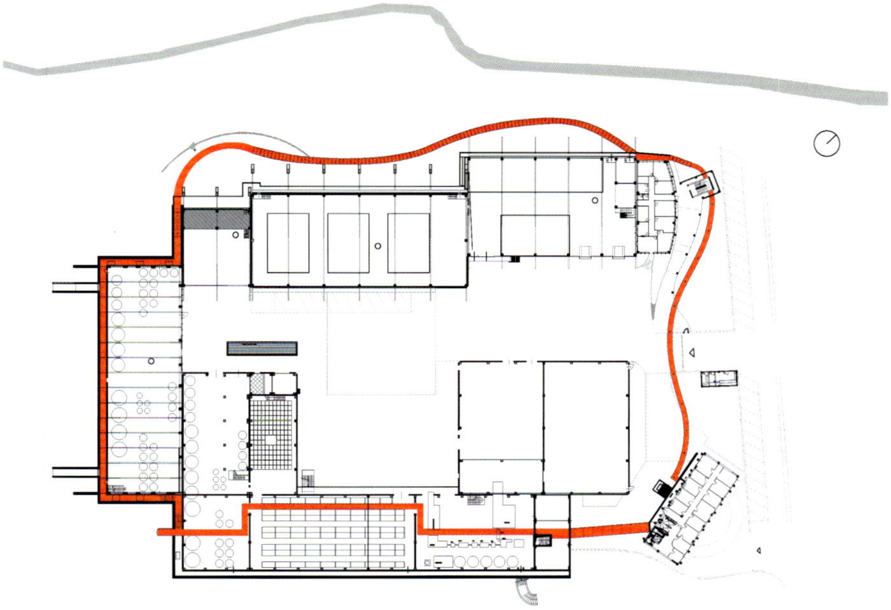

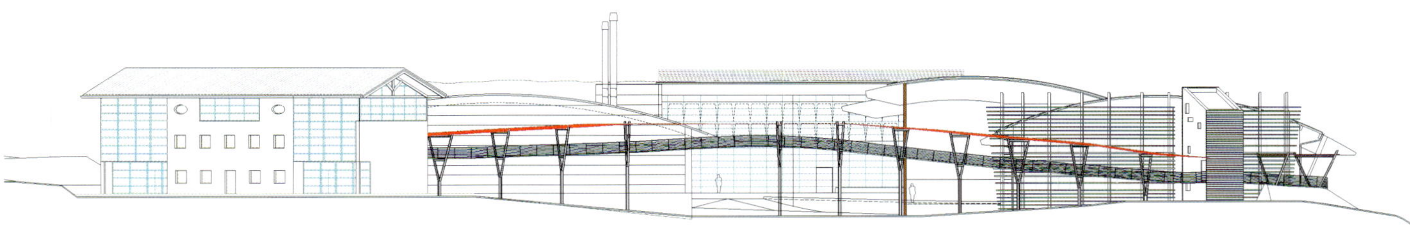

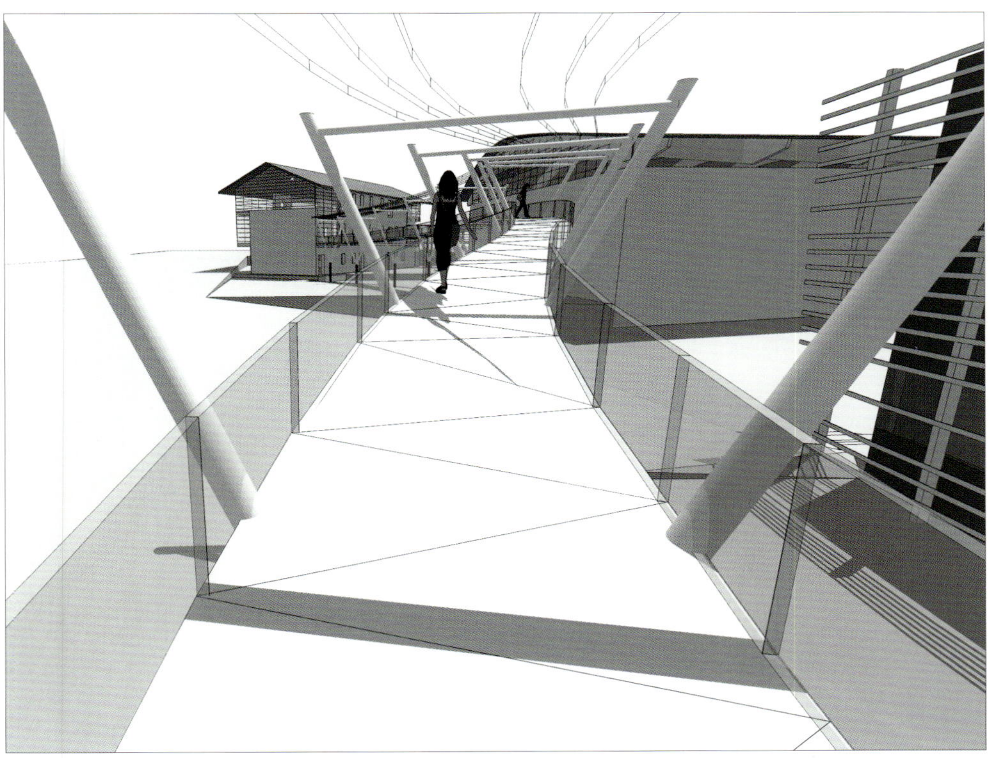

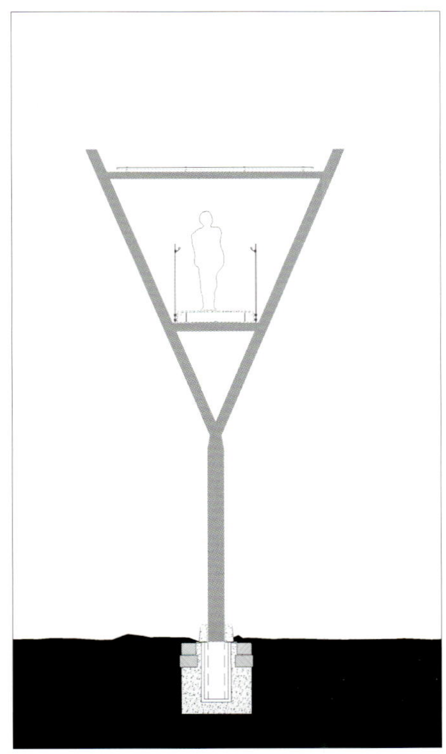

THE GHOST

This is not one of the many transparent buildings that characterize contemporary architecture,

Project for the
Ex-Arsenale
Cuneo

It is a ghost, the spectre of the avenue on the Napoleonic ramparts,

OF NAPOLEON AVENUE

because everything that is built for fashion has its *raison d'être* in the ephemeral dimension.

back to tell an almost forgotten story once again.

NAPOLEON BONAPARTE

ordered and devised the piano regolatore of 1802 for Cuneo, the city's first town-planning scheme based on a modern vision. He envisioned an elegant place, increasing the scenic elements and creating attractive trajectories with broad avenues and public spaces.

One of these avenues, which runs past the residential complex, was supposed to have two lines of trees providing shade for the promenade along the line of the demolished city walls. The town council only planted one. The other was to be created two centuries on as an act of homage to history.

This project was inspired by something Peggy Guggenheim once said when looking out across Canal Grande and musing that "the only imagine capable of competing with Venice is its reflection in the water". Anybody coming to Cuneo from Mondovì and crossing the bridge over the River Gesso will see a sequence of trees where the old city walls used to stand, with a backdrop of houses façades and the optical illusion of the outline of the trees being actually part of those façades. This effect can be captured at certain times of day when the sun projects the branches of trees onto the walls of the houses, creating seamless continuity between the natural and virtual backdrops.

The project actually came from this idea or, in other words, it inspired the design of the building facing onto the Avenue, whose outside bearing structures are shaped as if they were a projection of the trees incorporated in the façade, not just as a graphic symbol for its own sake and hence merely decorative, but as a reflection of a distinctive naturalistic feature unifying this cornice in the old city centre.

l'Arca no. 259, June 2010

Napoleon's city plan for Cuneo 1802

Photo of the façade
Arnaudo Archives

"...WE BECOME PRISONERS OF THE PAST THROUGH THE LOSS RATHER THAN THE WORSHIP OF MEMORY..."

Paolo Portoghesi
(*Dopo l'architettura moderna*, Laterza, Bari 1980)

Forgetting history

CREATES NON-PLACES, "COLD" AREAS OF THE CITY, DESERTED OR ILL-FREQUENTED, IN GLARING CONTRAST TO AREAS PERCEIVED AS "HOT", WHERE THE IMPRINT OF HISTORY HAS BEEN PRESERVED.
THIS IS EVIDENT IN THE AREA OF THE FORMER CATTLE MARKET IN CUNEO, AS IN OTHER CITIES, AND DOES NOT DEPEND ON THE PRESENCE OR ABSENCE OF GREEN SPACE WITH TREES BUT ON THE INSTINCTIVE PERCEPTION OF A PLACE AS DEVOID OF A SOUL AND ANY CENTRE OF INTEREST.

AS THE WINNER OF AN INTERNATIONAL COMPETITION HELD BY THE CITY OF CUNEO, IT WAS MY DREAM TO TRANSFORM A NON-PLACE INTO AN IDEA CAPABLE OF TURNING THIS STRETCH OF THE ANCIENT RAMPARTS INTO A CULTURAL CENTRE, CONNECTING THE MUSICAL CONSERVATORY WITH THE CONSTRUCTION OF AN AUDITORIUM ON THE AXIS OF ONE OF THE OLD NAPOLEONIC AVENUES, THE MEMORY OF WHICH IS IMPRINTED IN THE GLASS OF THE ENTRANCE.
COUNTLESS EXPERIENCES DEMONSTRATE THAT THE CREATION OF CULTURAL OPPORTUNITIES THROUGH THE REDEVELOPMENT OF PLACES THAT MAY ALSO HAVE SERVED A VERY DIFFERENT ORIGINAL PURPOSE, LIKE THE ZOLLVEREIN COAL MINE INDUSTRIAL COMPLEX IN THE RUHR, IS A SURE AND SUCCESSFUL WAY OF INJECTING VALUE, ALSO IN ECONOMIC TERMS, INTO AREAS DESERTED IN THE EVERYDAY LIFE OF THE PEOPLE.

THIS WAS THE DREAM FOR MY CITY...

The project was
the winner of
the competition
"La porta della città"
Gianni Arnaudo
in collaboration with
Studio AI - Turin

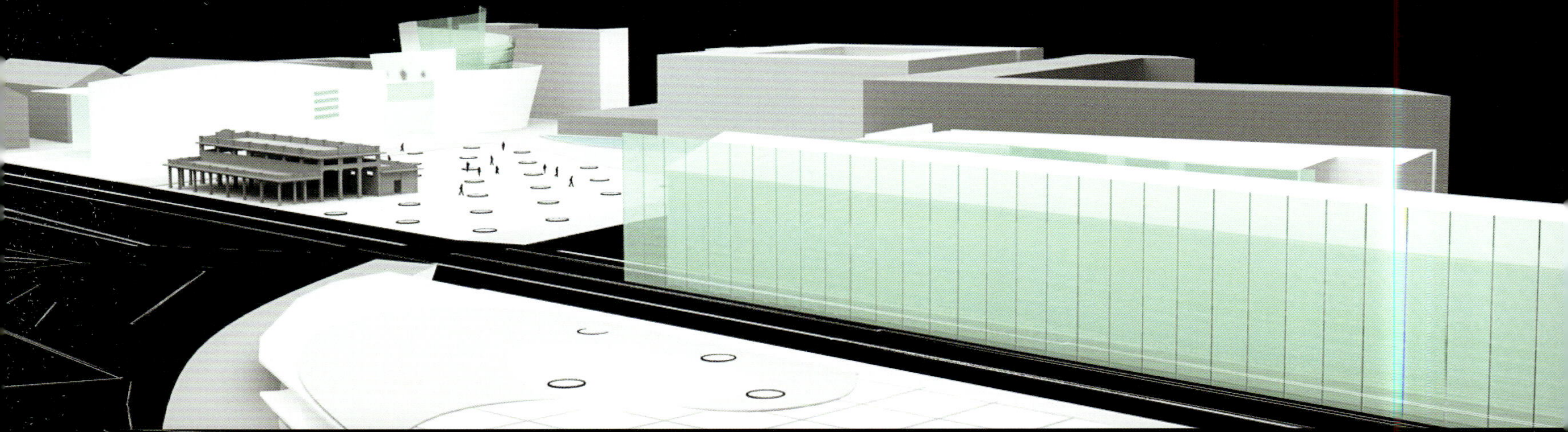

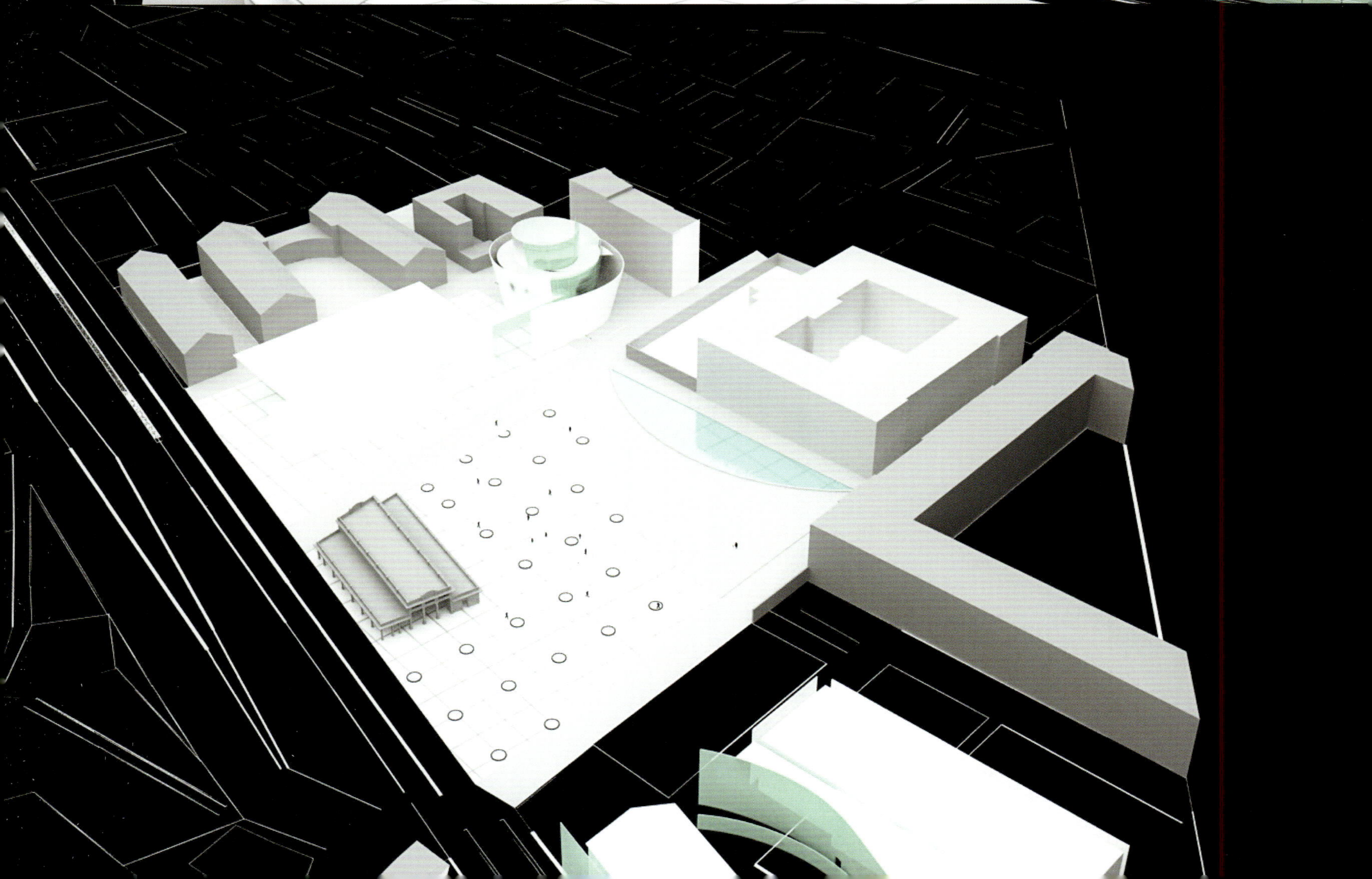

THEN IT WON THE COMPETITION BUT WAS LEFT ON THE DRAWING BOARD

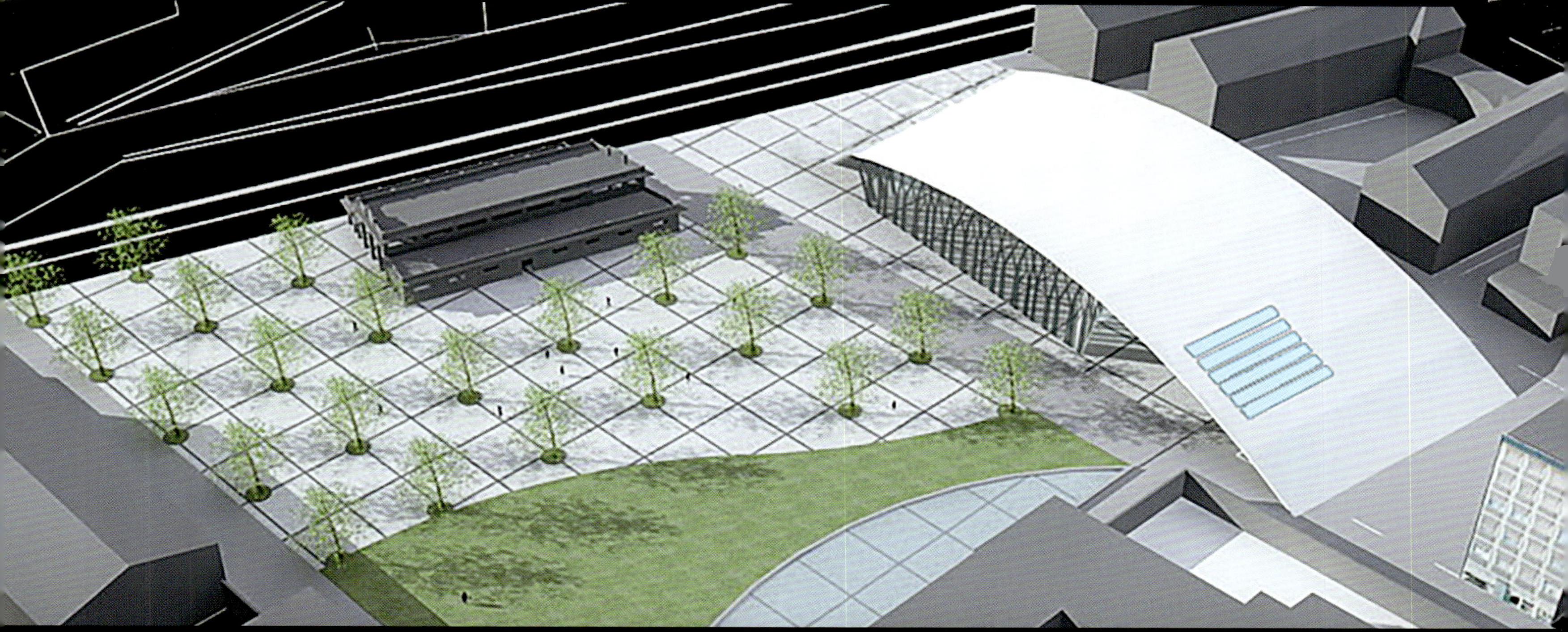

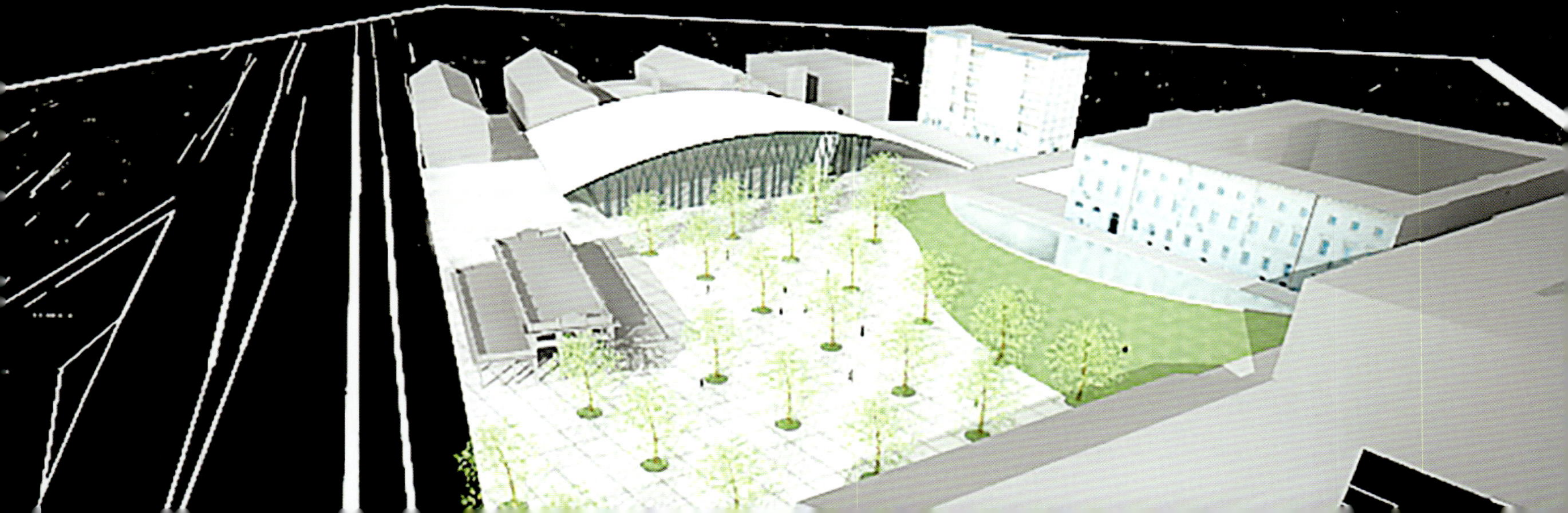

The project for Piazza
Foro Boario
Cuneo
2008–12

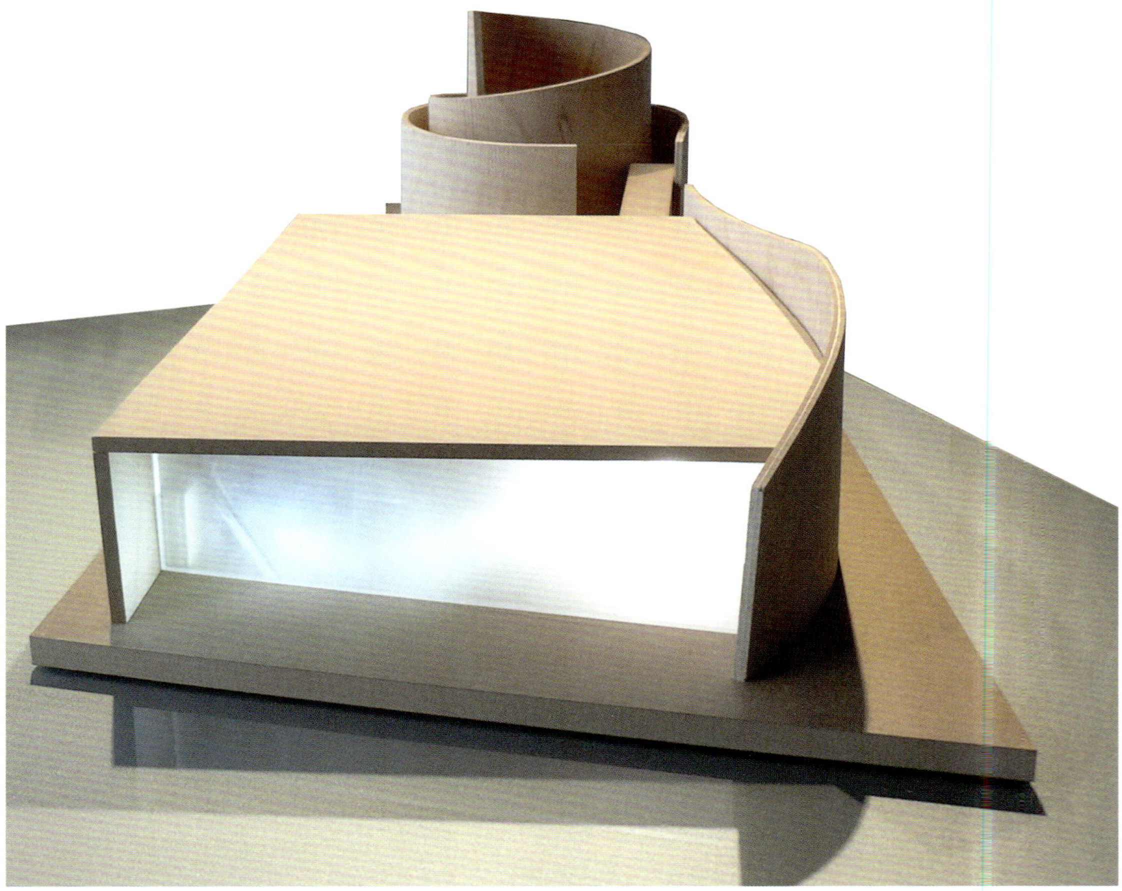

L'Île Rousse was a small harbour used by Corsican pirates and so I called it... La Marine Corsaire

Working in partnership with La Marine Corsaire, Gianni Arnaudo has transformed a suburban void into a place where local inhabitants can identify with their own history. Île Rousse, in Corsica, is an old fishing village in the north west part of the island, where history has left visible traces on the urban typology of the old town centre. There is also a port, once visited by pirates and a character like Pasquale Paoli, who, back in 1700, came up with the very modern town-planning idea for what is now the current fabric of the old village. Four parallel roads, an indoor market and a town square redesigned during the Napoleonic era, all surrounded by age-old sycamore trees and tall, harsh-looking buildings. A network of roads and backdrop constructions help breakup the wind.

Arnaudo's project is based on a clear and simple sign resulting from "tipping" the axis of the old town centre by 90° to create a large square acting as a new focus of local life. The fabric, surrounding buildings, and even the sheer size of the spaces, are a philological reproduction of the town plan devised by Paoli. The harsh elegance and simplicity in proportions of the building features of the housing translate the old-fashioned conventions once defining the façades, empty spaces, solid structures, heights, distances, internal pathways and traditional local materials into a very cutting-edge idiom.

Gianni Arnaudo
l'Arca International no. 116, January/February 2014

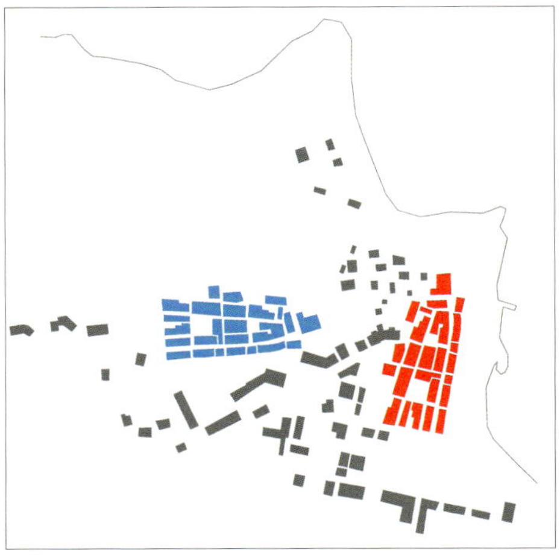

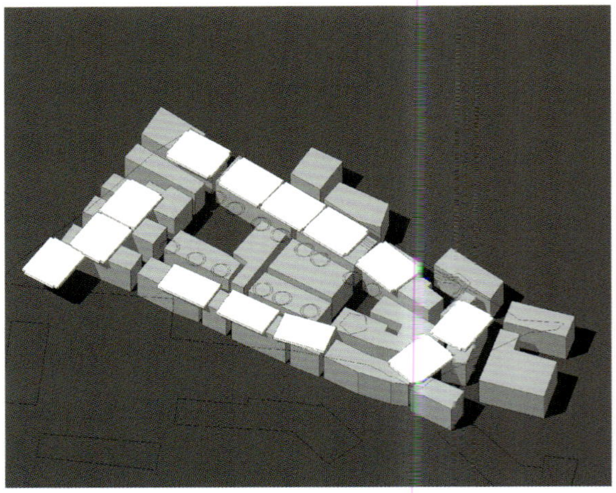

It was precisely a mirror that I used for designing, because I took the photo of the old centre of Île-Rousse and tilted its axis 90°.

The French always find a place to play *pétanque* wherever they may be, on the banks of the Seine in Paris or in the Camargue. It's part of their soul. This is why I conceived the Place de la Pétanque as the focal point of my design for the urban space.

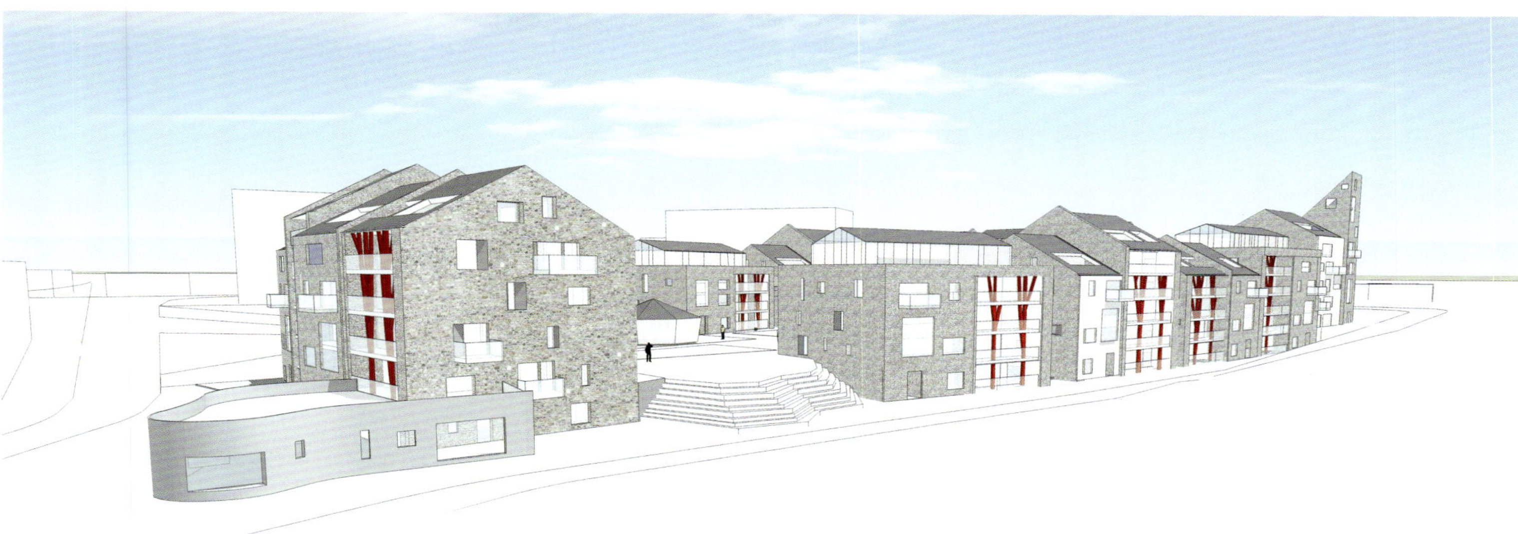

Napoleon's plane trees invaded France and, of course, Corsica too

Torre Pastor

The buildings in Montecarlo have an extraordinary capacity for appearing unclassifiable from the qualitative point of view. It is possible, within the Principality, to discuss architecture and confront the cultural consistence of its patrimony, in conjunction with the on-going debate in neighbouring European countries or in university and professional ambiences across the Atlantic.
In this small coastal territory, the environment is of a totally artificial nature: construction and territorial infrastructures have completely substituded every reference to the natural orographical conformation to the point of completely identifying itself with it.
For the subjects of the modern and tolerant Pricipality, Montecarlo's architectural heritage constitutes a renovated natural element and, as such, it is this heritage that sustains all human activity, as is the case, in different circumstances, in the rapport peasants have with the land, and fishermen with the sea.
In this extreme condition of dependence, architectural quality is a rather vague notion: the quality of a building depends on the kind of activity being practiced and on the potential for sufficient response to the financial expectations of those responsible for its realization. It is therefore not surprising that, seen from the outside, without entering into the unusual logic of the Principality, the architecture that has gone up inside its borders has not left any comment in its wake: there prevails a complete indifference to the built-up environment, reconciling the concrete effects of this international capital with our basic human condition by means of conferring a newfound dignity to all financial activity tied up with the construction sector.
Nevertheless, recently, in this world abounding in profound contradictions between the realizations of a visibly ostentatious opulence, a desire for renewal and the need to recuperate a credible image have been expressed with a series of new references, tied to several large projects, such as the extension of the Fontvieille area, the realization of a new tourist port and the urban reconstruction of the Condamine area and the railway lines that longitudinally cut across the Principality.
It is in this context that Gianni Arnaudo's project for a multifunctional building has been collocated. Some of his previous work in Montecarlo, such as the restructuring of the Engeco Pastor and Lamborghini Chrysler office blocks, served as preparatory experience and, in a way, as the definition of a programme, a linguistic expression. This new "unconventional architecture", realized a thousand kilometers from Parisian "transparency" in a world that is a long way off from the turmoil of cultural debate, has the subversive strenght characteristic of much of new architecture thanks to a generalized "diminishing" of the weight of each tectonic element of the building, which lends fresh lifeblood to an architectural image reduced to the minimum; to the point of rendering functionally efficient a building of simple yet dramatic contours, characterized by an impeccable and organic essentiality.
One cannot but notice, in the complex volumetric rapports, and particularly in the configuration of the topmost point of the vertical connections block; references to various realizations influenced by the mark of that branch of contemporary architecture which is most future-orientated, of which the project reproposes, in a newfound lean leitmotif, the unusual and innovative dovetailing of geometric volumes; whereas the structural geometry of the edifice appears to derive from a simple but precise "memory" of the lightness of sails, or the keels of ancient sailing vessels, while the steel trusses and pyramidal needle call to mind the masts of the old ships of the Grimaldi princes.

Alessandro Gubitosi
l'Arca no. 69, March 1993

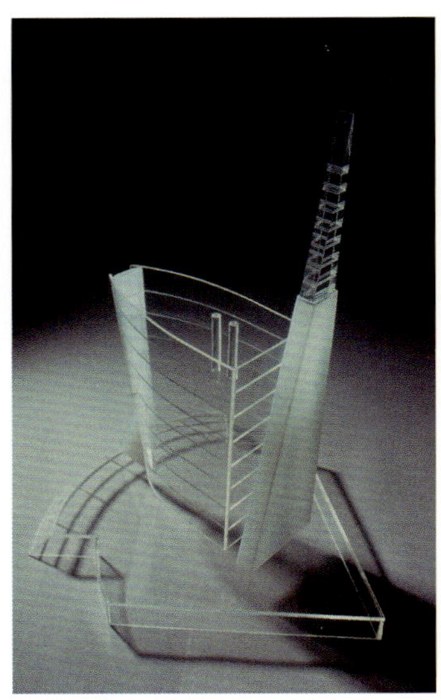
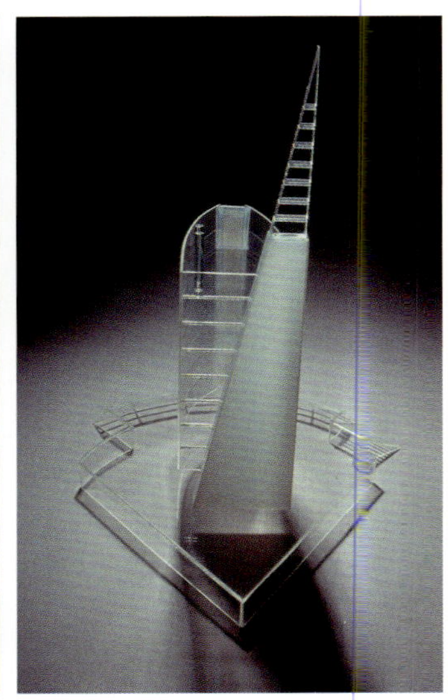

La Grande Halle de la Villette, Paris
SIAE 1992
Photo: Gianmario Cerato

Photo: Gianmario Cerato

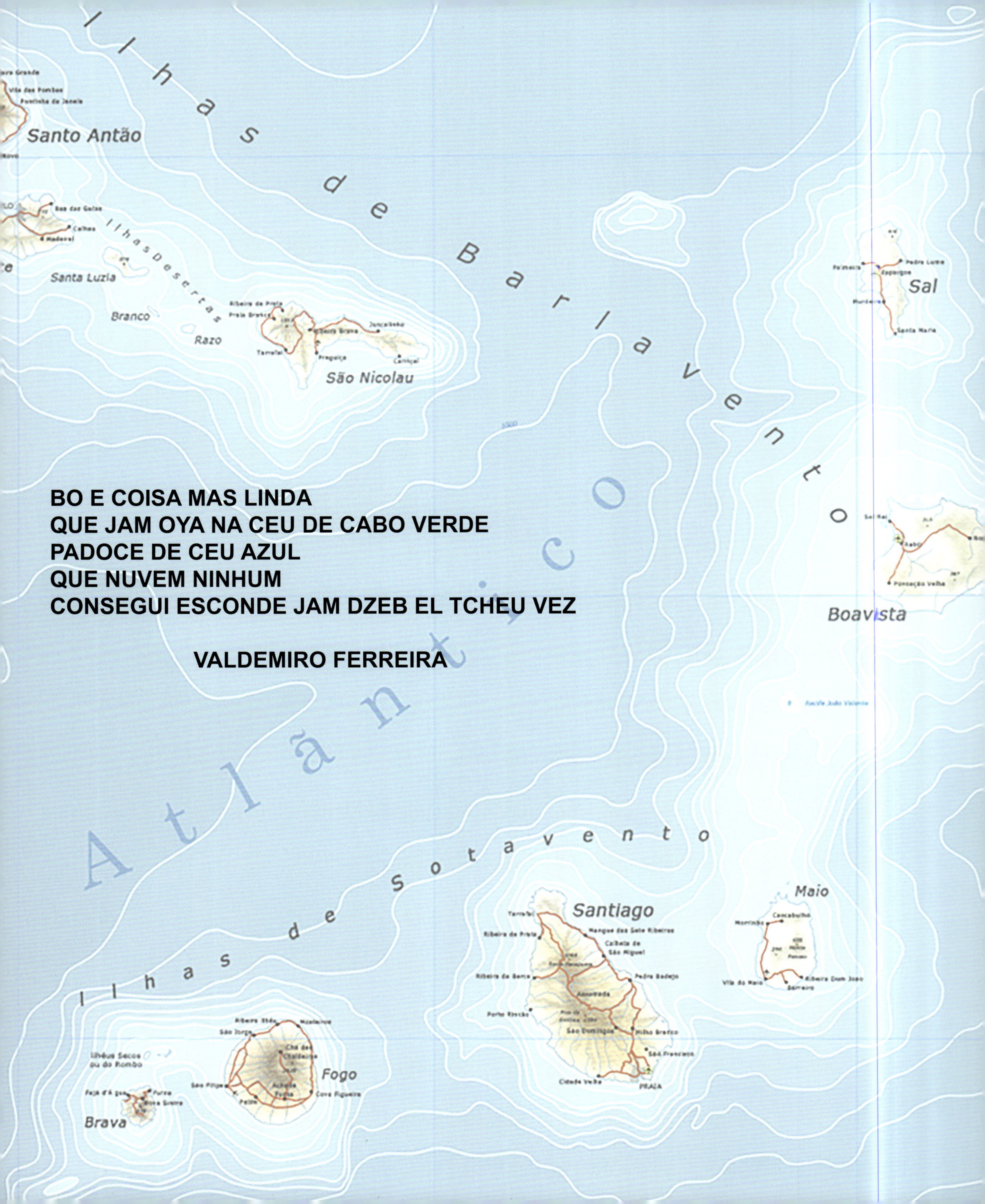

BO E COISA MAS LINDA
QUE JAM OYA NA CEU DE CABO VERDE
PADOCE DE CEU AZUL
QUE NUVEM NINHUM
CONSEGUI ESCONDE JAM DZEB EL TCHEU VEZ

VALDEMIRO FERREIRA

Stone, wood and volcanic rock

As a perfect stopping point for ships sailing between Europe and America, Cape Verde was a major hub for the trade in African slaves for a few hundred years as from the end of the 15th century.

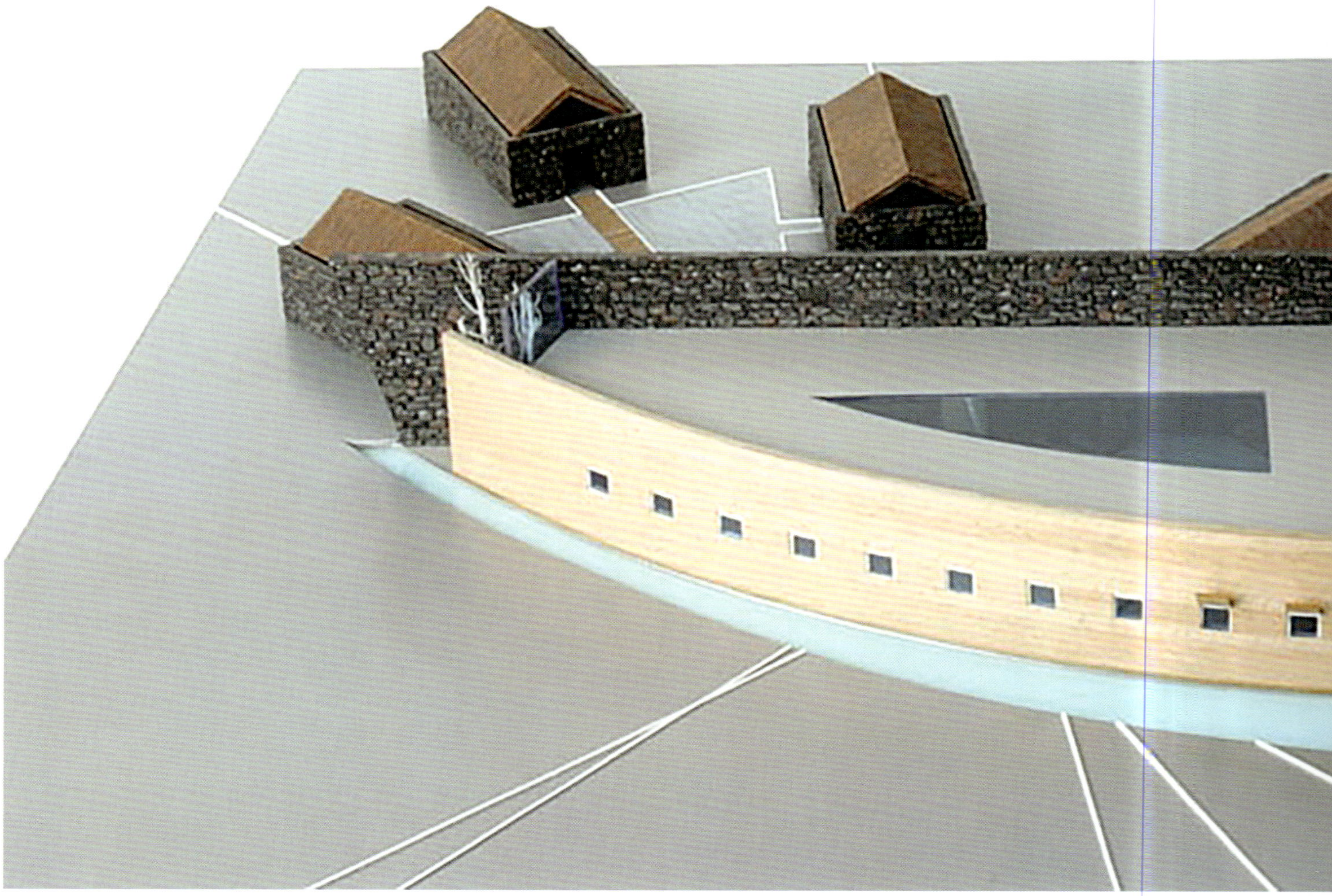

To ensure that this part of its history is not forgotten, the façade of the Cape Verde Museum is designed like the curved side of a ship with narrow windows to recall the despair of those who watched their homeland vanish in the distance.

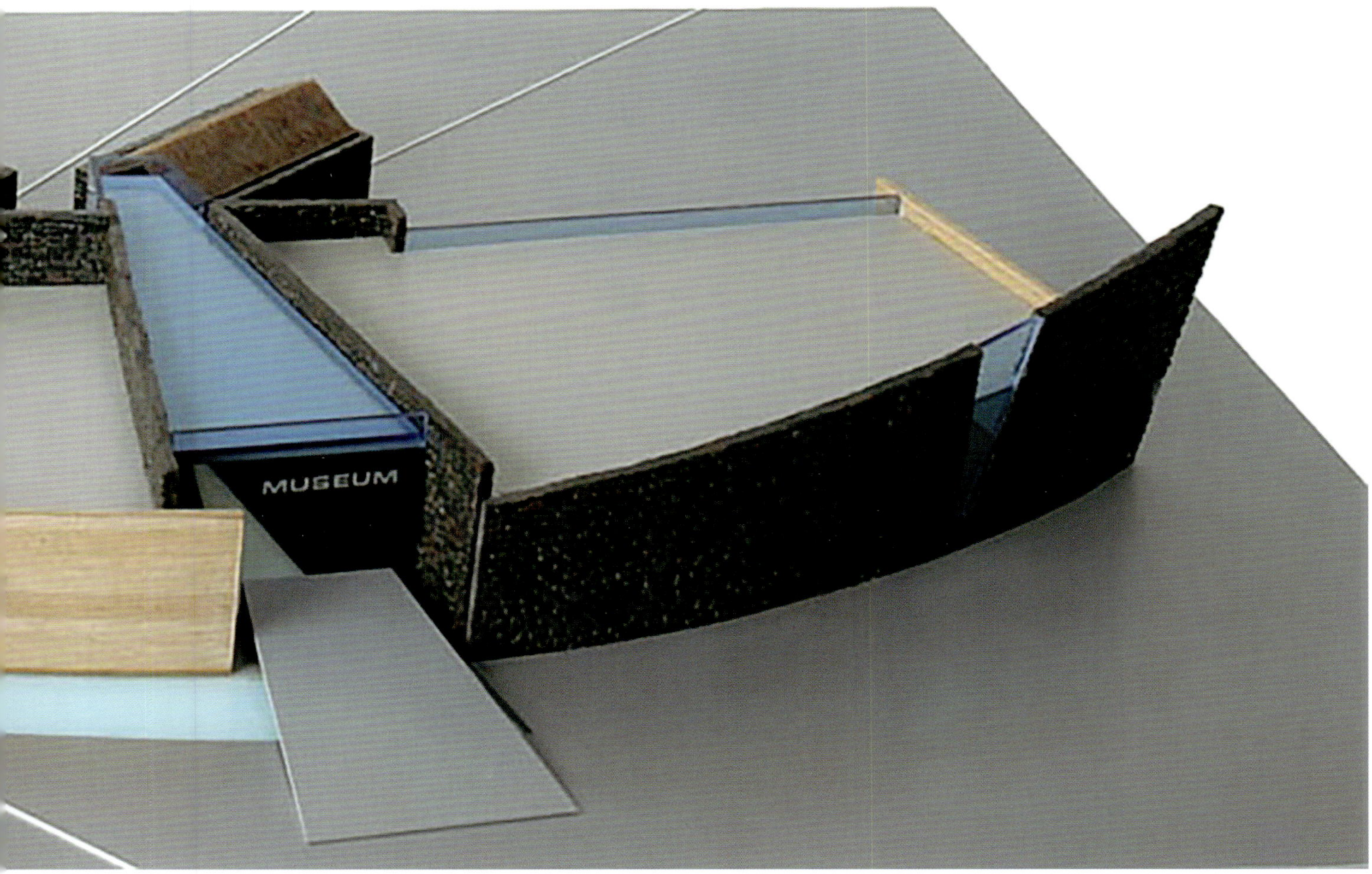

The islands of Cape Verde are very different from one another as regards geology and landscape, volcanic like Fogo or characterized by tropical flora like Mindelo.
The island of Sal, as its name suggests, presents desert-like salt flats lashed by hot winds. For many years it was the only harbour for visitors to the archipelago, who seldom reached the other islands, however, not least because of the poor connections.
The idea of the museum was born in order to give visitors some idea of the extraordinary heritage of a place and a people whose past deserves to be better known.
The building occupies an area of 800 square metres and develops in accordance with the architectural idea of a spiral path winding from the atrium through the display rooms at different levels, the library, the photographic and digital archives all the way to an upper deck offering a panoramic view of the salt flats in an almost metaphysical environment.
The small houses are laid out to reflect the position of the islands they represent, whose characteristics are illustrated to visitors in each. They are built in accordance with the architecture and materials typical of housing in the archipelago.

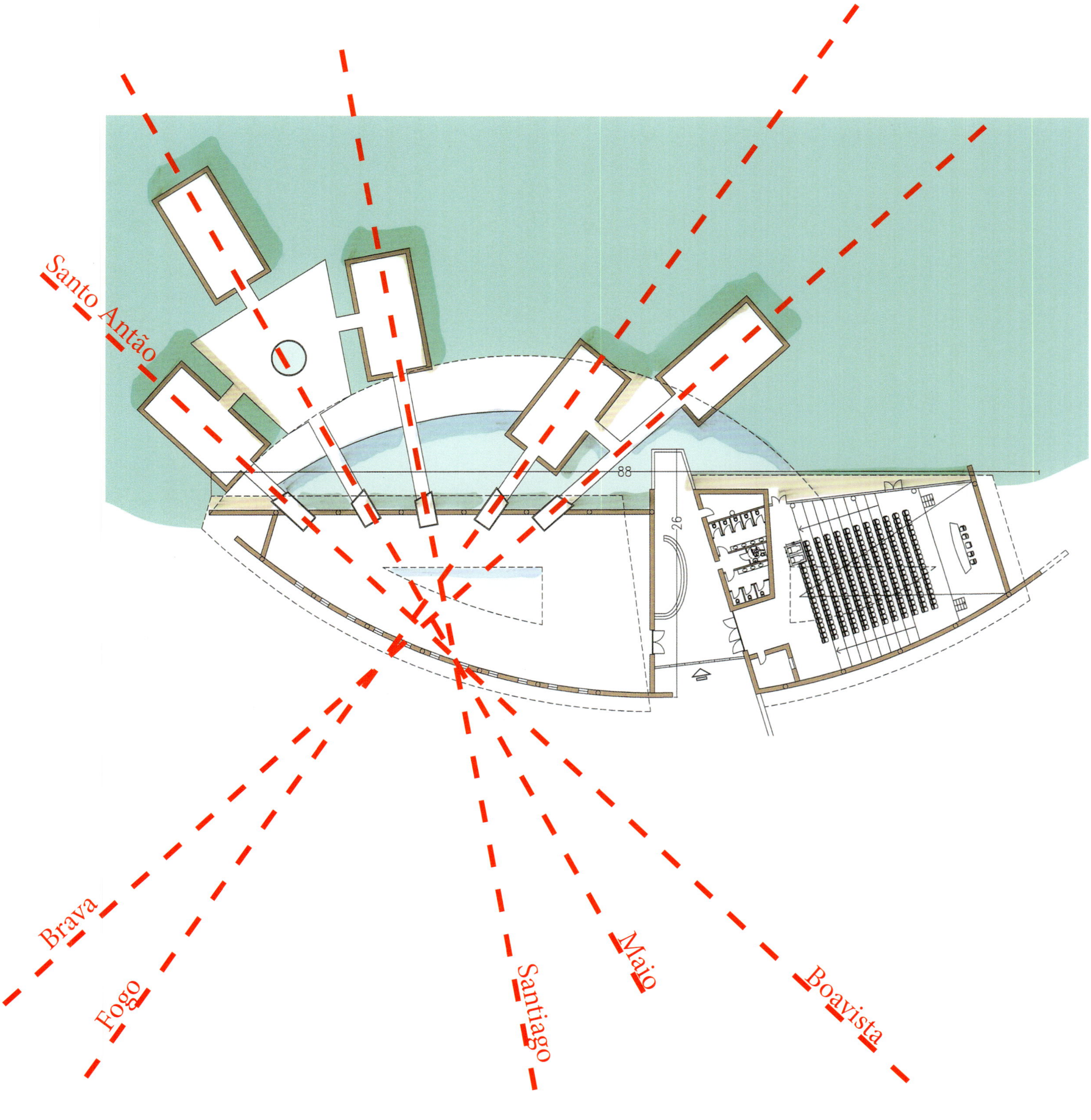
Santo Antão
88
26
Brava
Fogo
Santiago
Maio
Boavista

The Dromont plant

With the onset of industry, many enlightened businessman saw the architectural design of their factories as an important opportunity to enhance their own image and make their products more easily identifiable. For this reason they took quality architecture not just as a means of adapting to the latest requirements of their own manifacturing systems, but also as a way of conveying their own updated corporate philosophy, based on the concept of innovation, creativity and an awareness of external market demands.
As in many other cases, which now belong to the history of architecture, businessman set out to turn their own place of work into a powerful cultural landmark.
These are the underlying reasons characterising the aims and purposes of the Dromont company in Grinzane Cavour. The factory manufactures high-precision mechanical and electronic machinery for manufacturing industrial dyes and paints using everything from the kind of major production lines associated with multinationals to the automatic mixers used in paint shops and factories for creating different colours.
The project involved extending and upgrading an existing building, constructed quite recently but no longer able to cope with the manifacturing requirements and rather dated and post-modern looking in terms of its outside appearance. The idea was to create an extremely powerful architectural design connected to an "addition" (with a metal surface on the main side of the factory) to create a "strip", a sheet of metal abandoned on a green lawn up in the hills. A curved metal façade was created using "Alucobond" painting, exploiting its adaptability and flexibility.

The Dromont plant
Grinzane Cavour
2002
Archivio Arnaudo

It has been called the “Guggenheim of the Langhe”

The existing part of the complex was connected to the new section by a glass “skewer” which “perforates” the structures to create a compositional sequence.
This section, made entirely of structural glass, creates a suspended bridge for handling both the staff and utilities.
The guiding idea behind the project was to dematerialise the past: this operation was successfully achieved thanks to the help of wide glass surfaces built using Metra construction systems and Saint-Gobain glass.

l'Arca no. 259, June 2010

A wingbeat and its shadow

The airport of Cuneo-Levaldigi
Architectural design
by Gianni Arnaudo
Structural engineering
by Carlo Criscuolo
2004
Arnaudo Archives

The airport of Cuneo-Levaldigi

Meeting Centre of the Provincial Administration of Cuneo

Meeting Centre of the Provincial Administration of Cuneo
Cuneo
1996
Photo: Paolo Mussat Sartor

Model of the Meeting Centre of the Provincial Administration of Cuneo

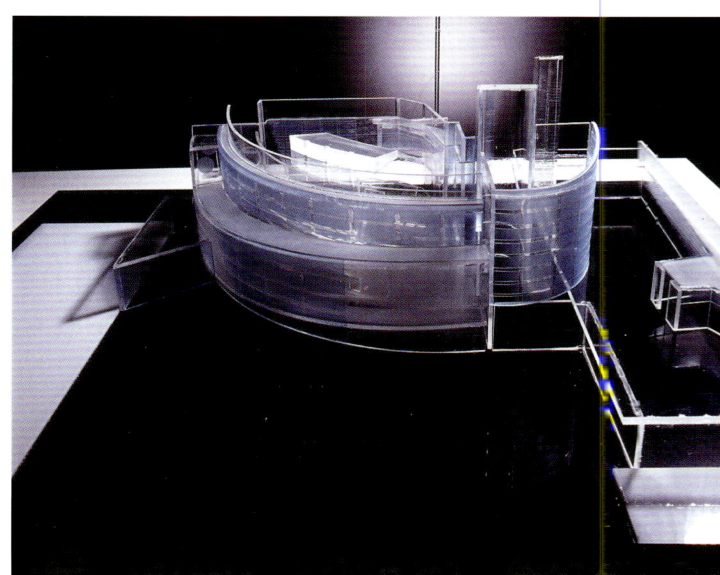

Meeting Centre of the Provincial Administration of Cuneo
Cuneo
1996
Photo: Paolo Mussat Sartor

The hills of Monferrato

This building is actually a Winery up in the hills of Monferrato. The main idea behind the design was to dematerialised its structures, placing them in dialectical contrast with a large exhibition space resulting from the geometric interaction between a light "leaf" of curved steel and the opaque parts of the complex.
This was created from a combination of wide glass surfaces and laminated wooden structure producing unexpected and extraordinary effects of light and transparency.
One of the distinctive problems involved in this design was to bring an industrial container into harmony with an important piece of landscape, bearing in mind certain decisions made by the client, particularly as regards the function and purpose of the interiors and the production-based layout of surfaces geared to a specific manufacturing cycle, which the architectural forms had to comply with.
Another important consideration, bearing in mind the these premises, was to dematerialise the resulting "weights" and structures through strategically chosen materials and building types. The resulting design came from interaction between surfaces and structures, opacity and transparency, which simultaneously characterise the overall sense of vitality and dialectical relations between the various components.
In a nutshell, the project involves designing a "strip" fitting in sealmlessly with the contours of the hills.
The first section, which looks onto a busy road, constitutes the area designated for selling the Winery's products: this roof surface then vanishes into the ground to create a wine conservation space before re-emerging again in the production section.
All the spaces are joined together by a walkway, which begins in the first section of the complex to create an overhead walkaway for visitors and providing the chance to study the various stages in the production of wine and, in the outside section, to admire the land from which this new creation emerges.
The cellar where the wine is left to mature calls to mind the belly of a cargo ship, like those which used to wait to be loaded with the product which has made Monferrato so famous, in the Port of Genoa.

l'Arca no. 259, June 2010

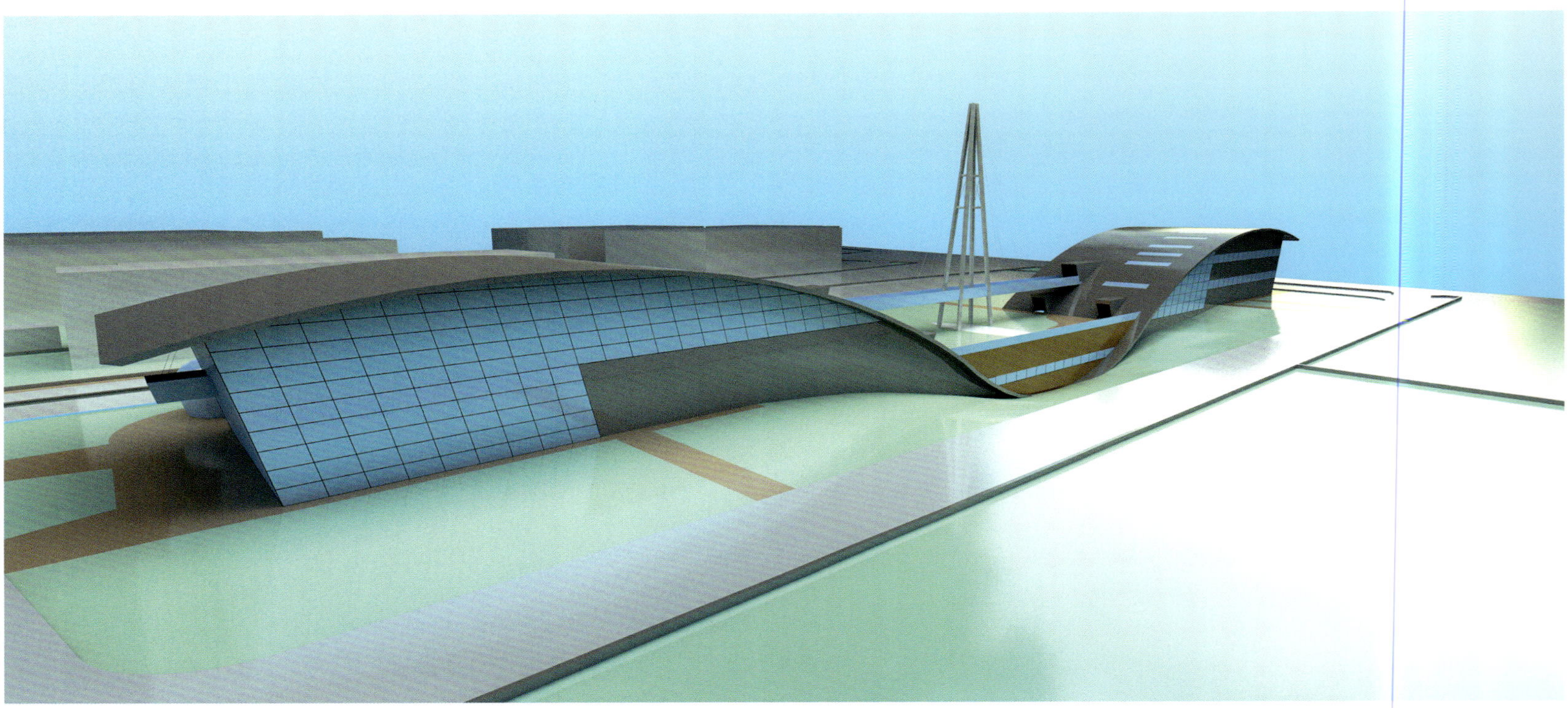

Project for the Nizza
Monferrato Winery
2007

A productive building

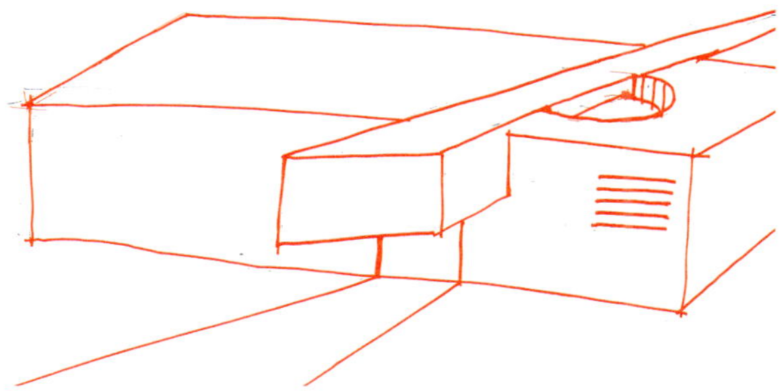

Industrial plant
Cuneo

Photo: Dario Fusaro

V2 plant
Racconigi
2002
Photo: Dario Fusaro

V2 plant

The complex designed by Gianni Arnaudo for V2 Elettronica, a factory manufacturing high-precision electronic components, is located in the outskirts of the city of Racconigi (Cuneo), midway across the flatland plain separating Turin from the Alps and the place where the Savoy decided to build one of their most distinctive works of architecture, an interesting complex, castle and park now safeguarded by UNESCO.

The factory faces onto an old avenue that acts likes a monumental backdrop to the castle façade. One of the main design issues was the problem of knitting an industrial building into a striking historical setting and piece of landscape, bearing in mind certain constraints set by the client, such as the use of a prefabricated structure and the arrangement of surfaces to cater for a production process based on a specific work cycle that the architectural forms had to accommodate.

Taking these considerations into account, another important factor was the need to dematerialise the "weights" and structures this entailed, thanks to carefully selected materials and building types.

This resulted in the idea of bringing together the surfaces and structures, opacity and transparency, injecting life into the design and, at the same time, creating dialectical relations between the various components.
As their business has boomed, some enlightened entrepreneurs have taken advantage of new buildings to create and convey something extra about their company image and the manufacturing operations they are involved in. They have discovered that high-quality architecture does not just meet the need to adapt spaces to new requirements and new production systems, but also provides a means of conveying their corporate philosophy based on the concept of creativity, innovation and an awareness of outside input from the market.
As in many cases now part of the history of architecture, this businessman wanted to use his own place of work to embody a strong desire to change and, at the same time, to create a new cultural landmark. This inevitably led to the construction of a "powerful sign" giving concrete shape to these goals.

The main idea behind the design was to dematerialise the structures by bringing them into dialectical relation with a large exhibition space produced by a geometric encounter between a "leaf" of gently curving steel and the opaque part of the complex.
This effect was created by the wide glass surfaces and the use of a laminated wooden structure: this resulted in an unexpected feeling of lightness and transparency and other striking effects.

One final crucial touch was provided by the lighting effects making the complex more eye-catching at nighttime: this allowed the new industrial premises to convey further messages with the same force and energy.

After twilight the building is transformed, bringing to life an object vaguely reminiscent of a spaceship whose LEDs and other startling effects express a desire to "take off" in the quest to conquer new spaces, thanks to the kind of business expertise allowing creativity and a different way of carrying out business to emerge even during crisis periods.

Gianni Arnaudo
l'Arca no. 209, December 2005

Villa Vola, Alba

The new shell around a small pre-existing building.
The new surfaces fragment and "fly away" towards the plain.

Photo: Dario Fusaro

A project for major distribution

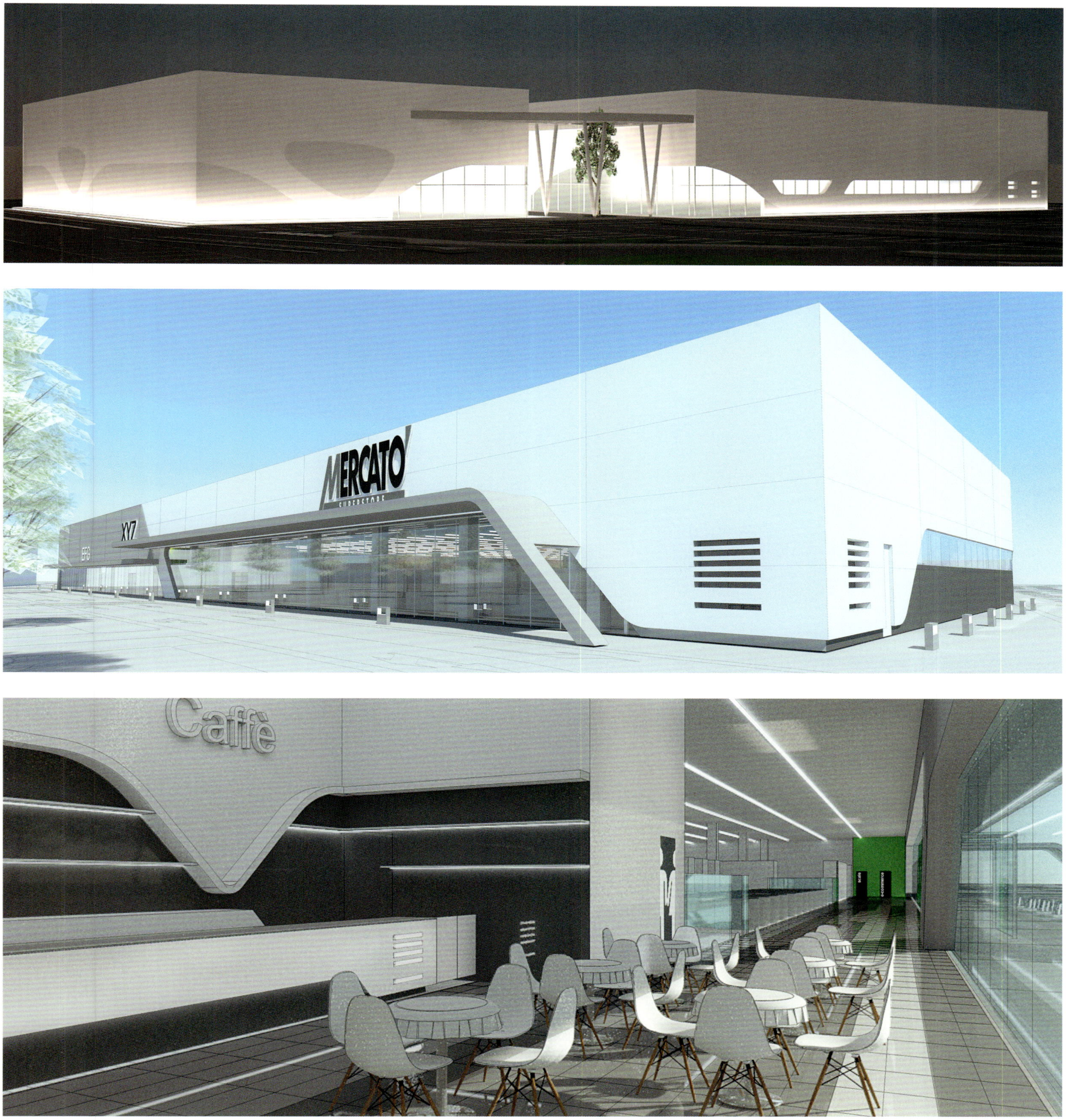

The first design for the new image of a great company: Mercatò (Dimar), Fossano (Cuneo)

Lightness, dematerialization and a return to nature

New plant for Bertolotto Porte

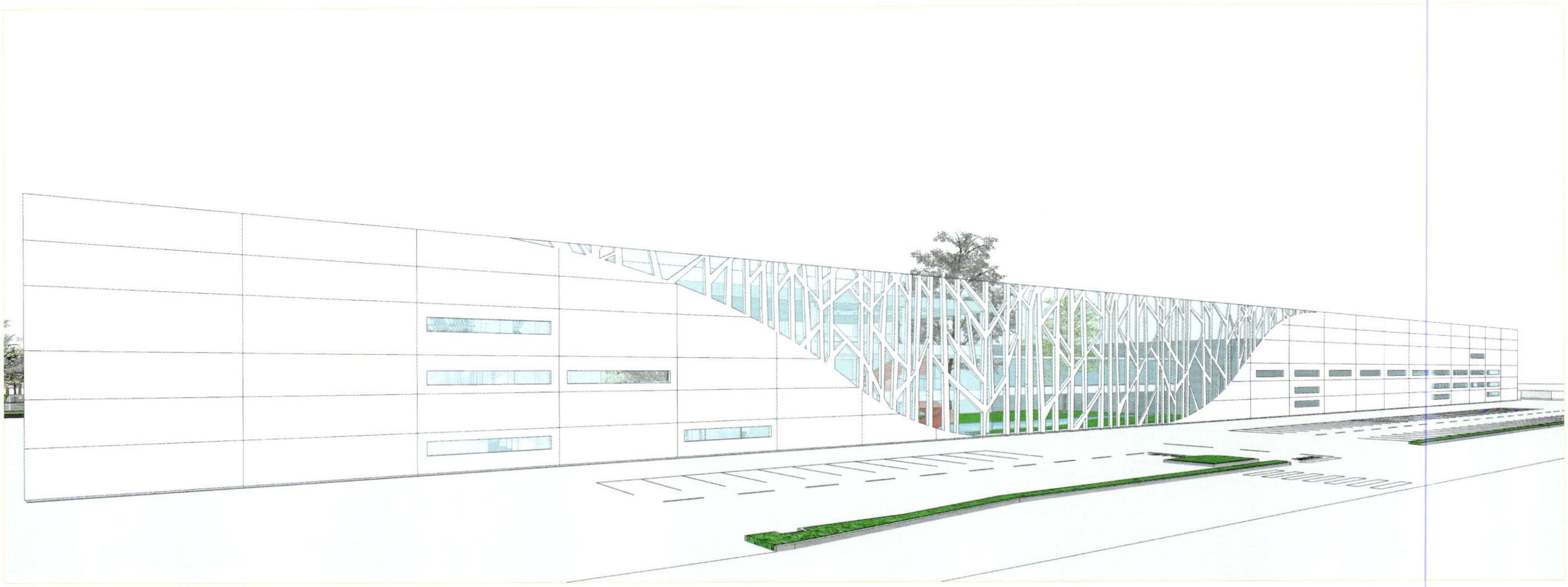

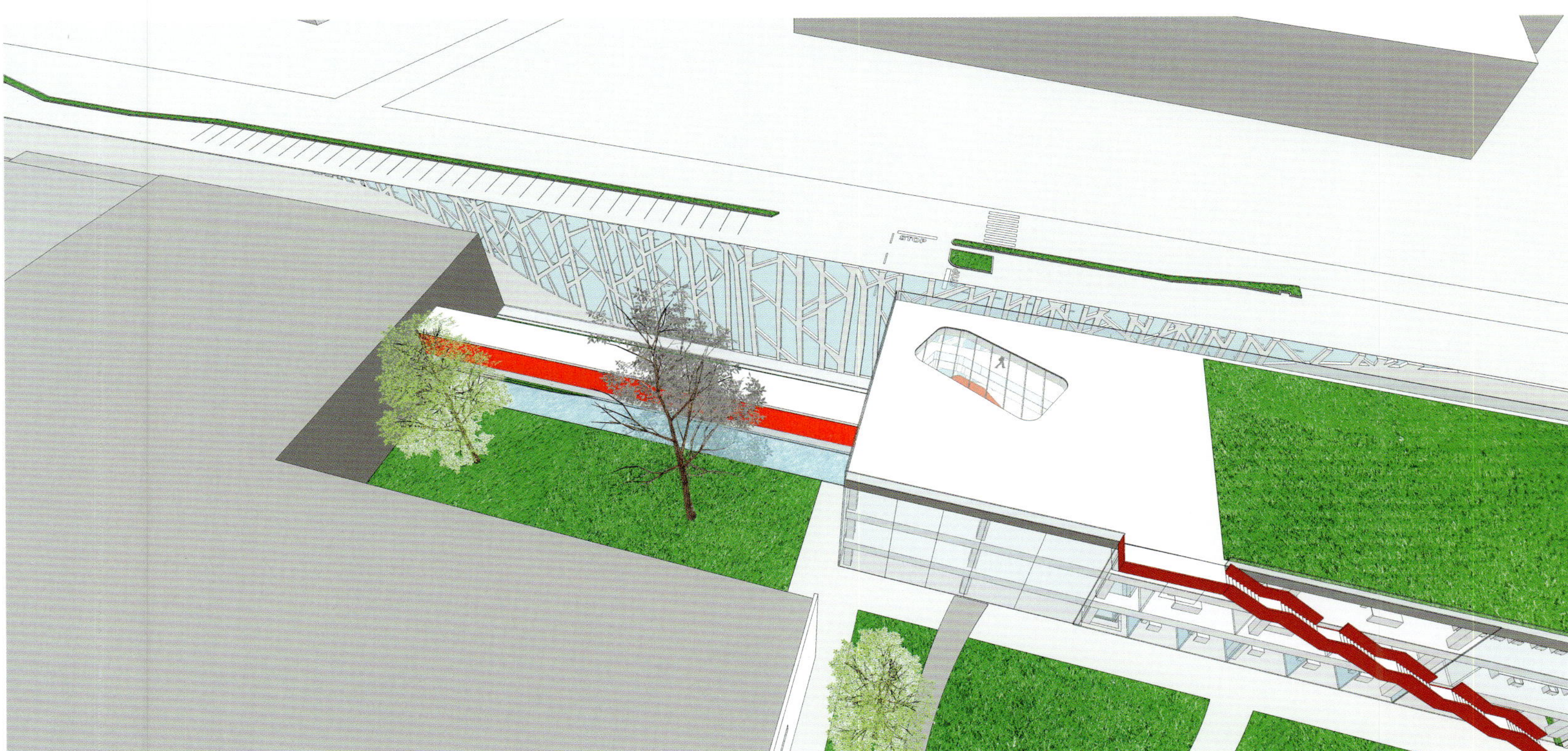

The Birth of Venus

Sandro Botticelli, c.1485
Gallerie degli Uffizi,
Florence

The Birth of Milo

Gianni Arnaudo, 2008
Unique work, artist's proof
Gufram factory
Arnaudo Archives

Soft sculpture, contrast between appearance and reality

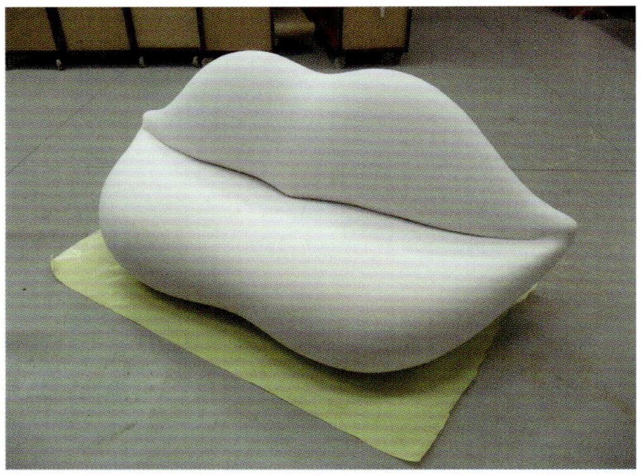
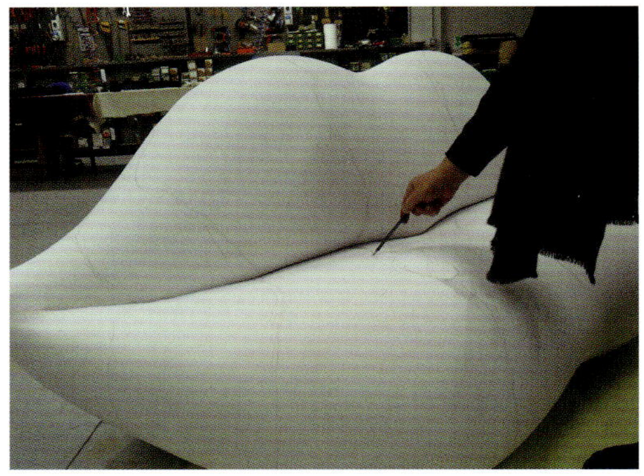

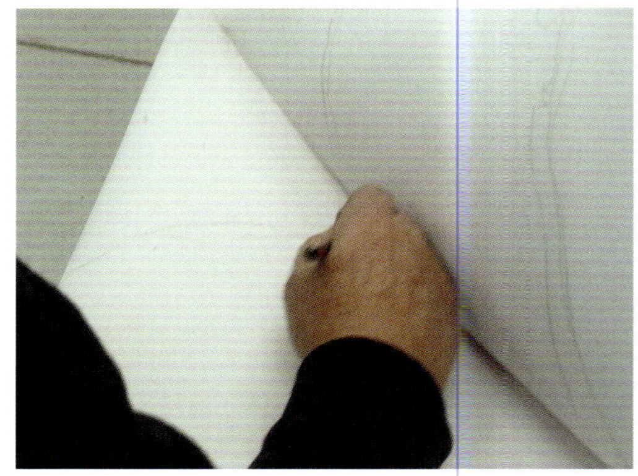

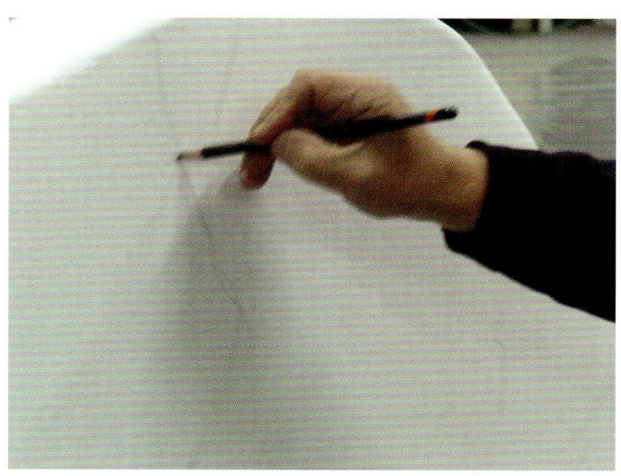
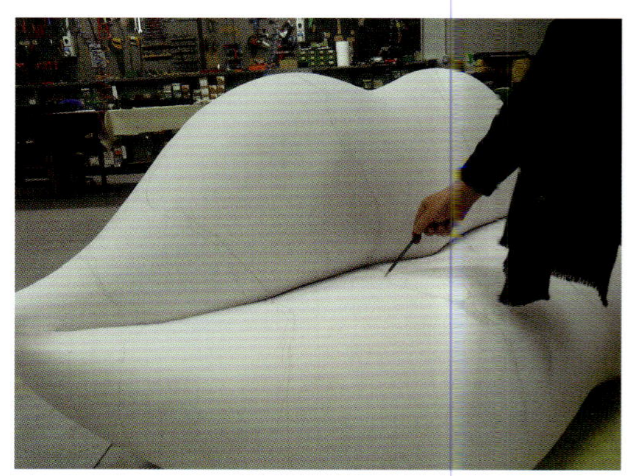

Marble is a shoulder...

The illusion of the senses

Struck by a marble statue of a young female figure seen in the museum on Samos, I was prompted to create a playful transposition based on the juxtaposition of material: cold marble and soft polyurethane.

It is interesting to witness the surprise of those who sit down on what they expect to be cold and hard but find it soft and cosy.

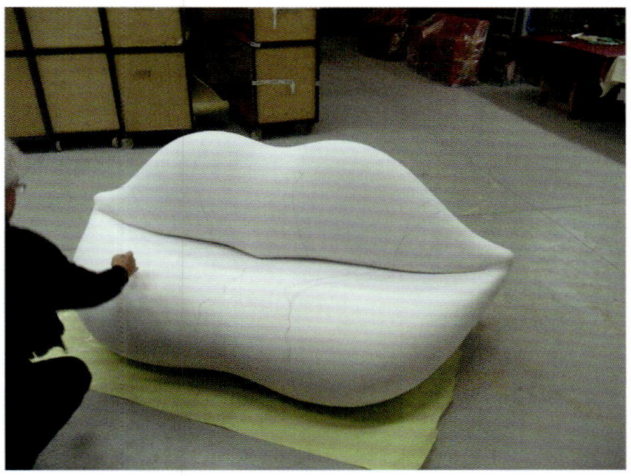
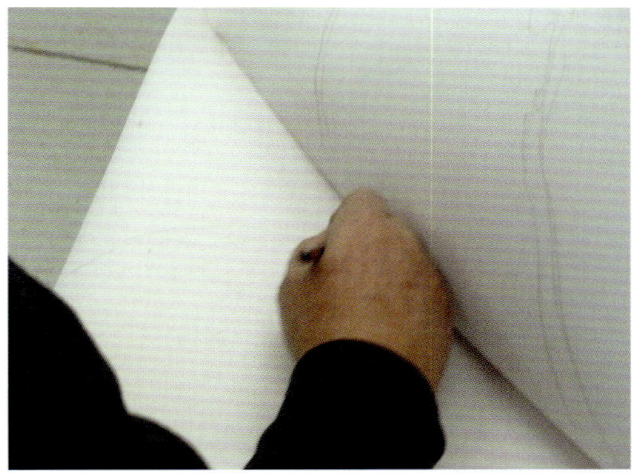

Creation of Milo
Gianni Arnaudo
in the Gufram factory, 2008
Arnaudo Archives
Artist's proof

...to carry time (García Lorca)

Ma questo non
è un regesto...

The exhibitions and the museum (despite everything)

MUSEE, NIVEAU 5

Pour la première fois, le Centre Pompidou présente ses collections sous une forme thématique, interdisciplinaire et non chronologique. Réalisée à partir des œuvres de la plus grande collection d'art moderne et contemporain en Europe, *Big Bang* associe les arts plastiques, la vidéo, la photographie, l'architecture, le design, la littérature et confronte les œuvres et les tendances du début du XXe siècle à nos jours. Cette exposition exceptionnelle s'appuie sur une thématique originale : le « big bang » moderne, ou le lien entre destruction et création dans l'art du XXème siècle. Sur un parcours de 4500m2, le Centre Pompidou propose une lecture renouvelée des phénomènes culturels du siècle.

Big Bang, Destruction and creation in 20th century art
Paris, Centre Pompidou
June 15 2005 – March 06 2006

COMMUNIQUÉ DE PRESSE

BIG BANG AU MUSÉE NATIONAL D'ART MODERNE

DESTRUCTION ET CRÉATION DANS L'ART DU XXe SIÈCLE

Centre Pompidou
Direction
de la communication
75191 Paris cedex 04
directrice de la communication
Roya Nasser

Responsable du service presse
Emilia Stocchi
téléphone
00 33 (0)1 44 78 42 00
télécopie
00 33 (0)1 44 78 13 02
e-mail
emilia.stocchi@cnac-gp.fr

attachée de presse
Coralie Sagot
téléphone
00 33 (0)1 44 78 12 42
télécopie
00 33 (0)1 44 78 13 02
e-mail
coralie.sagot@cnac-gp.fr

Direction des éditions
attachée de presse
Evelyne Poret
téléphone
00 33 (0)1 44 78 15 98
e-mail
evelyne.poret@cnac-gp.fr

Five Angels for the Millennium, 2001
Bill Viola
© Bill Viola, D.R.
© Photographe Kira Perov
© Centre Pompidou, MNAM, Paris/ Tate, London/ Whitney Museum of American Art, New York (achat conjoint)

MUSEE, NIVEAU 5

Pour la première fois, le Centre Pompidou présente ses collections sous une forme thématique, interdisciplinaire et non chronologique. Réalisée à partir des œuvres de la plus grande collection d'art moderne et contemporain en Europe, *Big Bang* associe les arts plastiques, la vidéo, la photographie, l'architecture, le design, la littérature et confronte les œuvres et les tendances du début du XXe siècle à nos jours. Cette exposition exceptionnelle s'appuie sur une thématique originale : le « big bang » moderne, ou le lien entre destruction et création dans l'art du XXème siècle. Sur un parcours de 4500m2, le Centre Pompidou propose une lecture renouvelée des phénomènes culturels du siècle.

The "historic" moment of the signing of the work immortalized

Vitra Design Museum

The consigning of *Déjeuner sur l'arbre* painting to Mathias Schwartz-Clauss, curator of the Vitra Design Museum, Basel, 2012

Construction of the exhibition Pop Art Design

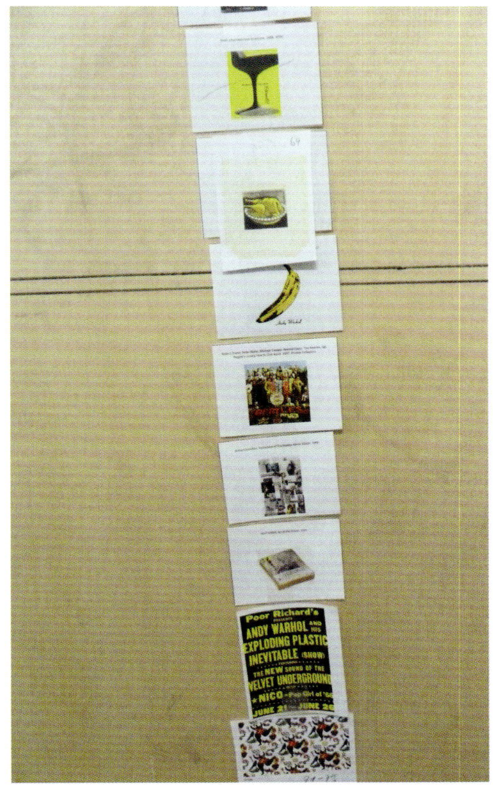

Preparation of the exhibition *Pop Art Design* Vitra Design Museum, Basel, 2012

And this was the result

Gianni Arnaudo and
Mathias Schwartz-Clauss,
curator of the exhibition
Pop Art Design
Vitra Design Museum,
Basel
Evening of inauguration

Vitra Design Museum

Mr
Gianni Arnaudo
Piazza Europa, 16
12100 Cuneo
Italien

Weil am Rhein, October 30th 2012

Pop Art Design

Caro Gianni,

the public response to our Pop Art Design exhibition and catalog is really fantastic. Thank you once again for your valuable contribution to this success!

Enclosed please find your voucher copy of the catalog in English. It is a great pleasure to working with you!

I am sending my best regards and greetings, Yours

Mathias

Mathias Schwartz-Clauss
Curator

The exhibition and its format in numerous museums...

Lousiana Museum,
Copenaghen
22 02 2013 – 09 06 2013

Moderna Museet,
Stockholm
29 06 2013 – 22 09 2013

Barbican Center, London
22 10 2013 – 09 02 2014

Henie Onstad
Kunstsenter, Oslo
04 06 2015 – 06 09 2015

EMMA, Espoo Museum
of Modern Art, Finland
18 02 2015 – 10 05 2015

Museum of Contemporary
Art, Chicago
19 12 2015 – 27 03 2016

Brillo

79 BABILONIA 79
STUDIO 65

Turin World Design Capital

Turin was the World Design Capital in 2008. The events that I planned together with Luisa Bocchietto, president of the ADI, included an exhibition at the former silk factory in Caraglio (Cuneo). This was the embryo of the one held at the Vitra Design Museum.

Pop Design. Fuori scala, fuori luogo, fuori schema
10 May – 14 September 2008
Filatoio di Caraglio (Cuneo)
Photo: Tommaso Mattina, Turin
Exhibition design: Gianni Arnaudo
Curator: Luisa Bocchietto

and everyone asks, "Where is Caraglio?"

Metropolitan, New York

THE METROPOLITAN MUSEUM OF ART

Visit | Exhibitions | Collection | Events | Learn | Research | Give and Join | About the Museum | Blogs | Shop

The Collection

"Capitello" Chair
Studio 65
(Italian)

Manufacturer: Gufram (Italian, founded 1952)
Date: 1970
Medium: Self-skinning polyurethane foam
Dimensions: H. 26 1/2, W. 40, D. 44 1/2 in. (67.3 x 101.6 x 113 cm)
Classification: Furniture
Rights and Reproduction: © Gufram s.r.l.

Louvre, Paris
Le design des années Pop

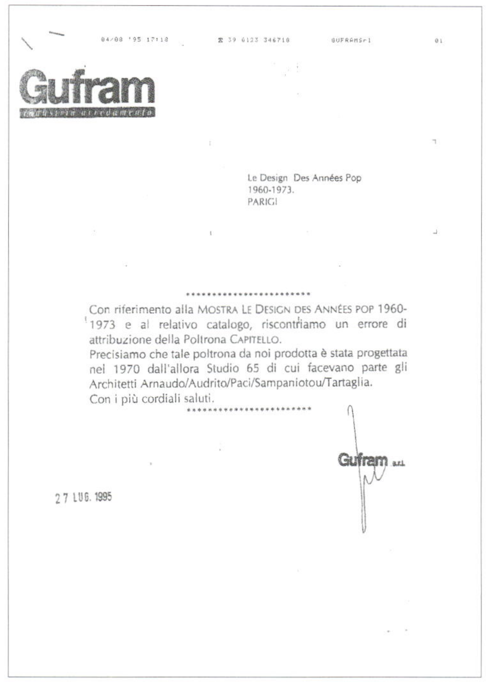

Gufram

Le Design Des Années Pop
1960-1973.
PARIGI

Con riferimento alla MOSTRA LE DESIGN DES ANNÉES POP 1960-1973 e al relativo catalogo, riscontriamo un errore di attribuzione della Poltrona CAPITELLO.
Precisiamo che tale poltrona da noi prodotta è stata progettata nel 1970 dall'allora Studio 65 di cui facevano parte gli Architetti Arnaudo/Audrito/Paci/Sampaniotou/Tartaglia.
Con i più cordiali saluti.

Gufram s.r.l.

27 LUG. 1995

Promenade dans les collections du musée

Promenade dans les collections du musée
Paris, Musée du Louvre, 1998

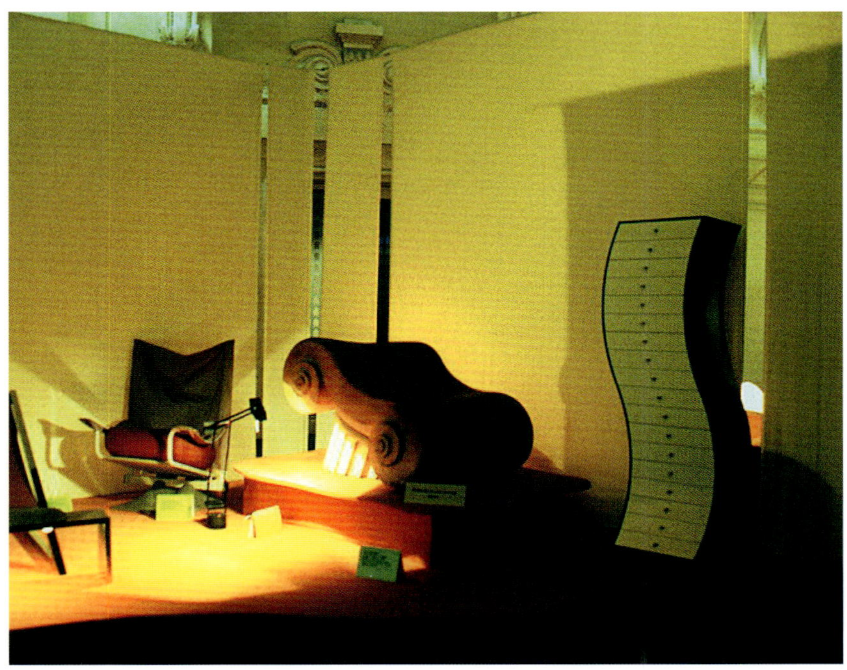

Centre Pompidou, Paris

Renouvellement complet de la Collection Permanente du Centre Pompidou, Paris
2002–2003
Colonna di piatti
Gianni Arnaudo

Capitello and Baby-Lonia
Gianni Arnaudo / Studio65
Arnaudo Archives

Castello di Rivoli

The Rock Furniture
Il design della Gufram negli anni del rock

Castello di Rivoli Museum
Curator Franco Mello
2002

Un dovuto omaggio all'amico Gianni che ha partecipato a scrivere la storia del design italiano.

Giuseppe Gugliermetto

Giuseppe Gugliermetto
and Guido Drocco Gufram
designers, at the opening
of the exihibition

Galleria TOT, Padua

Il grande A. Loos

Extract from the catalogue
Asparagus Age
Ennio Chiggio
and Giulia Laverda,
Padua, Galleria TOT
September 1984

La fischiata XXXIII

Extract from
Asparagus Age
Ennio Chiggio
and Giulia Laverda,
Padua, Galleria TOT,
September 1984

One evening, gathered together in the studio, we were talking about the Bocca sofa and how wonderfully "baroque" it was.
I suggested using Gian Battista Marino's lines on 17th-century poetry as a comment on it.
The idea was taken up enthusiastically and put into effect.
The poetics of Studio65 were enriched with the idea of wonder.

Triennale, Milan
Uomo, ambiente, colore

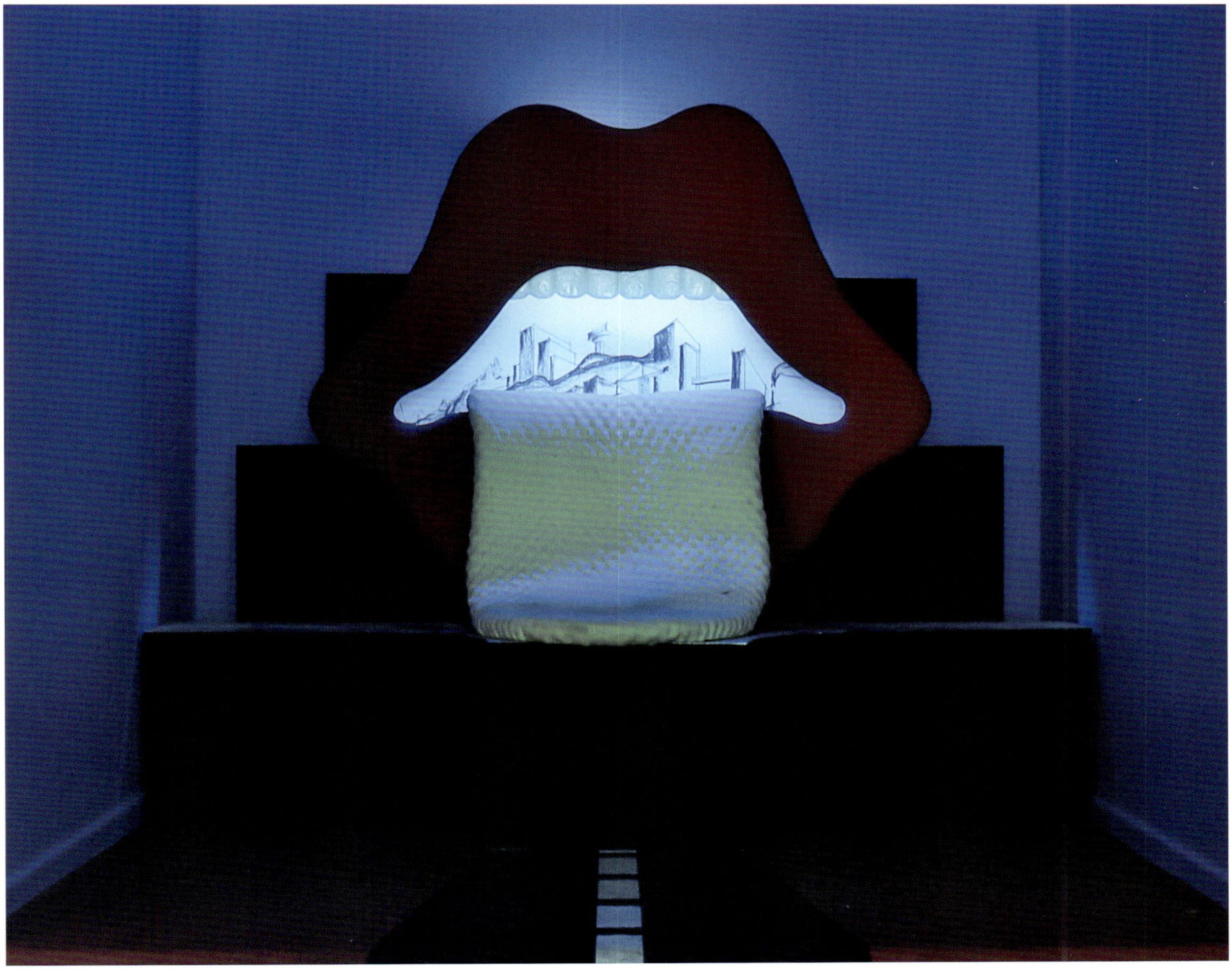

Foto Arnaudo
Archivio Arnaudo

1972

The Triennial organized an exhibition entitled *Uomo, ambiente, colore*.
We took part and could hardly believe we were rubbing shoulders with superstars of Italian architecture like Gae Aulenti, Albini, Sottsass and Zanuso.

Our space was dominated by a huge mouth that had devoured the city with its symbols.
The exhibition area was reached by the main staircase with 1:1 scale photos of the leading figures on the steps to accompany your visit to their ideas.

Fiera, Verona
Cantiere Italia

Inauguration
Pietro Lunardi and
Gianni Arnaudo
Verona Fiera
Exhibition design:
Gianni Arnaudo
Electronics and special
effects by Marco
Camisani Calzolari
2005

Nobody would recognize the lively, ironic young man from the Sunday morning TV programme *Unomattina in famiglia* on Rai Uno in this photo.

Palazzo Barolo, Turin

Design in everyday life

Palazzo Barolo with
Giorgetto Giugiaro
on the You Welcome sofa
designed by Gianni
Arnaudo for Poltrona Frau
Turin

Baby-Lonia
Gianni Arnaudo / Studio65

Palazzo della Ragione, Padua
La grande svolta anni ’60

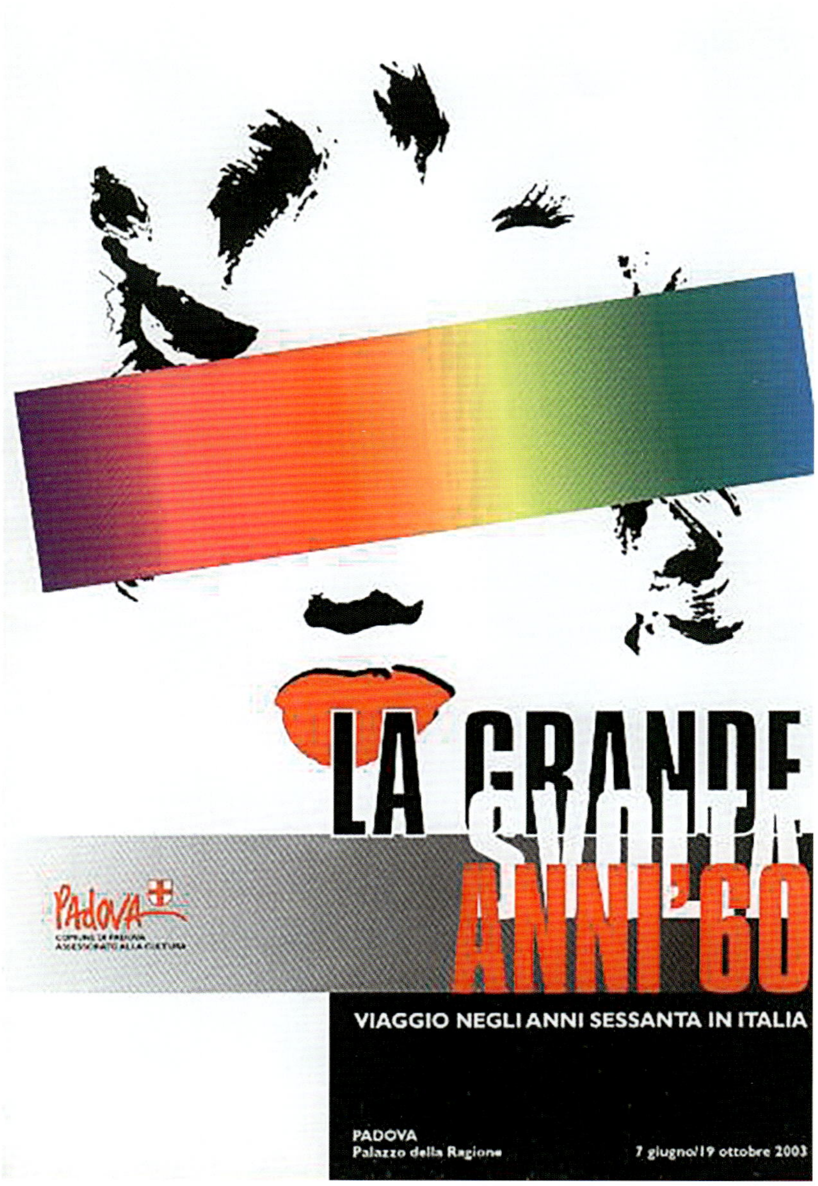

Exhibition, *La grande svolta anni ’60*
Official poster
Padua
2003

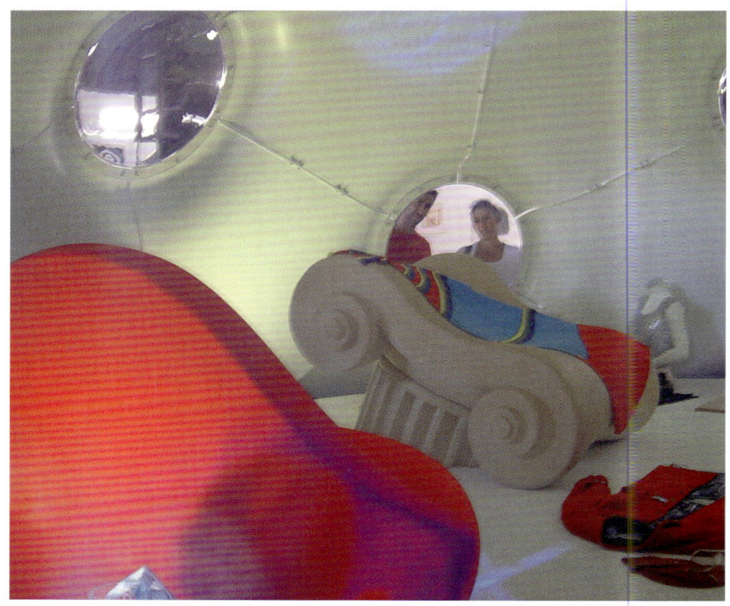

Ex Ansaldo, Milan
Fragments of history

Slide Installation – Spazio Ansaldo, Fuori Salone Milano Design Week, 2008
Rococo chaise-longue produced by Slide

Salone del Mobile 2002, Milan

That year, in order to demonstrate its ability to use leather for over-the-top designs far removed from its traditional production, Poltrona Frau asked three designers to create three different articles of seating.

Jean Nouvel on the Va Pensiero armchair designed by Gianni Arnaudo
Salone del Mobile 2002
Stand Poltrona Frau

GAM, Turin 2015

Delivery of the painting
Déjeuner sur l'arbre
to the GAM, Turin, 2015
Permanent collection

Triennale 2016, Milan

The Capitello (Studio65) becomes an icon of Italian creativity.

Papì, Fizzz and Déjeuner sur l'arbre at Eataly

Gianni Arnaudo and Oscar Farinetti, founder of Eataly, at the inauguration of Eataly Ostiense in Rome

Gianni Arnaudo and Carlo Petrini at the inauguration of Eataly Ostiense in Rome

When Oscar saw the Papì before the inauguration of Eataly Ostiense in Rome, he wanted it immediately, not least because it truly expressed his own idea of Italy: creativity and immediacy in the transmission of a message of infectious joy.

The Dedalo Minosse Prize

a prize awarded to HEROIC commissioners of projects together with their architects.

2003

Dedalo Minosse Prize
Dromont Project
Vicenza, Basilica Palladiana

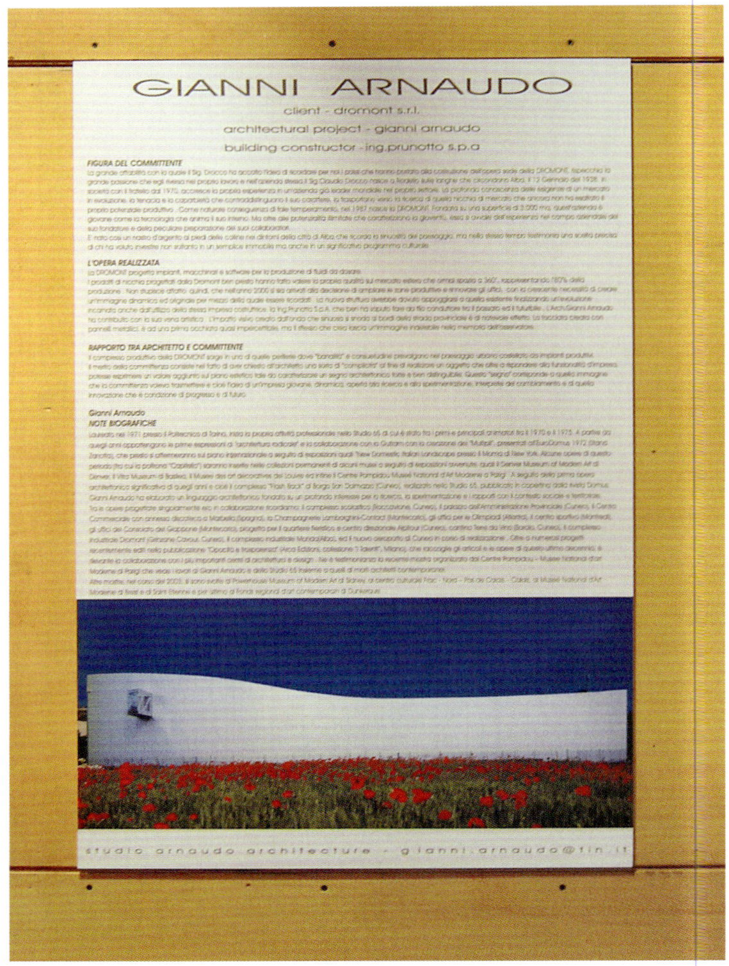

Gianni Arnaudo with Kisho Kurokawa during the award ceremony

2006

Dedalo Minosse Prize
Terre da Vino Project
Vicenza, Basilica
Palladiana

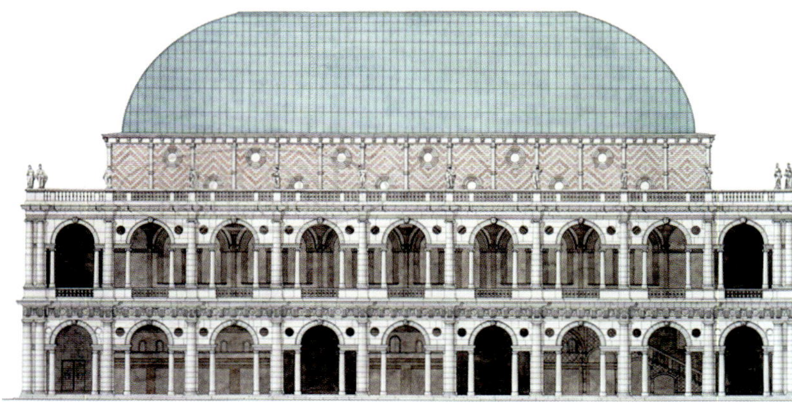

Venice Biennales of Architecture

2004 Biennial
Building in Monte Carlo
IX Venice Biennale -
Arsenale, *Le città d'acqua*

la Biennale di Venezia
11. Mostra Internazionale di Architettura

2008 Biennial
Le Cattedrali del Vino
Terre da Vino winery
XI Venice Biennale

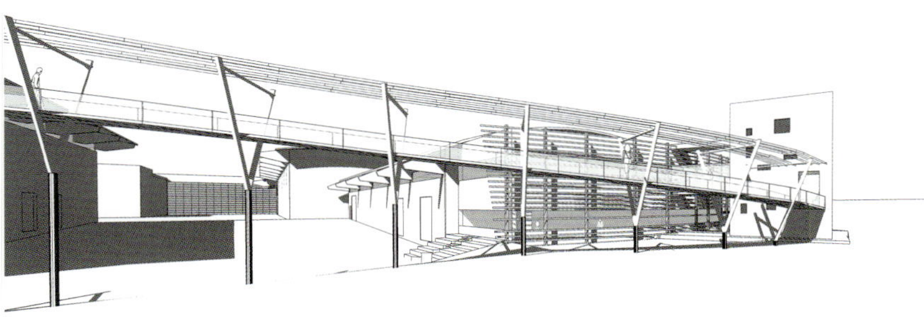

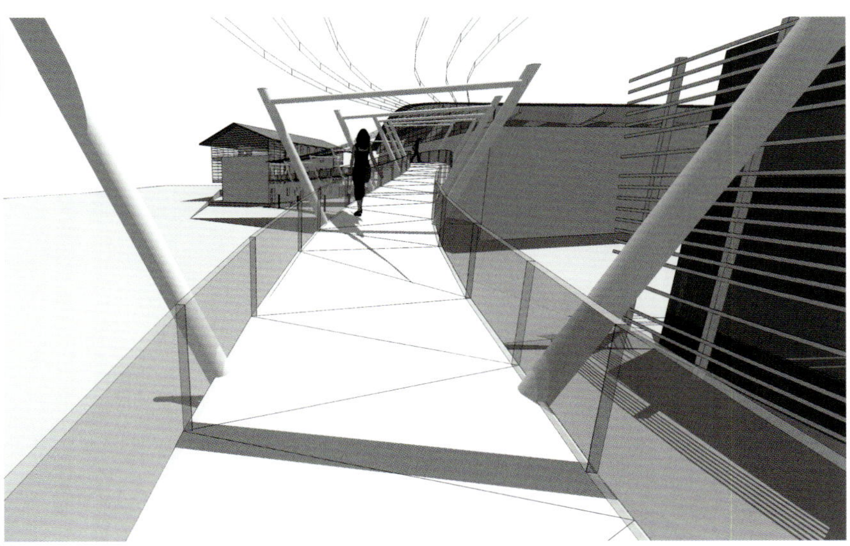

Arnaudo's two designs for wineries in Barolo were presented at this edition. Only two winery designs were selected for the Italian Pavilion, namely those of Arnaudo and Arnaldo Pomodoro, as examples of the cross-fertilization of art and architecture on a theme often addressed along wholly traditional lines.

2012 Biennial
Le Cattedrali del Vino
Pop Winery
Press conference
XIII Venice Biennale
Arsenale

2014 Biennial
Barbarella disco
Studio65, Arnaudo, Audrito,
Sampanioti, Tartaglia
Corderia dell'Arsenale
Photo: Paolo Mussat Sartor

The Rēgula Prize, "100 Progetti" Rome 2018

The Rēgula Prize, "100 Progetti" L'Astemia Pentita Winery Rome 2018

La Boîte de Nuit
Hyères, Villa Noailles
2017

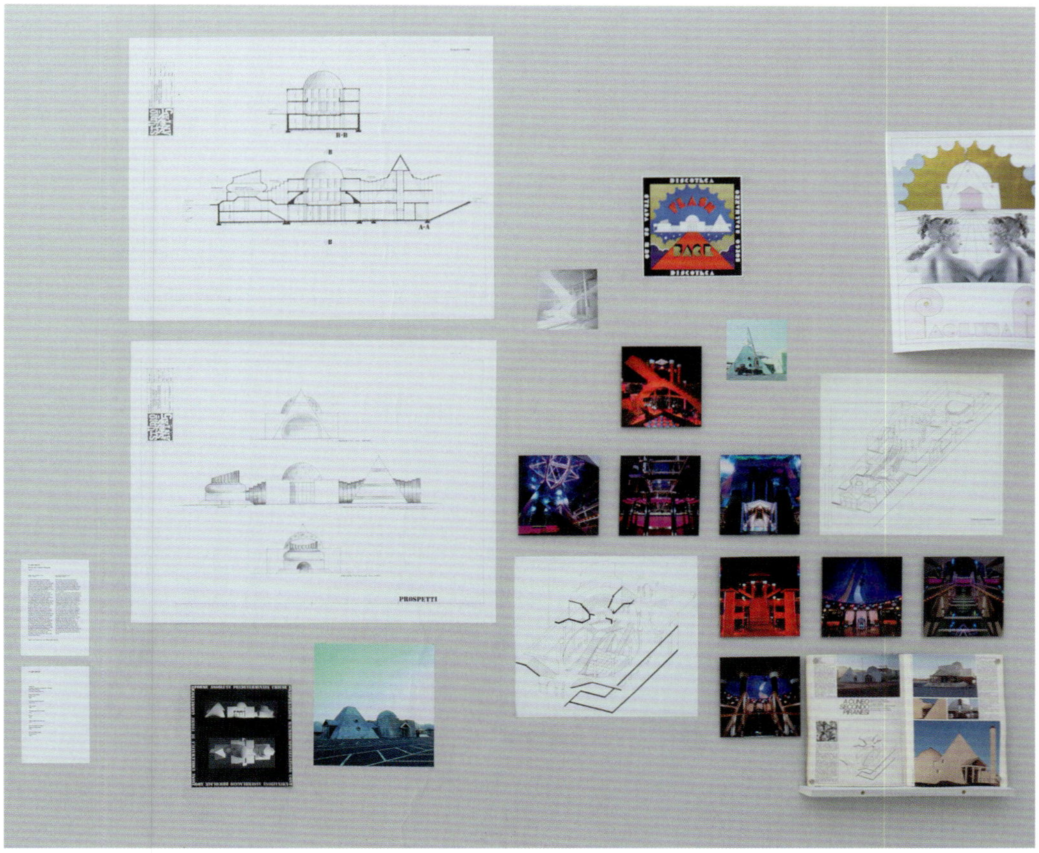

La Boîte de Nuit
Exposition d'architecture
Hyères, Villa Noailles
Flash Back-Paolina B disco
2017
Arnaudo Archives

FLASH-BACK
Studio 65 / Gianni Arnaudo
1974
BORGO SAN DALMAZZO, ITALIE
PROJET RÉALISÉ

Rencontre anachronique de ces éléments architecturaux, Flash-Back est un temple post-moderne dévolu au disco. Une pyramide et une colonne tronquée flanquent une villa palladienne ; une même couleur blanche unifie l'assemblage en apparence fortuit de ces archétypes issus de passés dissonants et l'intrication des échelles incohérentes. Dans ce bâtiment de quatre niveaux, la discothèque occupe le sous-sol. À l'étage, une grande colonne ionique abrite un espace d'écoute et la plinthe contient une galerie. À l'intérieur, la complexité provenant de la rencontre des volumes et l'enchevêtrement d'escaliers et de colonnes rappellent les *Prisons imaginaires*, des estampes de Gian Battista Piranesi (1743-1778). Toutefois l'atmosphère sombre et énigmatique de Piranesi cède la place à un univers pop composé de couleurs acidulées et de pistes de danse lumineuses. L'usage excessif de références multiples et contradictoires témoigne de l'attitude irrévérencieuse et profanes des architectes post-modernes envers les formes historiques.

Compagnia di San Paolo Dronero, “99 città” Award 2005

Compagnia di San Paolo
“99 città” Award
Dronero, Municipal
Theatre
2005

Turin Polytechnic

In the great abandoned factory Binario 18 Torino Mirafiori

Binario 18
05–12 May 2016
Turin, Spazio Mirafiori
Turin Polytechnic,
course of Architecture,
Construction and City
with professors Massimo
Crotti e Angelo Sampieri

Lectio Magistralis

Laurea Magistrale in Architettura Costruzione Città
Master Degree in Architecture Construction City

Lezioni di Architettura Costruzione Città
Lectures of Architecture Construction City

Politecnico di Torino_Lingotto_Aula Magna
Lunedì 27_04_2015_h 18,00
Via Nizza 230

Gianni Arnaudo

Architettura e territorio: il caso delle Langhe/Unesco

© Foto Murialdo _ "La Stampa"

Night Fever. Designing Club Culture

Vitra Design Museum, Basel
ADAM Design Museum, Brussels
Centro per l'Arte Contemporanea Luigi Pecci, Prato
Victoria and Albert Museum, Dundee

Night Fever
Designing Club Culture
Vitra Design Museum, Basel
17 03 - 09 09 2018

ADAM Design Museum, Brussels
21 11 2018 - 05 05 2019

Centro per l'Arte Contemporanea Luigi Pecci, Prato
07 06 2019 - 06 10 2019

Espressioni d'arte di Torino a Martigny

STUDIO SESSANTACINQUE

Componenti: Gianni Arnaudo - Franco Audrito - Nanà Sampaniotou - Ferruccio Tartaglia.
Laureati alla Facoltà di Architettura di Torino operano nel campo dell'architettura e del design con sede a Torino nell'atelier di via Bogino n. 15.
Lo studio ha esposto la sua produzione in numerose mostre tra le quali: Vienna, presso Section-n; Eurodomus tenuto a Torino nel 1972; Colonia, presso Laden 55; a Parigi e a Kortrijk.
Ha vinto nel 1971 al concorso PRINT un premio speciale per altra cultura. La sua produzione è stata pubblicata su numerose riviste e quotidiani italiani e stranieri tra cui: « Domus », « Casa Vogue », « In », « Casabella », « The Sunday Times », « Elle », « Die Presse », « Die Weltwoche » ed altre ancora.
Collabora tuttora con alcune ditte quali: la Gufram di Nole, la Ditta Colli di Torino, la Cyrus Company

Membres: Gianni Arnaudo - Franco Audrito - Nanà Sampaniotou - Ferruccio Tartaglia.
Diplômés à la Faculté d'Architecture de Turin, ils travaillent dans le domaine de l'architecture et du design.
Ils ont présenté leurs oeuvres dans de nombreuses expositions parmi lesquelles celle de Vienne, section-n ; celle d'Eurodomus qui s'est tenue à Turin en 1972 ; et celles de Cologne (laden 55), de Paris et de Kortrijk.
Ils ont obtenu en 1971 au concours PRINT un prix spécial. Leurs travaux ont été publiés dans de nombreuses revues et journaux italiens et étrangers parmi lesquels : « Domus », « Casa Vogue », « In », « Casabella », « The Sunday Times », « Elle », « Die Presse », « Die Weltwoche » et d'autres encore.
Ils collaborent encore avec quelques firmes dont La Gufran de Nole, La Firme Colli de Turin, La Cyrus Company

Divano Bocca - produzione Gufram
Poltrona Capitello - produzione Gufram
Poltrona Chiocciola - produzione Gufram

LUCE. Lampade 1968-1973:
il nuovo design italiano

Indice dei designers

I numeri rimandano alle fotografie e alle schede, la lettera n alle note delle schede e la lettera p alle pagine.

134

Nella costruzione del suo «Olimpo al quarto piano» lo Studio 65 esalta, tra gli arredi, gli oggetti illuminanti che sfuggono all'ovvia funzione di sorgente luminosa per assurgere a un loro status di protagonisti primari del progetto.

39.

40.

A.

39. STUDIO 65, «NUVOLA», 1971, PEZZO UNICO PER CASA CANELLA, TORINO.
40. STUDIO 65, «SATURNO», 1971, PEZZO UNICO PER CASA CANELLA, TORINO.
A. PROGETTO PER «UN OLIMPO AL QUARTO PIANO».

Emotional Fragments

Gianni Arnaudo with
Giovanni Michelucci
Arnaudo Archives

GIOVANNI MICHELUCCI

Caro Arnaudo, fra un pacco di lettere che ho trovato al mio ritorno a Fiesole dopo vari giorni di assenza vi è la tua, graditissima, alla quale rispondo con ritardo. Purtroppo non posso venire a Torino dove vorrei fare una scappata per stare con te e di Salvato

"IL ROSETO" TEL. 59234 FIESOLE

FIRENZE - Galleria Uffizi
Piero della Francesca
Borgo S. Sepolcro 1415 - Borgo S. Sepolcro 1492
Federigo di Montefeltro Duca di Urbino
Fréderic de Montefeltro, Duc d'Urbin
Fredric of Montefeltro, Duke of Urbino
Friedrich von Montefeltro Herzog von Urbino

NOVA LVX

POSTE ITALIANE REPVBBLICA ITALIANA LIRE 25

FIRENZE FERR. CORRISP. 25.12.67 -21

Grazie della incisione e degli auguri, che ricambio con affetto
Giovanni Michelucci
Dic. 67

Eg. Sig. Gianni Arnaudo
12100 Cuneo
P. Europa 16

Ediz. Giusti di S. Becocci - Firenze
da Fotocolor Kodak Ektachrome

P. MARZARI S.R.L. SCHIO 227

Letters from Giovanni Michelucci
October 11, 1967
December 25, 1967

Fragments of graphic art

Gianni Arnaudo with the
director of the Mercedes
Museum in Stuttgart
Presentation of the poster

Poster designed for Mercedes
for the SL Pagoda meeting
in Lugano
21–23 August 1987
Gianni Arnaudo

Lamborghini
Contact Montecarlo poster
Opening of the
Lamborghini-Contact
Champagnerie
1990

Poster for the *Pop Design. Fuori scala, fuori luogo, fuori schema* exhibition
Torino World Design Capital
Caraglio, 2006

(for Carlo Petrini)
Poster Vini Piemontesi
Slow food
1990

it was the beginning of Slow Food

Disco in Fossano, 1985
Drawing by Gianni
Arnaudo

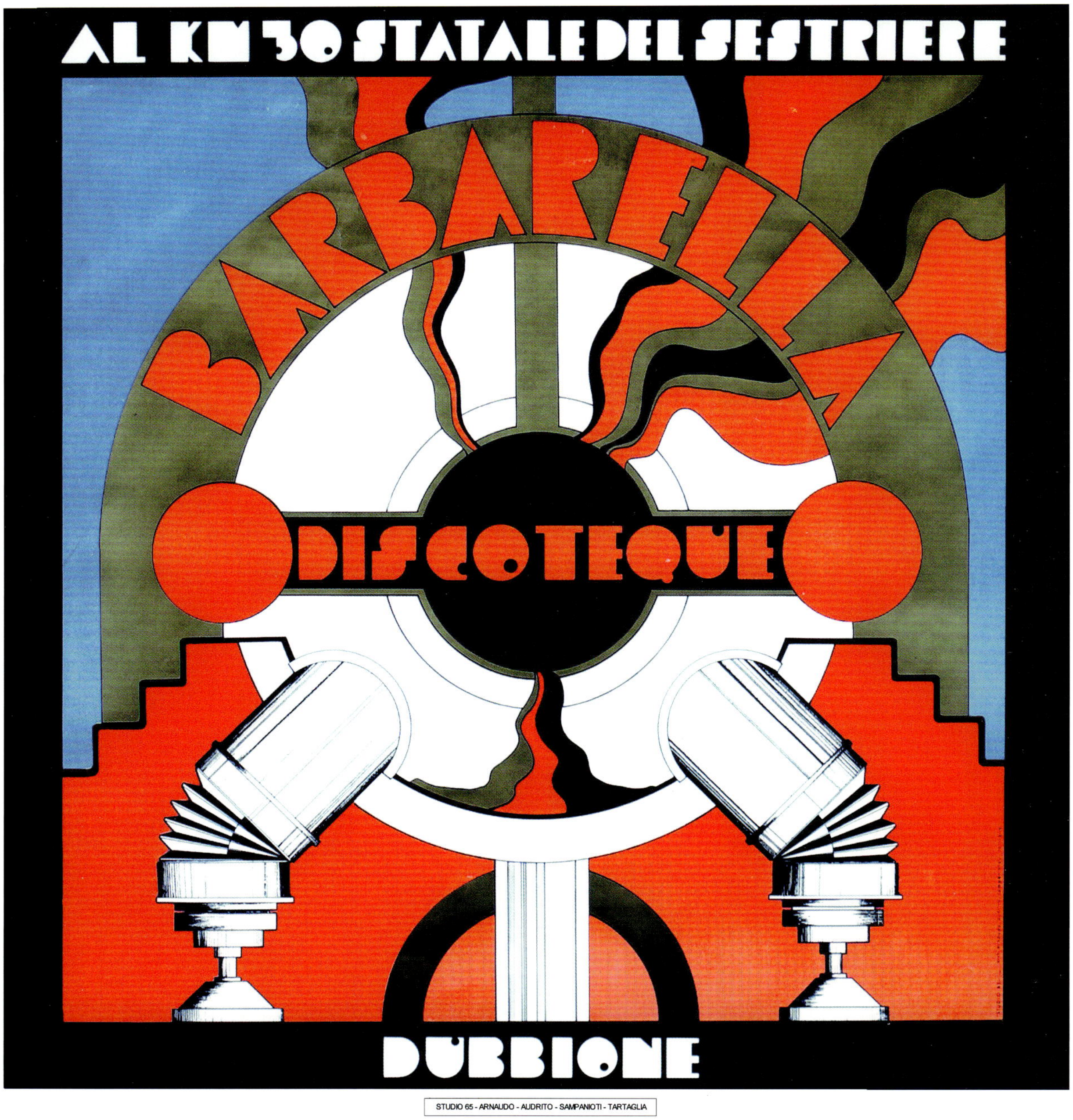

Poster of the Barbarella
disco in Dubbione
1972–73
Arnaudo, Audrito,
Sampanioti e Tartaglia
Arnaudo Archives

Poster for the Flash Back disco
Borgo San Dalmazzo
Design Gianni Arnaudo

Poster for the Paolina B disco
Borgo San Dalmazzo
Design Gianni Arnaudo

Poster of the
Salon International
de l'Architecture
Paris, La Grande Halle
de la Villette, 1992
Gianni Arnaudo

Four covers…

Bibliography

(for individual or shared works / per opere singole o in comunione)

1971
- *Casa Vogue*, July/ August: "Baby-Pop"
- *Domus* no. 504, November: "A Pordenone"
- *Casa Vogue*, December: "Se ne parla"

1972
- *Domus* no. 509, April: "Il tempio della Bellezza"
- *La Stampa*, May 19: "Un nuovo modo di abitare"
- *La Stampa*, May 21: "Babilonia made in Novara"
- *Gazzetta del Popolo*, May 26: "Babilonia"
- *Il Tempo*, June 4: "Babilonia"
- *Industrial Design*, June: "News"
- *Elle* no. 1389: "L'habitat de demain"
- *Domus* no. 512, July: "Eurodomus 4"
- *Casabella* no. 367, July: "Babilonia '72"
- *Casa Vogue*, July/August: "La colonna dissacrante"
- *Interni*, July: "Moderna Babilonia"
- AD, September: "Divano a fiore e bruco"
- *The Sunday Times*, October 1: P. Redford, "Radical Design"
- *Die Presse*, October 6: "Kultur"
- *Die Presse*, October 29: "Locales"
- *Die Weltwoche*; exhibition in Vienna, October 9
- *The Hanson Post*, November 30: "A Super Smash Exibit"
- *Life*: "The many moods of Marisa Berenson"

1973
- *Rassegna*, January/February: A. dal Lago, "America, America"
- *Casa Vogue*, March: "Casa Canella"
- *Fantazio*, April 17: "Due labbra rosse invitanti"
- *Casabella* no. 379, July: "Design e Mass Media"
- *Domus* no. 526, September: Barbarella
- *Casabella* no. 382, October: F. Raggi, "Radical Story"
- *Provincia di Torino*: "Espressioni d'arte di Torino a Martigny"

1974
- *Domus* no. 532, March: "La Gufram, al Centro Domus dal 12 al 17.11.1973"
- *Domus* no. 534, May: "L'Expo 74. L'Assemblage…"
- *Domus* no. 537, August: "Pelletterie Skin Up"
- *Hogares Modernos*, October: "Flash back"
- *Domus* no. 539, October: "Alì e Aladino Pop Soft"
- *Time*, November: "Design radicale"

1975
- *Domus* no. 546, May: "La Maison Introuvable"
- *Domus* no. 546, May: "Baby-lonia, un gioco"
- *Abitare*, June: "Maison Introuvable"
- *Casabella* no. 406, October: "Baby-lonia"

1976
- *Domus* no. 554, January: "Una casa palladiana"
- *Domus* no. 565, December: "Scaffale Press"

1977
- *Domus* no. 567, February: "A Cuneo secondo Serlio"

1978
- *Domus* no. 580, March: "Architettura radicale in Italia"

1979
- *Domus* no. 597, August: "A Cuneo secondo Piranesi: Flashback"
- *Panorama* no. 711, December 3: L. Berni, "Architettura" section – Cuneo - Borgo San Dalmazzo Expo '74

1980
- *Harpers*, December: “New Classical Again”

1984
- *Asparagus Age*: Ennio Chiggio and Giulia Laverda, exhibition catalogue, Galleria TOT, Padua
- *Gran Bazar*, March: “Un’importante collezione privata europea”
- *L’Unità*, March 30: “La loggia veneziana della lana”
- *La Stampa*, March 30: “La loggia veneziana della lana”
- Gufram catalogue, September
- *Domus* no. 654, October: Capitello

1985
- *Ulisse* 2000, April/June: “Italian Graffiti”
- *Gap Casa*, no. 30, August/September: Chiara Mantica, “I multipli Gufram”
- *Les Plastiques*, September: Sylvia Katz, “Sieges divers et portechapeaux”
- *Europeo* no. 40, October 5: Christina Morozzi, “Prego, si accomodi su questo sasso”

1986
- *La mia casa* no. 186, April: Gigi Grigioni, “Ironia postmoderna”
- *Gap Casa*, August/September: Lella Valtorta, Lucio Zolti, “Per Dilmos”
- *La Repubblica*, September 11: “Cactus e Capitelli”
- *Corriere della Sera*, September 18: Antonia Dettore, “Morbide nostalgie di ironie passate”
- *Corriere della Sera*, September 19: Antonello Mosca, “Questa è la stagione in cui fiorisce il design”
- *Air du Temps*, October 18: “Les arts plastiques”
- *IL*, October: “Les meubles mousse du Pop Art”
- *Le Figaro Magazine*, October 18: “Mobilier Pop Art: vertiges de mousse”
- *Le Journal de la Maison*, October: “Reedition - La vie en mousse”
- *Le Nouvel Observateur*, October: “Mythologies 86”
- *Maison Francaise* no. 400, October: “Denise Bosselet fait mousser le Pop Art”
- *Brava Casa*, October: “In mostra a Milano”
- *City Magazine International* no. 26, October: “Gufram. Multipli Studio65”
- *La mia casa* no. 191, October: Rosaria Miraglia Zucconi, “Tra storia e futuro”
- *Anna* no. 43, October: Cristina Pauly, “I multipli per stupire”
- *MODO* no. 93, October: “Omnibus”
- *L’ambiente cucina* no. 55, November/December: “Tra un Cactus e un Capitello”

1987
- *Modern Forniture Classics*: Miriam Stimpson, Whitney Library of Design, Watson Guptill, New York
- *Grand Bazaar* no. 12/1, December/January: “Riedizioni di un successo”
- *La Stampa*, June 28: “Discoteca che passione!”
- *Liberation*, July 7: Pascaline Cuvelier, “Le post-chip gènèration”
- *Disco Dancing*, December: “Il teatro del mondo”
- *Towards Postmodernism*: Michael Collins, A New York Graphic Society Book/ Little, Brown & Company, Inc., New York & Boston

1988
- *Rassegna* no. 32: C. Benigni, “Una nuova idea dello spazio”
- *Abitare Italia*: Giuseppe Raimondi, “Anni Settanta”, Fabbri editore, Milano

1989
- *Sourcebook of Modern Furniture*: Jerrill Habegger and Joseph H. Osman, W.W. Norton & Company, New York
- *Design Now. Industry or Art?*: Volker Fischer, Prestel Publishing, Munich

1990
- *Il design del mobile italiano dal 1946 a oggi* (“Guide all’Architettura Moderna”): Anty Pansera, Laterza, Bari
- *Möbel aus Kunststoffl*: Alexander von Vegesack, exhibition catalogue, Vitra Design Museum, Basel

1991
- *l’Arca* no. 45, January: Albert Stevens, “Il SIA di Parigi”
- *Progressive Architecture*, February: Barbara Shortt, “Salon International de l’Architecture à Paris”
- *Les classiques du mobilier contemporain*: Charlotte and Peter Fiell, Thames & Hudson, London
- *Le design du meuble au XXe siècle*: Peter Gössel, Gabriele Leuthäuser and Klaus-Jürgen Sembach, Taschen, Cologne
- *Mobili italiani 1961-1991. Le varie età dei linguaggi*: Claudia Donà (edited by), exhibition catalogue, Milan Triennale, S. e. Publisher, Milan, - Milan Triennale
- *l’Arca* no. 54, November: “I multipli dello Studio65” – Salone dell’Architettura, Milan
- *L’Europeo* no. 21: “Works on show at the Milan Triennale”
- *Design in Italia 1950-1990*: Stefano Casciani and Giacinto Di Pietrantonio (edited by), Giancarlo Politi Editore, Milan

1992
- *l’Arca* no. 64, October: Paolo Righetti, “La Scuola del Sole”
- *La Stampa*, October 24: “Gianni Arnaudo Architetto”
- *Domus* no. 742, October: “La porta a scomparsa” – Porta Proteus

1993
- *l’Arca* no. 68, February : “Il V Salon International de l’Architecture”
- *l’Arca* no. 69, March: Alessandro Gubitosi, “Il lavoro ribelle” – Torre Pasteur in Montecarlo
- *l’Arca* no. 70, April: Mario Antonio Arnaboldi, “Un gioco stupendo”
- *Vitra Design Museum*: Alexander Von Vegesack, GA Design Center, Tokyo
- *Modern Chairs*: Charlotte and Peter Fiell, Taschen, Cologne

• *Storia del design industriale italiano* ("Grandi Opere"): Anty Pansera, Laterza, Bari

1994
• *l'Arca* no. 79, February: "A Cuneo un laboratorio d'idee"
• *Interni* no. 439: "Gli oggetti ci parlano"
• *Progetto e cronache*, January 1: "Villa a Mondovì"
• *Histoire du design 1940-1990*: Raimond Guidot, Hazan, Paris
• *L'utopie du tout plastique*, 1960-1973: Fondation pour l'Architecture, Brussels

1995
• *l'Arca* no. 90, February: Mario Antonio Arnaboldi, "Un vascello fra le colline"
• *Le design des anneès Pop. Parcours dan le collections du musée*: exhibition catalogue, Musée des Arts décoratifs, Palais du Louvre, Paris
• *MODO* no. 165: "Studio65 a Parigi"
• *Casanostra, Arte, architettura e tecnologie per l'abitare* no. I/1: "Una villa a Mondovì"
• *Casanostra, Arte, architettura e tecnologie per l'abitare* no. I/2: "Un cuneese al Louvre"
• *100 Chefs-d'oeuvre de la collection du Vitra Design Museum*: Peter Dunas and Alexander Von Vegesack, exhibition catalogue, Vitra Design Museum, Basel
• T*orino design. Dall'automobile al cucchiaio*: Giorgio De Ferrari (edited by), exhibition catalogue, Allemandi Editore, Turin
• *Design: An Illustrated Historical Overview*: Thomas Hauffe, Barrons, New York

1996
• Dictionnaire international des arts appliqués et du design: Arlette Barré-Despond (edited by), Editions du Regard, Paris
• *35 anni di design al salone del mobile. 1961 1996*: Laura Lazzaroni, Cosmit, Milan
• *l'Arca* no. 110, December: Maurizio Vogliazzo, "Grugliasco: fabbrica e immagine"
• *l'Arca International* no. 8: Maurizio Vogliazzo, "Grugliasco: l'industrie et son image"
• *Masterworks: Italian Design, 1960-1994*: R. Craig Miller (edited by), exhibition catalogue, American Federation of Arts, New York

1997
• *1000 Chairs*: Charlotte and Peter Fiell, Taschen, Cologne
• *Plastics + Design*: Florian Hufnagl, Arnoldsche, Stuttgart
• *Sourcebook of Modern Furniture*: Jeryll Habegger and Joseph H. Osman, Norton & Company, New York
• *l'Arca* no. 121, December: Walter Bianchi, "Un caposaldo della città"
• *l'Arca Plus* no. 14: "1987-1997. 10 anni di Architettura in Italia"
• *Abitare* no. 367, November: "Nuova generazione: 50 progetti di architetti italiani" –Meeting Centre of the Provincial Administration of Cuneo
• *Dimensions of design. 100 classical seats*: exhibition catalogue, Vitra Design Museum, Basel,
• *Il look del secolo*: Michael Tambini, Mondadori, Milan
• *Sogno e segno. Il Centro congressi della provincia di Cuneo*: Walter Bianchi, l'Arca Edizioni, Milan
• *The Chair, an Appreciation*: Sarah Colombo, photos by Guy Ryecart, Laurel Glen, san Diego

1998
• *Design, an Illustrated Historical Overview*: Thomas Hauffe, Barron's, New York
• *L'Espresso* no. 23, June 11: "Italians do it better"

1999
• *Acciaio Arte Architettura* no. 1, May: Michela Tosatto, "Un guscio d'acciaio per la fabbrica del futuro" – Dromont plant
• *Spazio Casa* no. 5, May: Renato De Marco, "Una lezione di semplicità nel lavoro di famosi progettisti"
• *Op to Pop. Furniture of the 1960's*: Cara Greenberg, Bulfinch Press, New York
• *Gianni Arnaudo. Opacità e trasparenza*: Maurizio Vogliazzo, l'Arca Edizioni, Milan
• *Il design in Italia dell'arredamento domestico*: Paola Biondi e Giuliana Gramigna, Allemandi Editore, Turin
• *Elle Decor*:"Commencez votre collection de sieges miniatures Vitra"
• *Positionen des Designs die 60er*: Gerda Breuer, Andrea Peters, Kerstin Plüm (edited by) Wienand, Cologne
• *Dictionnaire du design. Italie*: Seuil, Paris
• *World Design: The Best in Classic and Contemporary Furniture, Fashion, Graphics and More*: Christian Pixis and Uta Abendroth, Chronicle Books, San Francisco

2000
• *Modulo* no. 261, May: "Premiata la cultura dell'alluminio" – Portarossa
• *l'Arca* no. 144, January: "Bianco lucente, Portarossa complex, Cuneo"
• *l'Arca* no. 149, June: "Premi a trenta realizzazioni", Portarossa
• *Abitare* no. 396, June: "Metra = alluminio"
• *Modernism* vol. 3, Fall: "Adventures in the furniture trade"
• *Design for Living: Furniture and Lighting 1950-2000*: David A. Hanks and Anne Hoy, Flammarion, Paris
• *Vinum*, December 2000:"Terre da Vino - eine Kellerei für die Zukunft"

2001
• *Panorama*, March 22: Silvia Bombelli, "Fermentare è bello. Tra le botti elementi hi-tech e architettura rurale"
• *Barolo & Co*, March:"Un rudere riprende vita"– Terre da Vino winery
• *l'Arca* no. 160, June: Elena Cardani, "Oltre Le Colline" – Terre da Vino winery
• *Presenza Tecnica* no. 172, June: Raffaella Chierici, "Seguendo L'orizzonte" – Terre da Vino winery

- *Der Feinschmecker*, no. 2, June:"Durchblik dank gewagter Architektur" – Terre da Vino winery
- *l'Arca* no. 163, October: "In bocca al comfort"
- *Arkitekton* no. 3, October: Luciana Ceresini, "Di rispetto e fantasia" – Terre da Vino winery
- *Domus* no. 841, October: "Legno lamellare e acciaio" – Terre da Vino winery
- *Civiltà del bere* no. 10, October: "Affascinanti costruzioni già inserite nel paesaggio" – Terre da Vino winery
- *La collection de design du Centre Georges Pompidou*: exhibition catalogue, Centre Georges Pompidou, Paris
- *Le catalogue de vos rêves*: Pierre Marchand and Hervé Tardy, Hachette, Paris – San Fin
- *Modern Furniture Classics: Postwar to Post-Modernism*: Charlotte and Peter Fiell, Thames & Hudson, London

2002
- *Materia* no. 37, January/April: "Gianni Arnaudo stabilimento 'Terre da Vino'" – Terre da Vino winery
- *Panorama*, February 28: Silvia Bombelli, "Baciami, Frau"
- *Luce, lampade 1968-1973, il nuovo design italiano*: Fulvio e Napoleone Ferrari, Allemandi Editore, Turin
- *Il design italiano dell'arredamento domestico*: Paola Biondi e Giuliana Gramigna, Allemandi Editore, Turin
- *The rock furniture. Il design della Gufram negli anni del rock*: Franco Mello, exhibition cataologue, Castello di Rivoli. Museo d'Arte contemporanea, Rivoli (Turin)
- *Abitare* no. 415, March: Maria Giulia Zumino, "Gianni Arnaudo a Barolo" – Terre da Vino winery
- *Metra*, no. 2, March: "Il complesso Portarossa di Cuneo: una nave che guarda l'altopiano"
- *Presenza Tecnica* no. 185, October: Raffaella Chierici "Giochi di luce e colori" – Dromont plant
- *Aeronautica e Spazio* no. 11, November: Paolo Giovannini, "Cuneo, la nuova aerostazione"
- *Der Feinschmecker* no. 4, December: Ralf Frädtke, "Heilige Hallen" – Terre da Vino winery
- *Intramuros* no. 104, December: "Réserves à découvert"
- *Techniques et architecture*, December: "Débats, déballages – 3e Biennale de Design, novembre 2002"

2003
- *l'Arca* no. 177, January: Michele Bazan Giordano, "La metamorfosi dell'edificio" – Dromont plant
- *l'Arca International* no. 50, February: Michele Bazan Giordano, "La métamorphose du bâtiment", – Dromont plant
- *Acciaio Arte Architettura* no. 15, June: Marzia Urettini, "Funzione e personalità, il nuovo stabilimento Dromont"
- *Area* no. 69, July/August: "Stabilimento industriale Alba, Cuneo" – Dromont plant
- *Materia* no. 41, May/August: "Stabilimento industriale Dromont, Grinzane Cavour, Italia" – Dromont plant
- *Campagna Amica*, March/April: Carlo Raspollini "Cantine incantate, dimore del vino a regola d'arte"
- *Casabella* no. 712, June: "Zen"
- *Specchio* no. 381, July 12: "Anni '60. La fantasia al potere"
- *Acciaio Arte Architettura* no. 16, September: Laura Cristiana Bertola, "Cenando sulle Langhe"
- *Gambero Rosso* no. 141, October: "Se la cantina la fa l'architetto" – Terre da Vino winery
- *Elementi del progetto. Porte. Il design della migliore produzione*: Carlo Vannicola (edited by), Federico Motta Editore
- *Ottagono* no. 164, October: Floriana Morrone, "Passerella sulle botti"
- *Domus* no. 864, November: "Zen – design: Gianni Arnaudo"
- *Abitare* no. 434, December: "Metra: sistema d'autore" – Dromont plant
- *Design, carrefour des arts*: Raymond Guidot, Flammarion, Paris
- *La grande svolta anni '60. Viaggio negli anni Sessanta in Italia:* Virginia Baradel, Ennio Ludovico Chiggio, Roberto Masiero, Skira, Milan

2004
- *Infiniture*, distributed with *Interni* no. 3, March: Katrin Cosseta, "The doors"
- *Il Nuovo Cantiere* no. 3, March: Sandra Lasagni, "Il nastro d'argento" – Dromont plant
- *Specchio* no. 414, April: "Etichette d'autore" – Terre da Vino winery
- *Domus* no. 870, May: "Facciata in alluminio – Design: Gianni Arnaudo" – Dromont plant
- *La Stampa*, May 28: "Aeroporto di Cuneo-Levaldigi"
- *L'industria italiana del cemento* no. 798, May: Portarossa
- *Modulo* no. 302, June: "Aeroporto di Cuneo-Levaldigi firmato Arnaudo" – Cuneo-Levaldigi airport
- *La Stampa*, July 27: "Premio Dedalo Minosse"
- *Ottagono* no. 172, July: "Produzione a Palazzo" – Dromont plant
- *Cantine. Architetture 1990-2005*: Marco Casamonti, Vincenzo Pavan, Federico Motta Editore, Milan
- *Presenza Tecnica* no. 202, September: Maria Chiara Garavini, "Battito d'ali" – Cuneo-Levaldigi airport
- *Il Sole 24 Ore*, October 16: "Arredare casa con pezzi da museo"
- *La Stampa*, October 31: Mario Bosonetto, "L'architetto che progetta città d'acqua"
- *l'Arca* no. 198, December: Remo Dorigati, "Capelli al vento"
- *Wineries with Style*: Peter Richards, Mitchell Beazley Publishers, London
- *D'Architettura* no. 25, September: "100 Progetti"; and "Rassegna Italiana" – V2 Elettronica plant
- *Dis-moi le design*: Claude Courtecuisse and Anne de Boissieux, Isthme Éditions, Paris
- *Le Design*: *Histoire, principaux courants, grandes figures*: Anne Bony, Edition Larousse, Paris Anne Bony, Larousse, Paris

2005
- *Italy Builds - Italia Costruisce*: Paolo Portoghesi (edited by), l'Arca Edizioni, Milan – Terre da Vino winery
- *Barolo & Co.*, March: "Un rudere riprende vita", a project with the students of Turin's Turin Polytechnic
- *Vanity Fair*, April: "Terapia di gruppo"
- *Interni* no. 30, June: Roberto Ciminaghi "360° di ironia"

- *Class* no. 229, May: “Le Cattedrali del Vino” – Terre da Vino winery
- *Glamour* no. 159, May: Terre da Vino winery
- *Grazia Casa*, distributed with *Grazia* no. 26, June 28: Deborah Piana Agostinetti “In movimento”
- *Architetture per il vino* no. 6, July: Elena Riboldi, “Il connubio tra architettura e vino…” – Terre da Vino winery
- *Architetture contemporanee per paesaggi vitivinicoli*: Alessandro Sondini, Edizioni Unicopli, Milan
- *Acciaio Arte Architettura* no. 23, June: Marzia Urettini, “The Phantom of the Church” – Savigliano
- *Abitare* no. 452, July/August: “Gufram – Déjeuner sur l’arbre”
- *Domus* no. 884, September: “Arbre Magique – Design: Gianni Arnaudo”
- *Arca Plus* no. 14, June: “Grugliasco, Torino – Bitron plant”
- *l'Arca* no. 204, June: “Salone Internazionale del mobile e dintorni, Milano 2005”
- *l'Arca International* no. 65, July/August: “Design et ses alentours”
- *Case da Abitare* no. 88, June: Arbre Magique
- *Il Giornale dell’Architettura*, no. 31, July: Gioco Studio65
- *Specchio* no. 475, July 9: “Quando Arbre Magique diventa ispirazione l’arte incontra il design”
- *Imbottigliamento* no. 6, July: “Architetture per il vino” – Terre da Vino winery
- *L’Officiel* no. 3, June: “1000 modèles design” – Arbre Magique
- *Gap Casa* no. 195, September: Raffaella Capretti “Appuntamento al Fuori Salone”
- *AD* no. 292, September: “Luoghi divini” – Terre da Vino winery
- *Elle UK*, September: Arbre Magique
- *I Viaggi di Repubblica*, October: Terre da Vino winery
- *Il Giornale dell’Architettura* no. 34, November: “Progetto per una fabbrica a Racconigi” – V2 Elettronica plant
- *l'Arca* no. 209, December: “Confronto con la storia” – V2 Elettronica plant
- *MODO*, October/December: “Per un design impuro”

2006
- *Abitare* no. 457, January: “Il Museo nazionale di Capo Verde”
- *Corriere della Sera Magazine* no. 7, January 16: Davide Perillo, “Il Rinascimento del vino è iniziato con il metanolo” – Terre da Vino winery
- *Flair* no. 4, March: Monica Baio “Tutti a Milano (a vedere il design)”
- *l'Arca* no. 212, March: “Un riferimento per il progettista” – Maligno Industries plant
- *Presenza Tecnica* no. 216, March/April; “Forme di luce” – V2 Elettronica plant
- *Must*, April: “Terre da Vino”
- *Materia* no. 50, May/August: “Around ’50”
- *AD* no. 300, May: “Quando la natura diventa artificio”
- *A+D+M Magazine* no. 4, June: “La porta del vento per volare verso il mondo” – Aeroporto di Cuneo-Levaldigi
- *Risorse CRC* no. 5, June: “Il recupero dell’ex Bertello a Borgo San Dalmazzo” – Bertello
- *Elementi del progetto. Facciate a secco*: Alessandra Coppa and Barbara Borello, Federico Motta Editore, Milan – Dromont plant
- *In Vite Qualitas* no. 5, June: Francesca Bizzarri “L’opaca trasparenza del vino” – Terre da Vino winery
- *Il Modo Italiano: Design et avant-garde en Italie au XXe siècle*: Giampiero Bosoni (edited by), exhibition catalogue, Skira, Milan
- *La Stampa*, September 4: “Gianni Arnaudo in Cina”
- *Provincia Oggi*, October: “Il vino che guarda verso il futuro” – Terre da Vino winery
- *Interni* no. 11, December: “Il Modo Italiano”
- *A+D+M Magazine* no. 6, December: Renzo Ricasso “Irriverente ricerca tra Pop Art e ironia”, front cover and interview
- *Ulisse* no. 268, December: Massimo Locci “Gli architetti di Bacco” – Terre da Vino winery
- *Risorse CRC* no. 6, December: “Il nuovo auditorium ‘Città di Borgo San Dalmazzo’”

2007
- *Provincia Oggi*, January: “Un polo culturale nel cuore di Borgo” – Bertero
- *Materia* no. 53, March: Jacopo Maria Giagnoni, “V2 Elettronica Productive Plant”
- *Il Giornale*, April 8: “L’angolo del design”
- *Interni*, n. 39, April: “Voglia di design”
- *l'Arca* no. 226, June: “Qualità molteplici”, News section
- *Casabella* no. 756, June: “Serramenti Porte” section
- *AD* no. 313, June: “Design News”
- *A+D+M Magazine* no. 8, June: “Design”
- *l'Arca* no. 226, June: “Qualità molteplici”
- *Riabita* no. 6, June: “Nuove tecnologie”
- *Casabella* no. 758, September: “Rococò – Snake”
- *OFARCH* no. 97: “Lualdi”
- *D’Architettura* no. 34: “Casa ad appartamenti a Cuneo” – Via Tornaforte
- *A+D+M Magazine* no. 10, October: “Una cantina come una nave” – Nizza Monferrato winery
- *ADI Design Report 07*: Allemandi Editore, Turin
- *Amedeo Albertini. Fantasia e tecnica nell’architettura*: Guido Montanari, Skira, Milan, foreword by Gianni Arnaudo
- *Wineries II / Bodegas II: Architecture & Design / Arquitectura y Diseno*: Antonio Corcuera, Kliczkowski Publisher – Terre da Vino winery

2008
- *Arredamento & Design. Interiors & Design 2008-2009*: Aurelio Magistà, *La Repubblica* “Grandi Guide”
- *A+D+M Magazine* no. 13, March: Luisa Craviotto “Nuovi paesaggi per il pensiero” – Castello di Montaldo
- *Le case del vino. Elementi linguistici del paesaggio vitivinicolo*: Gianni Arnaudo, foreword by Carlo Petrini, L’Artistica Editrice, Savigliano (Cuneo)
- *Elle*, May: “Oggetti col sorriso” – *Pop design* exhibition, Caraglio

- *La Stampa, Dossier Più*: "Evergreen Design"
- *Design italiano del XX secolo*: Aldo Colonetti, Elena Brigi, and Valentina Croci, Giunti Editore, Milan
- *Cantine*: Veronica Pirazzini (edited by), Federico Motta Editore, Milan – Terre da Vino winery
- *Hotel*: Veronica Pirazzini (edited by), Federico Motta Editore, Milan – Soul Farm Hotel, Castello di Montaldo
- *Area* no. 97, April: "40 anni di design"
- *A+D+M Magazine* no. 15, May: Riccardo Delfino "Una mostra all'insegna dell'ironia" – *Pop design* exhibition, Caraglio
- *Tende da sole e schermature solari*, June: Fabio Sciacca "Tra tecnologia e tradizione" – Villa Torre San Giorgio (Cuneo)
- *AD France*: I.M., "Les grands éditeurs revoient leurs classique"
- *Guida del Piemonte. Architettura del Novecento*: Maria Adriana Giusti and Rosa Tamborrino (edited by), Allemandi Editore, Turin – Terre da Vino winery, Dromont plant, V2 Elettronica plant, Cuneo-Levaldigi airport, Castello di Montaldo
- *Presenza Tecnica* no. 236, June 2008: "Nel mondo del vino" – Terre da Vino winery
- *Brava Casa*, August: "Sediamoci fuori"
- *ADI Design Report 08*: Allemandi Editore, Turin
- *Grazia Casa* no. 12, December: "Green design"
- *Benessere* no. 44, December: Rosa Marino, "C'era una volta…" – Castello di Montaldo
- *Pop Design. Fuori scala, fuori luogo, fuori schema*: Luisa Bocchietto, Anty Pansera, Vanni Pasca, Piero Dadone (edited by), exhibition catalogue, SilvanaEditoriale
- *The A-Z of Modern Design*: Bernd Polster, Claudia Neumann, Markus Schuler and Frederick Leven, Merrell, London and New York

2009
- *ADI Design Index* 2008: Oscar G. Colli (edite by), Editrice Compositori, Milan-Bologna
- *Elle Decor Italia* no. 1–2, January/February: Beatrice Rossetti , "Come nelle fiabe…"
- *Interni*, April: "Il tema centrale"
- *Case & Country* no. 187, April: Franca Rottola, "Viva la libertà" – Casa Massucco, Cherasco (Cuneo)
- *La Guida*, April 10: Enrico Giaccone , "Quattro ipotesi per il Foro Boario" – feasibility study on the area of Foro Boario (Cuneo)
- *AD* no. 334, March: "AD outdoor. 100 proposte per vivere all'aperto"
- *A+D+M Magazine* no. 22, April/May: Luisa Craviotto, "Il marmo è una spalla per portare il tempo"
- *Provincia Oggi*, May: "L'arte fa impresa con la creatività"
- *La Stampa*, May 25: "L'architetto cuneese amico di Capo Verde"
- *l'Arca* no. 248, June: Michele Bazan Giordano, "I Saloni 2009 Milano"
- *Idea*, June: "Il belvedere sul fiume" – Dronero
- *AD* no. 337, June: Capitello
- *Case & Stili*, July 2009: "In Giardino"
- *Cuneo 7*, July 28: Sergio Peirone, "Grande come piazza San Pietro" – Foro Boario
- *Idea* no. 21, September: "Architettura sostenibile. Una villa realizzata in legno e pietra di Langa"
- *Magnetti Murature*, December: "Aeroporto di Cuneo. Quando l'architettura vola alto"
- *Edilia*, December: "Aeroporto di Cuneo. Quando l'architettura vola alto" – Cuneo-Levaldigi airport

2010
- *Domus* no. 932, January: "FIZZZ by Gianni Arnaudo"
- *Triennale Design Museum. Che cosa è il design italiano? Le sette ossessioni del design italiano*: Silvana Annicchiarico and Andrea Branzi (edited by), Electa, Milan
- *Cuneo 7*, February 2: "Piazza Foro Boario, si discute se costruirci sopra o no" – Foro Boario (Cuneo)
- *Pocket Magazine*, March: "Nonpossoviveresenza"
- *Problemi di architettura albesi dal secondo dopoguerra ad oggi*: Alessandra Bertolino, Emanuela Giudice e Gabriele Proglio, L'Artistica Editrice, Savigliano (Cuneo) – Dromont plant
- *Cuneo 7*, April 17: Sergio Peirone, "Nell'ex Arsenale due palazzi"
- *La Stampa*, April 14: Lorenzo Boratto, "Ex Arsenale, no ai palazzi" – Ex Arsenale
- *Case & Country Class* no. 199, April: "Progetti al naturale" – Terre da Vino winery
- *Metrocubo* no. 102, May: "Architettura verso il cielo" – Cuneo-Levaldigi airport
- *l'Arca* no. 259, June 2010: guest editor Gianni Arnaudo
- *Kamchi Lighting*, June
- *Il Giornale*, July: "La regina delle gelatine e il sogno del Barolo" – L'Astemia Pentita winery
- *La Stampa*, July 2: Sergio Miravalle, "A Barolo un progetto che farà girare le scatole" – L'Astemia Pentita winery
- *Area* no. 111, July/August: Davide Cattaneo, "Slide progetti di luce e di colore"
- *Confidenze*, July: "Tutto in meno di 80 cm"
- *GDA International*, July: "Creations Slide"
- *Horeca Magazine*, October: "L'arredo esterno si illumina"
- *AD* no. 354, November: "Quadrature"
- *Cuneo 7*, December 7: Sergio Peirone, "Su piazza Foro Boario ci sono già tre progetti" – Foro Boario (Cuneo)
- *Cuneo 7*, December 7: Sergio Peirone, "Perché non il pizza di Cuneo" – Foro Boario (Cuneo)
- *Cuneo 7*, December 21: Sergio Peirone, "Le cattedrali del vino" – Terre da Vino winery
- *Collecting design*: Adam Lindemann, Taschen, Cologne
- *A+D+M Magazine* no. 31, December: "La trasformazione pop della cantina" – L'Astemia Pentita winery

2011
- *AD Russia*, January
- *Panorama*, February 3: "Extra"
- *Casabella* no. 800, April: "Contract sistemi di arredo"
- *Io Donna*, April: "Aspettando il Fuori Salone"
- *Arketipo, Il Sole 24 Ore*, May: "Tetti verdi e promenade" – Terre da Vino winery

- *Gazzetta degli Edili*, October: "La nuova nobiltà: Welness e Hotel in Castello" – Castello di Montaldo
- *AD*, October: "Capriccio romano"
- *l'Arca* no. 270, June: "Una copertura perfetta" –
- *Casabella* no. 804, August: "Aeroporto di Cuneo"
- *l'Arca* no. 272, September: "Storie di successo" – Terre da Vino winery
- *Toscano* no. 3: "Le cattedrali del vino" – Terre da Vino winery
- *La Stampa*, December 28: "Una tela di Arnaudo accanto a Le Corbusier"

2012
- *l'Arca* no. 277, February, "Gianni Arnaudo al Vitra"
- *l'Arca* no. 279, April: "È tutto design"
- *l'Arca International* no. 106, May/June: "Black is black"
- *AD*, June: "Lo stile libero del design"
- *La Stampa*, June 13: "Poltrone con toppe di poesia dell'architetto Arnaudo"
- *Casabella* no. 817, September: "Soul farm hotel" – Castello di Montaldo
- *Il Venerdì di* Repubblica, October 12: "La Pop Art diviene mobile"
- *AD* no. 378, November: "1972: Bocca, il divano pop"
- *Gambero Rosso* no. 251, November: "Cantine belle e buone"
- *Elle Decor Sudafrica*, August: Bocca sofa
- *Il Gazzettino*, September: "Cattedrali di vino – l'arte nelle cantine" – L'Astemia Pentita winery
- *Pop Art Design*: exhibition catalogue, Vitra Design Museum, Basel
- *La Stampa*, September 11: "Presidente Festival dell'Architettura"
- *Side Magazine* no. 10, October: "Kitsch di qualità"
- *Cuneo 7*, December 25: "Il genio di Gianni Arnaudo"
- *A+D+M Magazine* no. 37: " Gugliermetto Fratelli Multipli Experience"
- *La Stampa*, December 3: "Da Bacco alle Archistar" – L'Astemia Pentita winery

2013
- *Domus* no. 965, January: "Pop Art Design"
- *Area* 131, December: "25° by Arnaudo" – Bertolotto Porte
- *Elle France* online: Arbre Magique
- *Casabella* (edited by): "Casalgrandepadana Grand Prix" – Terre da Vino winery, Maligno Industries plant
- *AD* no. 383, April: " Il mobile è donna"
- *La Stampa*, April 14: "Quattro firme d'Italia per una rivincita pop"
- *La Stampa*, June 29: "Crea architettura e arte nel mondo"
- *Elle Decor* year 24 no. 9, August
- *Cuneo 7*, September 3: "Ripartire dalla cultura per crescere" – Foro Boario Auditorium
- *Salon* Russia no. 3
- *Ville e Casali* no. 10, October: "Nuove strutture"
- *L'Espresso* no. 40, October 10: "Abitare il futuro"
- *Interni* no.73, October: "100% Made in Italy"
- *Porte & Finestre*, September: "Fantasia dissacrante"
- *Excellence*, October: Gianni Arnaudo, "La grande architettura entra in cantina"
- *ASK*, November: "Gufram, a museum of furniture!"
- *Marie Claire Maison*, December: "Tendenze"
- *Le design: Histoire, principaux courants, grandes figures*: Anne Bony, Edition Larousse (second edition), Paris - Capitello
- *Area* no. 131, December: "25° by Arnaudo"

2014
- *Cuneo 7*, January 14: "Arnaudo al Beaubourg""
- *La Guida*, February 28: "Sette ville per Villa Sarah"
- *Il Sole 24 Ore*: "Vino, tra le sette cantine meraviglie svetta Petra, cantina di Terra Moretti" – Terre da Vino winery
- *Elle Decor*, year 25 no. 5, May: "Design news"
- *l'Arca International* no. 116, January: "La Marine Corsaire"
- *AD* no. 395, April: Bocca sofa
- *Interni*, Wining & Designing dossier: "Food Wine Design Week" – Terre da Vino winery
- *Elle Decor* year 25 no. 6, June: "Hi-Light"
- *La Stampa*, June 28: "Maina amplia lo stabilimento e aumenta la produzione"
- *Ville e Casali* no. 24: "Interior decorator"
- *Dentro Casa* no. 177, August: "Non solo rosa"
- *Interni* no. 10, October: "In News"
- *Percorsi* no. 30, *Casabella* special edition, December: Gianni Arnaudo, "Pop reloaded"
- *1968: Radical Italian Design*: Maria Cristina Didero and Dakis Joannou, photos by Maurizio Cattelan and Pieropaolo Ferrari, Deste Foundation for Contemporary Art / Toiletpaper
- *Gioia*, December: "Che ne dici di… 'labbra' d'autore?"

2015
- *Elle Decor* no. 2, February: "Guide d'eccezione"
- *Marie Claire Maison, Guida Design 2015*
- *La Stampa*, February 3: "Le Langhe si dividono sulla 'cantina pop'", L'Astemia Pentita winery
- *Corriere della Sera*, February 8: "Barolo in scatola, la cantina che piace all'Unesco"
- *Abitare* no. 542, March: "BiHome by Bertolotto"
- *Case Così*, April: "Bocca – L'originale, dal 1970, è solo Gufram"
- *Gioia*, May: "Unica"
- *Vogue Japan*, April: "Inspired by Ellen's The real Barbie"
- *Plastic Days. Materiali e design*: Cecilia Cecchini and Marco Petroni (edited by), Silvana Editoriale, Milan
- *The Story of Design: From the Paleolithic to the Present*: Charlotte and Pieter Fiell, The Monacelli Press, New York
- Il Sole 24 Ore, December 23: "Arnaudo firma la nuova sede Maina a Fossano"

2016
- *Piazza Grande*, February 25: "Dalla Maina una lezione di stile" – Maina plant
- *l'Arca International* no. 129, March: "Maina panettoni"– Maina plant
- *IoArch* no. 63, May: "Il nastro rosso delle feste Maina"

- *The Plan* no. 94, November: “Un fil rouge per osare e stupire” – Maina plant
- *Casabella* no. 867, November: “Fabbrica di panettoni Maina – Fossano, Cuneo”
- *Now>next*: Luigi Prestinenza Puglisi, Gian Maria Casadei, Federica Marchetti, and Maria Michaela Pani (edited by), LetteraVentidue Edizioni, Siracusa, Maina plant

2017

- *Area* no. 150, January/ February: “Maina. Gianni Arnaudo”
- *Corriere della Sera*, February 5:“La Francia a caccia di creatività scopre l’ironia del design radicale”
- *La Stampa*, February 26: Matteo Borgetto, “Da discoteche a luoghi fantasma”
- *l'Arca International* no. 135, March: “Hyeres, Villa Noailles, La Boîte de nuit”
- *The Plan* no. 99, June: “Un nastro tra presente e passato” – Dromont plant
- *ARK*, July: “Industrie Maina”
- *100 Progetti Italiani*: Riccardo Dell’anna Editore – Maina plant
- *La Repubblica*, October 19: Diego Longhin, “La città di grattacieli e nuovi quartieri” – Maina plant
- *Cantine da collezione. Itinerari di architettura contemporanea nel paesaggio italiano*: Luca Molinari (edited by), Forma Edizioni – Terre da Vino winery
- *Tutela del design*: Guardamagna e associati, Forma Edizioni, foreword by Gianni Arnaudo
- *Domus* no. 1019, December: “Retrofit per l’architettura”– Maina plant
- *Area* no. 155, December: “Contemporary Itinerary: Northen Italy” – Terre da Vino winery
- *La boîte de nuit*: Carlotta Darò and Jean-Pierre Blanc (edited by), exhibition catalogue, Association Villa Noailles, Hyeres

2018

- *Bagni*, February: “Italgelatine”
- *La Stampa*, March 15: “L’architetto che disegnava i templi della discomusic” – Flashback
- *Night Fever: Designing Club Culture 1960–Today*: Mateo Kries, Jochen Eisenbrand, Catharine Rossi and Katarina Serulus (edited by), exhibition catalogue, Vitra Design Museum, Basel
- *The Wall Street Journal*, March: “Nightclub at the Museum: Decades of Disco Design” – *Night Fever* exhibition
- *Abitare* online, March: “Vitra: in mostra le discoteche dagli anni Sessanta” – *Night Fever* exhibition
- *Elle Decor* online, April: “Dalle discoteche anni ’60 ai club dei millennials: la (silent) mostra ‘Night Fever’”
- *100 Progetti Italiani*: Riccardo Dell’Anna Editore – L’Astemia Pentita winery
- *Interni* no. 85, April: “Libertà di pensiero” – *Night Fever* exhibition, Flash Back
- *Triennale Design Museum, Il museo mutante*: Silvana Annicchiarico (edited by), Mondadori Electa, Milan
- *Domus* no. 1024: Flash Back,
- *The Plan* online, June: L’Astemia Pentita winery
- *La Stampa*, June 6: “Premiato a Roma il progetto della cantina a forma di casse di vino” – L’Astemia Pentita winery
- *Living Corriere*, September: “La sfida del Pop” – L’Astemia Pentita winery
- *Wallpaper**, September: “Crate Escape” – L’Astemia Pentita winery
- *Icon Design*, October 5: L’Astemia Pentita winery
- *Exibart* no. 102, October/December: Flashback
- *The Plastic Collection*: Anne Bony, Alexandra Midal and Richard Thommeret, ADAM Design Museum, Brussels *Exibart* no. 102, October/December: “Discos in the 80’s: un’estetica dell’edonismo”
- *Panorama Italiano*, vol. 5: The Plan Editions – L’Astemia Pentita winery

2019

- *Interni* no. 8, July/ August: “Evergreen” – Aliko
- *l'Arca International* no. 149, July/August: “Cantina L’Astemia Pentita”
- *YouBuild*, September: “Arte pop in cantina” – L’Astemia Pentita winery
- *IoArch* no. 84, November: “L’Astemia Pentita – Eco Bio e molto Pop”
- *AD* no. 458, November: Sonia S. Braga, “Mobili oltre la realtà” – *Objects of Desire exhibition* at Vitra Design Museum, Basilea
- *100 Progetti Italiani*: Riccardo Dell’anna Editore – Dromont plant

2020

- *La Repubblica*, January 30: “La rivincita del talento di Arnaudo”
- *Idea* no. 3, March: “Gianni Arnaudo – visione e sovversione”
- *IoArch* no. 86, March: “Un balcone sulle Langhe”
- *Tre bicchieri* no. 31, August: “Speciale guida per enoturisti. 10 itinerari per 10 cantine” – Terre da Vino winery
- *Sky tg24*, September: “Le 30 cantine vinicole di design più belle d'Italia” – L’astemia Pentita winery, Terre da Vino winery (online publication)
- *Harper’s Bazaar Italia*, October: “Cinque cantine moderne e di design da visitare nelle Langhe” – L’Astemia Pentita winery (online publication)
- *Grinzane Cavour – l’evoluzione di un territorio di Langa*: Luigi Cabutto (edited by), Edizioni Langhe Roero Monferrato, Alba (Cuneo)
- *IoArch* no. 90, November: “Pensare al restauro come un kintsugi” – Ex Frigorifero Militare complex, Cuneo

RICORDATI DI
COLTIVARE L'IRONIA
ANCHE SOLO PER
USO PERSONALE

"When someone says, I could do that too, it means that they could do it again, otherwise they would have already done it."

Bruno Munari

To find out more

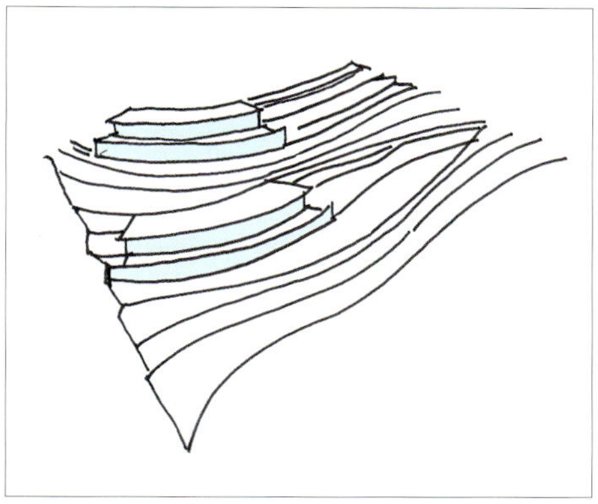

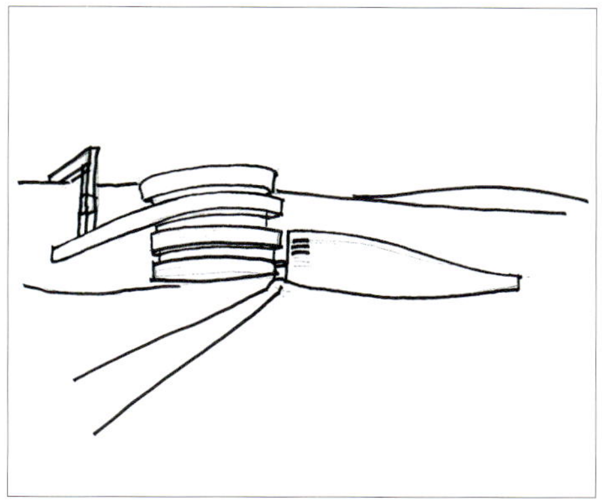

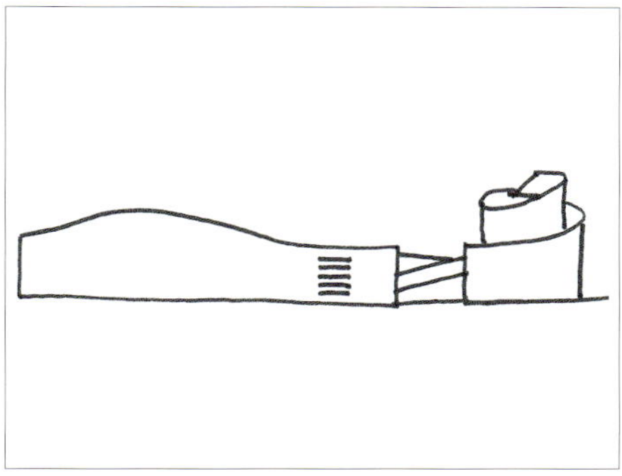

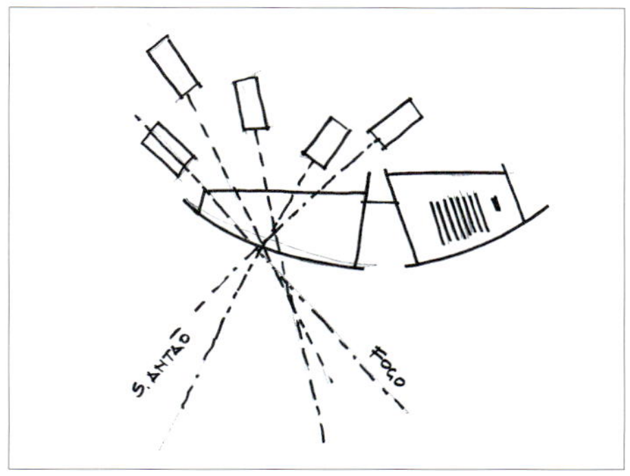

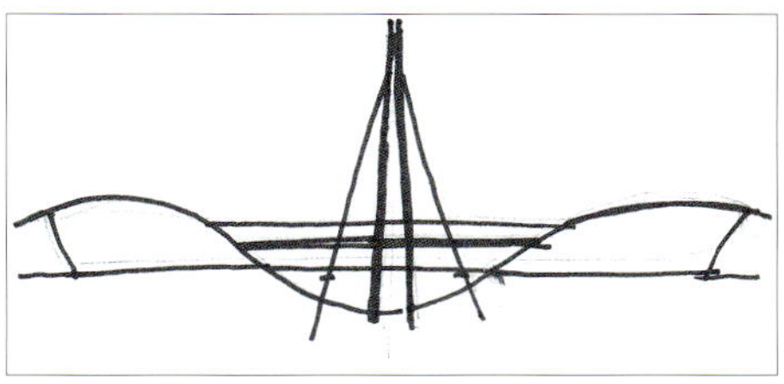

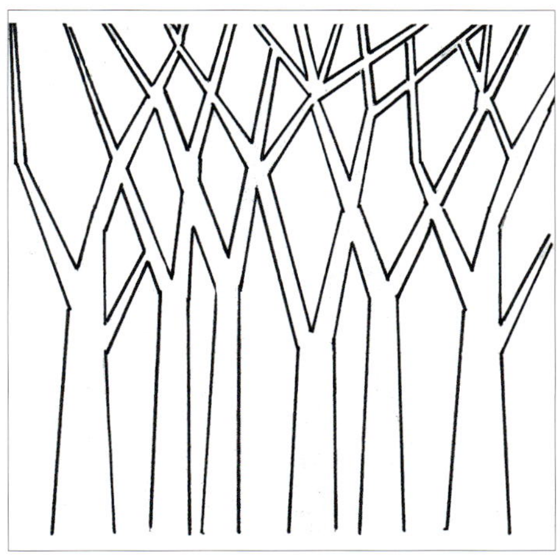

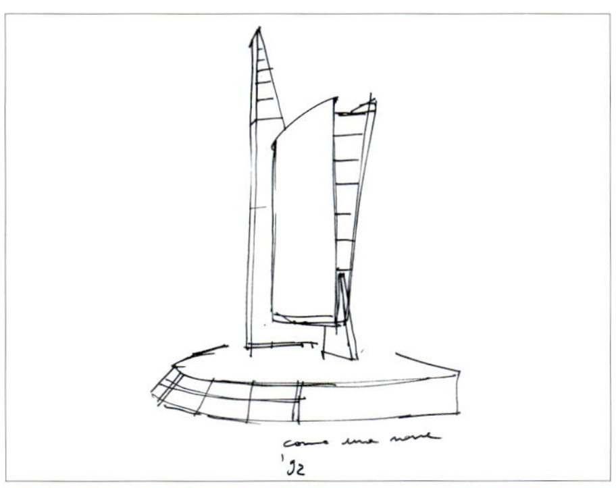

Every architectural work has
its own DNA,
its own *raison d'être*.
It's our task to discover it.
If there is none, then it's a copy,
or a mediocre banality.

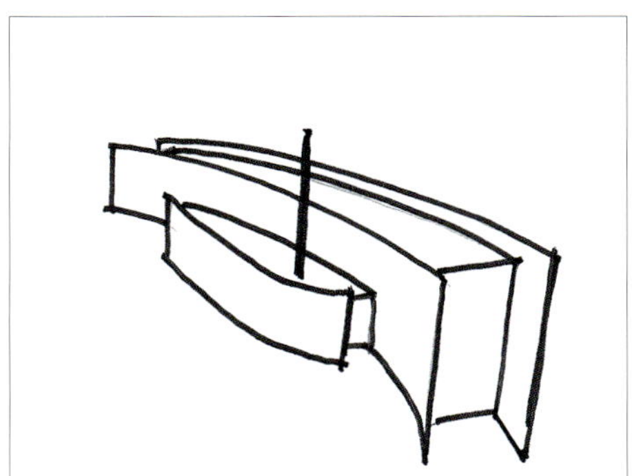

TESTI IN
ITALIANO

p. 5

DEDICATO A TUTTI GLI ARCHITETTI CHE HANNO CREATO PICCOLE BELLISSIME POESIE
MA NON HANNO LA FORZA PER COMUNICARLE

in ricordo di Otto Steidle

p. 7

ANTIMUSEALE
Storia senza cronologia di Gianni Arnaudo

p. 9

Prefazione
di Valérie Guillaume

Conservatrice, direttrice del servizio di Prospettiva industriale. Centre Georges Pompidou, Musée national d'art moderne / Centre de création industrielle.

Caro Gianni,

è stato a Salvador de Bahia, dove ho potuto constatare con un certo stupore – poiché lo notavo per la prima volta – che potevi prendere le distanze dall'architettura. Noi visitavamo la chiesa di São Francisco, le cui decorazioni barocche, scolpite e dorate in sovrabbondanza, non lasciavano nessuno spazio vuoto, nessu—na tregua visiva. Mi è sembrato a un certo punto che privilegiassi con costanza i silenzi dell'architettura. Un volume, una superficie lasciati liberi permettono la proiezione verso il passato e verso il futuro e lasciano all'immaginazione il piacere di completare la parte mancante. Il palinsesto di un oggetto o di un edificio suggerisce in questo modo sia la stratificazione storica precedente sia la fonte ispiratrice o una citazione. L'originalità del tuo percorso si riconosce in tutte le opere progettate dai primi anni settanta in seno alla Studio65 e successivamente, in epoca più recente, con il Déjeuner sur l'arbre, Milo, Rococò... Le tue creazioni rivelano in profondo le trasformazioni delle strategie e delle estetiche di progettazione e di produzione industriale. Tu esprimi nella creazione architettonica e di design un'estetica dell'ironia i cui echi e sviluppi interpretativi risultano sempre incisivi. L'ironia del frammento di un capitello (Capitello), di un'asta (Attica), o della base di una colonna (Colonna di piatti), quella del ribaltamento, del disequilibrio (Rococò), quella del collage (intervento dissacrate sul quadro di Manet con Dèjeuner sur l'arbre) e dell'assemblaggio/bricolage, creando delle figure di mezzo, delle pause intermedie tra la storia e il presente. L'oggetto partecipa a molteplici storie, all'architettura come alla scultura, così come a memorie e contestazioni collettive. La sua frammentazione ci porta verso l'idea dell'impermanenza, dell'effimero.

Recentemente, nel 2007, la messa in scena nello spazio dei processi temporali è comparsa nel progetto vincitore del concorso per la costruzione del museo nazionale di Capo Verde, sull'isola di Sal. Un lato della facciata, rivestito in legno e ritmato a intervalli regolari piccole aperture quadrate, ricorda il fianco di un galeone della tratta dei neri transatlantica. Un secondo insieme di facciate è realizzato in pietre vulcaniche locali, come le cinque casette espositive disposte a raggiera. Progettare un museo riporta a reintrodurre una parte di tempo e di storia in una situazione di vivere comune, per restituire all'avvenimento tutto il suo ruolo. In questi ultimi anni, il tuo lavoro non consiste nell'abbandono dei tuoi ideali radicali, bensì nel loro spostamento, dal politico verso l'etico. Sono impaziente di visitare in tua compagnia e di quella dei capoverdani questo nuovo museo. Dimmi infine, caro Gianni, quale sarà a tuo parere il modo migliore per sostenere questa costruzione?

"l'Arca" n. 259, giugno 2010

p. 12

L'Antimuseale
Ironia come metodo di demistificazione e di stimolo; il paradosso, la macroscopicizzazione, come strumenti di indagine sui fenomeni e sui significati, che vengono in questo modo resi più evidenti.
Dissacrazione per far saltare le contraddizioni dei processi e la banalità dei "luoghi comuni" a cui siamo abituati.

Dai primi lavori realizzati con lo Studio65, si definiscono tutti gli elementi caratterizzanti il mio modo di pensare: il progetto non è soltanto forma estetica, espressione tecnologica, ma deve essere uno strumento critico.
Questo modo di vedere, di indagare e di progettare induce un modo diverso di lettura della città, degli oggetti, nonché dei miti e dei riti che li circondano.
Basta anche soltanto cambiare il punto di vista e non accettare quello che viene proposto, per avere una realtà diversa. Basterebbe cambiare il cono ottico di ripresa delle immagini dei fratelli Alinari per riscrivere molti testi di storia dell'arte, ma soprattutto per creare una coscienza nuova sulle opere stesse.
L'esistenza di un'idea leggibile da chiunque diviene la ragione dell'architettura. Essa non deve essere soltanto uno strumento tecnico, che permette di creare forme prive di significati culturali e in alcuni casi esclusivamente autoreferenziali, ma al contrario essa deve diventare mezzo primario di diffusione della cultura stessa.
La leggibilità di una "formula di struttura di un edificio" deve essere accessibile a tutti, così come le sue ragioni, il suo carattere, la sua storia, perché le grandi idee sono idee semplici.

L'architettura che ci circonda è zeppa di luoghi comuni, frutto di regole indiscusse, che generano di conseguenza forme assolute, predeterminate, chiuse, tremendamente irreversibili, ove non esiste margine per il sogno.
La periferia delle città non è soltanto il luogo in cui il potere ha sperimentato il fallimento della sua prassi urbanistica, "the waste land" (per dirla come T.S. Elliot), la terra desolata dove nessuno si riconosce, ma diviene una categoria mentale per esprimere un infinito disagio sociale.
La maggioranza del patrimonio architettonico prodotto in questi ultimi anni è un manifesto di questo disagio, che annichilisce la memoria, la speranza e l'immaginazione.
"Periferia" è un'architettura priva di contenuti culturali, priva di DNA, di storia e ancor più di un'idea che ne costituisca l'ossatura, la formula di struttura e cioè la bellezza.
Nella realtà, in Italia e non solo, si sono costruit dal dopoguerra in avanti e, purtroppo in modo massiccio ancor oggi, milioni di metri cubi e quindi di volumi senza alcun DNA, e cioè in definitiva senza alcuna ragione, incrementando in modo smisurato i luoghi della bruttezza.
Molte di queste opere sono costituite da copie in tutto o in parte di altri edifici, di trapianti insensati di particolari per il tutto, dall'accanimento della poetica del "famolo strano", nella tanto affannosa quanto vana ricerca di sensazionalismo, di autoreferenza e di una omologazione nel firmamento cultural-intellettual-architettonico.
Anche nel "domestic landscape", dal razionalismo fino al minimalismo non sono stati in grado di cambiare l'associazione di idee che domina l'organizzazione domestica e soprattutto la relazione immutabile fra le varie component dell'arredo.

Questo è il riflesso interno di una banalità esterna, che ha fatto sì, ad esempio, che le ville californiane di Neutra siano state brutalmente trapiantate, fatte salve poche modifiche, ancora oggi, in ogni parte del mondo.

La brutale copiatura, spesso posta in essere senza capire le ragioni e i rapporti fra l'opera originale e il luogo ma motivata dalla pura necessità di imitazione, ha fatto sì che il territorio si sia arricchito di edifici "alla...", evidenza di un deprimente provincialismo, assolutamente estranei al contesto ambientale e storico in cui si collocano.

La città concepita secondo il metodo di un progetto critico deve avere per effetto una maggiore libertà, la creazione degli spazi, dove la gente si riconosca e possa ristabilire un rapporto armonico con l'ambiente in cui ha deciso di vivere.
Il significato sociale di questa "rivoluzione" indica una strada e un metodo per riappropriarci della città, ripensandola e riprogettandola secondo un approccio emotivo, che individui le parti "allegre" e le parti "tristi", evidenziando le cause di queste ultime e sapendo proporre una radicale trasformazione.

Questo approccio di lettura è fondamentale per identificare l'architettura copiata, in ultima analisi fonte di malessere e disorientamento culturale.
Ogni "luogo architettonico", sia esso un edificio o oggetto di design, dovrebbe essere prima percepito attraverso una "visione" emotiva, come avviene per la musica o per la poesia.
Molti oggetti, spesso bollati come kitsch, posseggono, al contrario, un'incredibile carica di allegria ed una notevole vitalità, cioè posseggono

"un'anima", che a dispetto di un certo snobismo culturale, ne ha garantito e ne garantisce la permanenza e la sopravvivenza nella storia.
Il progetto critico, tradotto nel campo del design, trae ispirazione dalla carica eversiva di questi oggetti, che sfuggono al condizionamento del sistema e del potere.
Sfuggono anche all'azione imbalsamatrice del museo, perché traggono la propria linfa vitale dall'anima popolare, che li ha generati.
In questi mesi una catena di grande distribuzione di mobili ha prodotto un messaggio pubblicitario nel quale si dimostra che da un modo diverso e libero di pensare uno spazio piccolo e costretto, come la cella di un carcere, può scaturire una speranza di vita.

Questo è un metodo che come un testimone viene consegnato a chi vede nell'architettura l'antiaccademia, l'antimuseo e l'occasione di stimolare chiunque a cercare nel progetto la motivazione, l'allegria e lo stimolo rivoluzionario per affrontare e distruggere quella mediocrità (in determinati casi assunta addirittura come valore) che ha generato tante "periferie" nel pensiero, nella produzione intellettuale, nel territorio.
Gianni Arnaudo

"l'Arca" n. 259, giugno 2010

p. 14

...IN REALTÀ NON CI CERCAVA PROPRIO NESSUNO

p. 15

"OPERA SOVVERSIVA"
UN MOVIMENTO STORICAMENTE CULTURALE nasce quando prende consapevolezza delle proprie idee e coscienza di sè

Con questo intento ho ideato per Studio65 la carta da lettere, che è ora diventata un esempio unico di comunicazione pop. Fa parte delle collezioni di alcuni musei d'Europa, tra i quali il Centre George Pompidou Musée national d'art moderne, Parigi, il Vitra Design Museum di Basilea, ed è stata esposta al Louisiana Museum di Copenaghen, al Moderna Museet di Stoccolma, al centro culturale Barbican di Londra, all'Emma Museum Hensinki, all'Henie Onstad Kunstsenter di Oslo e al Museum of Contemporary Art di Chicago.

Pubblicata sul catalogo *Pop Art Design* del Vitra Design Museum, Basilea, 2012 (p. 53), e sul catalogo *Asparagus Age*, Galleria TOT, Padova, 1984. Archivio Arnaudo

p. 16

ERA UNA DICHIARAZIONE DI GUERRA...
...ed è per questo motivo che in una di quelle cabine per autoscatto di fototessera ci siamo fatti delle foto e io ho creato quest'opera. La carta da lettere del nostro studio, che avrebbe dovuto essere la presentazione ai clienti, perché fossero ben consapevoli di cosa avremmo potuto fare... (e a cosa andavano incontro.)
Adesso è un esempio di "contro-selfie", non autocelebrazione, ma autodenuncia...

p. 17

...Il sottofondo scenografico di una azione TOTALE

p. 18

Prima di quel momento eravamo solo un gruppo di neolaureati e studenti che passavano in uno studio come continuazione dell'università e delle lotte studentesche iniziate nel 1967 al Politecnico di Torino.

p. 19

Non è nostalgia

per affermare la necessità di una cultura diversa, nuova e contemporanea. Era importante impegnarsi sul presente con il sogno di cambiare il mondo.

Il Gruppo I, di cui Arnaudo era leader, era una delle componenti di Città-Fabbrica nella grande inchiesta sull'abitare a Torino.
Mentre alcuni studenti si occupavano del centro storico e delle condizioni di vita precarie o disumane che si riscontravano, altri studiavano i quartieri operai della zona di Mirafiori Sud, di Nichelino, della Falchera o delle Vallette.

Il tema era formulare un'alternativa progettuale per una committenza alternativa a quella che aveva trasformato la periferia e il centro storico in un dormitorio.
Si combatteva per una cultura diversa, per una città diversa, ma anche per una Facoltà diversa, per dare spazio a nuove idee.

p. 20

Qualsiasi lavoro era concepito come "collettivo" e indifferenziato, tutti lavoravano per una causa...

p. 21

In quel momento le lotte studentesche si univano alle lotte operaie per il diritto alla casa.

Quarant'anni dopo, nel 2016, gli studenti del mio corso alla Facoltà di Architettura del Politecnico di Torino hanno riprogettato il vecchio quartiere operaio di Mirafiori, gettando le basi di una nuova città possibile.
Anche con loro l'obiettivo è la libertà di pensiero, la riconquista di una città.
Le loro proposte progettuali sono state esposte in una mostra nella fabbrica di Mirafiori.

pp. 22-23

L'ironia al potere, il potere dell'ironia: i graffiti

p. 25

Dopo quarant'anni...
Presentazione progetti di rinnovamento Mirafiori Sud al Politecnico di Torino

p. 26

Il metodo
Il '68 come metodo di investigazione sulla realtà.

Impegno per studiare di più, pensando che la nuova cultura diventasse la base per l'evoluzione di un nuovo linguaggio architettonico: stava nascendo il concetto di PROGETTO CRITICO.

Architettura come messaggio politico. La città doveva essere più vicina ai nostri ideali: diverso doveva essere il rapporto fra società e università. Questa è stata una delle motivazioni per cui sarei diventato professore al Politecnico di Torino.

p. 27

EURODOMUS 4
La CASA DELL'IMPERIALISTA
(la distruzione creatrice)

p. 28

Questo manifesto, che ho voluto facesse parte dell'esposizione e successivamente del catalogo della mostra "Pop Art Design" del Vitra Design Museum, è stato poi esposto al Louisiana Museum di Copenaghen, al Moderna Museet di Stoccolma, al centro culturale Barbican di Londra, all'Emma Museum Hensinki, al Henie Onstad Kunstsenter Oslo e al Museum of Contemporary Art di Chicago.
Archivio Arnaudo

p. 29

LA CASA DELL'IMPERIALISTA

Che cosa c'è di più "IMPERIALE" che abitare in una colonna, portandosi in casa tutti i simboli del potere da ostentare?

EURODOMUS 72
Nel 1972, una piccola ditta di Nole Canavese proprietà dei tre fratelli Gugliermetto, la Gufram, si appresta ad affrontare una nuova sfida per poter entrare, a buon diritto, nel panorama, oltre che nel mercato, del design italiano. L'Eurodomus, patrocinata dalla rivista "Domus" e organizzata da Giò Ponti insieme a Cesare Casati ed Emanuele Ponzio, lasciata Milano approda a Torino nei locali del Palazzo delle Esposizioni. Occasione di confronto aperto attraverso convegni e tavole rotonde, destinati ad accogliere proposte per il nuovo abitare, l'Eurodomus si distingue dalle manifestazioni collaterali anche per la sua apertura alle istanze artistiche del periodo.
Le aziende produttrici di arredamento, molte delle quali ancora a carattere artigianale, intravedono nella manifestazione la possibilità reale

di tentare il salto verso la produzione industriale. Oltre alla Gufram, tra gli espositori più importanti, parteciperanno Kartell, Zanotta, FontanaArte, Poltrona Frau, Brionvega, Giovannetti, De Padova e Abet Laminati, B&B (allora C&B), Acerbis, Cristal Art, Colli, Boschis, Saportiti. Prendendo parte all'Eurodomus, la Gufram avrebbe potuto comunicare la propria filosofia aziendale ma anche, e soprattutto, proporre un nuovo e possibile modello abitativo, fortemente condizionato da giovani designer intemperanti ma creativi, usciti dalle lotte studentesche per affermare una nuova cultura. Esse, da poco concluse, avrebbero creato le basi per un decennio colorato, segnato dall'ottimismo della cultura giovanile, dalla nuova musica e dalla moda alternativa, terminando tuttavia con una inattesa mobilitazione politica, spontanea e inaspettata. Non ci si limitava a guardare le cose, i processi storici e politici, ma si cercava di capire ciò che "ci stava dietro", il perché, la causa, il DNA, per poter più facilmente "colpire, distruggere, demistificare e riaffermare nuove idee". Accanto al "good design" (il design per bene di alcuni stand dell'Eurodomus) fanno capolino coloro che avrebbero presto posto le basi di ciò che sarà definito "design radicale".

Torino è una città in pieno fermento culturale: attorno alla Facoltà di Architettura gravitano una serie di gruppi vicini al mondo intellettuale, alcuni decisamente attratti dall'attivismo sindacale e comunque dal mondo politico in mutamento. Tra questi il Gruppo Strum, Studio65, ma anche A.ba.co, formatosi attorno a Giuseppe Raimondi e il gruppo Libidarch, i Vikinghi, "Le rane verdi". La cultura torinese si confrontava con il contemporaneo pensiero di altri gruppi presenti all'Eurodomus, quali Archizoom, Superstudio, Gruppo 999, Ufo.

Per tutti vale un concetto esprimibile attraverso l e parole del Gruppo Strum, per cui "operare nell'architettura diviene un modo di partecipare agli antagonismi e alle lotte che le divaricazioni tra bisogni di spazio e spazio realmente prodotto e disponibile generano".

Per questo l'edizione dell'Eurodomus del 1972 ha rappresentato l'occasione per manifestare critiche precise nei confronti della società e della disciplina architettonica. A dar voce a queste operazioni sono i componenti dello Studio65 che, a proposito della manifestazione, dichiaravano:

"...Considerato il luogo – L'Eurodomus – come santuario del design, il nostro atteggiamento, nei confronti di questa ricerca, si carica in termini provocatori, fino al limite di assumere il kitsch stesso come bandiera demistificante, laddove i diversi aspetti della comunicazione ideologica (culturale l'uno, sottoculturale l'altro) vengono a bella vista distrutti e tenuti separati, ottenendo l'effetto di filtrare e demistificare i messaggi: noi abbracciamo l'atteggiamento sottoculturale come sfida lanciata dalla cultura di serie B contro quella di serie A, della cultura plebea contro quella aristocratica. Un'assunzione tattica e demolitoria nel santuario della Cultura...".
Emanuela Giudice
Ricerca sulla Gufram
2011

pp. 30-31

...DOPO LA FACOLTÀ INCONTRAMMO DEGLI EROI, MOLTO PIÙ MATTI DI NOI

p. 32

Eurodomus 4

p. 33

Allo Studio65 la Gufram affida il progetto del proprio stand dell'Eurodomus 72: le lampadine colorate, sistemate a mano pazientemente, racchiudono in un arco la prospettiva che inquadra i Puffi, il Cactus, il modello Fantico e poi il divano Bocca, che qui non è più prototipo, ma sostanzialmente modificato in collaborazione tra azienda e designer (rifacimento struttura e copertura in stoffa, quella utilizzata per i costumi da bagno) può essere finalmente commercializzato.

Studio65 è da poco entrato a far parte del gruppo di progettisti che lavorano per la Gufram. Usciti dalla Facoltà di Architettura di Torino, per lo più tra il 1970 e il 1972, trasformano subito la produzione di design dell'azienda con una dose massiccia di ironia. La manifestazione di una dissacrazione ricercata e necessaria per stravolgere un sistema contestato fin dagli anni universitari si ritrova nel progetto del proprio stand Babilonia '72, realizzato da Zanotta (con grande coraggio) e presentato all'Eurodomus torinese. A questa edizione dell'Eurodomus partecipano, oltre a Gufram, altre aziende di importanza internazionale tra cui Abet Print con i suoi laminati, la Arclinea che avrebbe realizzato il prototipo del braciere di Giove, la Nonwoven di Milano per la pavimentazione e le moquettes.

Il compito, per ognuno, è quello di cercare alternative proponendo nuovi ambienti in cui vivere.

Studio65, accanto al Gruppo Strum, è, all'interno della Gufram, il gruppo con la maggiore esperienza contestativa e con la più acuta volontà costruttiva di nuovi modelli sociali.
Per quanto riguarda il tema della casa, in Babilonia '72 si introduce, nel progetto dello spazio espositivo, lo stesso spirito provocatorio utilizzato nei prodotti di design.

"...Abbiamo così imparato a svolgere l'unico ruolo che si presenta oggi a chi produce cultura: quello di celebrare, con forme più o meno nuove, il capitalismo imperiale. E questo nostro unico ruolo lo abbiamo assunto fino in fondo, senza complessi, senza mistificazioni, a tal punto che la nostra celebrazione viene letta come parodia, il nostro humor come sarcasmo, fino al punto di diventare operazione demistificante, contribuendo alla chiarificazione del senso dell'operare architettonico a livello di linguaggio. I nostri progetti diventano così essi stessi metaprogetti, la nostra architettura un discorso sull'architettura..."

Il progetto presentato da Studio65 per Zanotta ha per titolo, dunque, "Babilonia '72" e per forma una colonna ionica, o meglio, la sua base, proponendo in essa uno spazio continuo in cui quattro luoghi simbolici fondamentali, quattro oggetti capaci di connotare il livello sociale di vita del fruitore, hanno la possibilità di raccontare un possibile cambiamento.

Così la colonna che contiene lo spazio domestico, ciondolo macroscopicizzato, si apre e diventa la forma giusta per comunicare da un lato la falsità dei valori propugnati per sortire l'effetto di vendere il bene casa, dall'altro per fare il verso a quei valori tipologici che la cultura propone all'architettura come liberatori (spazio aperto, continuo, polifunzionale, attrezzato, concentrazione dei servizi in spazi serventi, componibilità).
Emanuela Giudice
Ricerca sulla Gufram
2011

p. 36

L'idea era quella di riprodurre il tiro a segno delle fiere di paese.

p. 38

LA PASSIONE C'ERA.
POTEVA ESSERE MUSICA,
È STATO DESIGN
(Giuseppe Gugliermetto)

p. 39

Foto di eroi: i fratelli Gugliermetto

p. 40

Con il poliuretano espanso abbiamo "smontato" totalmente l'idea dell'oggetto di arredamento e lo abbiamo reso un manifesto della nostra forma di dissacrazione, privandolo di una ossatura portante, di un rivestimento e di tutte le sue valenze borghesi.
Gianni Arnaudo

pp. 42-43

PER PASSARE DA QUESTO... A QUESTO... CE NE VOLEVA DI CORAGGIO...

p. 44

ORDINATISSIMO / BABY-LONIA
(Studio65 / Gianni Arnaudo)

Il falegname Quinto di Torino era una brava persona, ormai così avanti negli anni da perdonare le intemperanze di un gruppo di giovani architetti, che proponevano mobili e oggetti molto lontani dalla sua tradizione artigianale.

Aveva però messo a nostra disposizione la sua formidabile perizia tecnica, che aveva reso possibile la realizzazione di tanti prototipi.
I buoni rapporti con la ditta Abet avevano consentito la fornitura a basso costo di alcuni fogli di laminato, con colori e tipologie – alcuni dei quali non più in uso – che tuttavia costituivano la base del nostro linguaggio architettonico.
Nacque così un mobile – l'Ordinatissimo – che ricordava i giochi dei "legnetti" utilizzati dai bambini nei giardini d'infanzia, con la differenza che questi volumi multicolori erano cresciuti di scala e si erano trasformati in un armadio, compartimentato all'interno, per ospitare oggetti di dimensioni diverse.
Il nome "Ordinatissimo", che esprimeva un programma, ironizzava fortemente con il concetto di ordine borghese (ogni cosa al suo posto, un posto per ogni cosa).
Dalla fonte di ispirazione dell'Ordinatissimo al Baby-lonia il passaggio fu breve, tenendo conto delle necessità dei destinatari di avere nella propria cameretta un teatrino smontabile e rimontabile a piacimento per assecondare la propria fantasia e creare la scenografia delle proprie fiabe.

"Il figlio del capitalista doveva essere sempre... ORDINATISSIMO"

p. 45

In ricordo del falegname Quinto (anche lui è stato un eroe)
Il gioco Baby-Lonia è stato derivato dal mobile Ordinatissimo, realizzato in laminato plastico autentico.
Per il figlio del capitalista ecco la sua cameretta trasformata in Wall Street, con tutti i simboli del potere e quello del dollaro nel centro del frontone dedicato al Dio Denaro.
"L'ordine è" (Louis Kahn): l'ordine è il criterio informatore per la stanza del pupo che un giorno sarà presidente.

p. 46

KANAL BRUXELLES
sede satellite del CENTRE POMPIDOU
2019

KANAL - Centre Pompidou nasce dalla convinzione che arte e cultura sono fondamentali per far incontrare le persone in una società sempre più divisa. L'idea è quella di offrire un centro culturale e di scambio aperto a tutti, per dare attenzione alla scena creativa di Bruxelles e contribuire alla crescita dell'appeal culturale della capitale.
KANAL - Centre Pompidou ospita non solo un museo d'arte moderna e contemporanea, ma anche ricche collezioni di architettura e urbanistica. Inoltre è dotato di molti spazi pubblici con diverse funzioni.

p. 47

SKIN UP
"Il curioso negozio di pelletterie Skin Up progettato dallo Studio65 a Torino. È una grande scatola nera in cui son disposti e montati pezzi di costruzione per bambini in formato gigante, che costituiscono il portale d'ingresso, il teatrino di prova e le scalinate per l'esposizione.
Il divano è la 'Chiocciola' della Gufram, lo specchio è della Cristal-Art, la scultura bianca è una copia della Venere dei Medici."
("Domus" n. 537, 1974
Per gentile concessione di Editoriale Domus S.p.A.)

Inventai io il nome del negozio,
che pressappoco voleva dire:
"soprattutto pelle"
(la Venere però era nuda)

p. 48

IL CAPITELLO AL MUSEO DELLA TRIENNALE MILANO
per la Storia ora è design radicale,
segno forte, unico, eroico, dissacrante.

p. 49

Helmut Newton

non lo volle il divano Bocca, e me lo disse chiaramente mentre eravamo seduti per terra a casa sua a Montecarlo a esaminare il mio progetto di interni del suo nuovo appartamento.
Per lui era solo una fotogenica copia del divano ideato da Dalí per la stanza surrealista del volto di Mae West; mentre il Capitello, quello sì che era davvero originale, ironico ed eversivo, una vera icona Pop.

Sono passati quarant'anni e sono molte le versioni della nascita di un'icona, ma ciò che conta è che il Capitello, più di ogni altro oggetto prodotto dalla Gufram in quegli anni, rispecchia l'intento dissacratorio dell'idea di design e di architettura.

La forma non ha alcuna importanza in sé e nemmeno ce l'ha la funzione dell'oggetto: ciò che conta è che trasmetta in chiaro il messaggio irridente "delle voglie represse e delle ambizioni frustrate" di chi ancora vuole un mondo senza ironia e senza immaginazione e cioè un PROGETTO CRITICO.

Questa è rimasta la ragione della mia opera e dei miei progetti.

p. 50

IL PROGETTO CRITICO
tutto il mio lavoro è un "progetto critico"
Come il critico manifesta il proprio pensiero attraverso le proprie parole o Bansky con gli stencil, così l'architetto si esprime con i progetti. Essi sono composti di segni, simboli, invettive, denunce.

Il progetto diventa una forma di analisi e quindi un discorso sull'architettura. Non è invenzione di nuovi linguaggi – o meglio – l'adozione di linguaggi nuovi non è fine a se stessa o strumentale per creare clamore mediatico (...purché se ne parli).

Guardare un'architettura vuole dire individuare il DNA che l'ha creata e di qui il pensiero dell'architetto.

Il "progetto critico", cioè l'architettura militante contro il luogo comune e la banalità, ha costantemente fatto parte del mio DNA.

GLI STRUMENTI

Ironia
Dissacrazione
Provocazione
Trasgressione
Paradosso
Decontestualizzazione
Decostruzione del linguaggio
Assemblaggio di simboli
Sovversione

p. 51

IL MAUSOLEO
delle voglie represse e delle ambizioni frustrate venne costruito vicino a Cuneo e fu un progetto provocatorio, un vero esempio di forte decontestualizzazione critica.

È L'ARCHITETTURA RADICALE

Questa architettura sarà allo stesso tempo anticipazione e antitesi al movimento post-moderno che sarebbe nato anni dopo.

p. 52

La razionalità dell'assurdo

Avevo un cliente (amico di mio padre, anche lui architetto) che vendeva piastrelle a Borgo San Dalmazzo, vicino a Cuneo.

Un giorno mi si era presentato dicendomi che voleva rinnovare l'esposizione di piastrelle e sanitari e mostrandomi una sua idea di cosa desiderasse: era la sagoma di una grande balena con la bocca aperta verso la strada statale, che collega Cuneo alla Francia.

Ho pensato subito che questo fosse il committente giusto a cui raccontare le idee che sviluppavo con lo Studio65.

Il cliente ottenne quello che voleva: tutti gli archetipi del potere e della cultura, ironia e provocazione.
Un'idea fortemente innovativa era quella di pensare a questa nuova esposizione come luogo di incontro, di musica per giovani, e quindi, da possibile esposizione di piastrelle... divenne il Flash Back.

Avendo già lavorato nel campo delle discoteche (il Blue-Hill a Lequio Tanaro), inventai una distribuzione interna degli spazi assolutamente inconsueta, collocando la postazione del dj in alto, al di sopra della pista da ballo, sopra un ponte che collegava il tempio della musica con quello delle piastrelle.

A completamento di questo spazio, venne utilizzata la Colonna realizzata da Zanotta per Eurodomus, facendo una prima grande operazione di "riciclo" dell'architettura.

Questo "riciclo" consentiva di esprimere meglio il "non senso" di un progetto assurdo, che meglio di ogni scritto avrebbe spiegato il nostro pensiero sull'architettura. Siccome la nascita di un movimento culturale corrisponde alla definizione di un pensiero compiuto solo quando acquisisce coscienza di sé – come disse Gramsci –, il progetto del Flash Back costituisce la base di lettura del pensiero dello Studio65, nel periodo in cui abbiamo progettato insieme.

La Colonna di Zanotta non subì alcun incendio, ma semplicemente il degrado di tutta la struttura lignea, dovuto all'uso di una vernice protettiva non adeguata, che ne consentì il deterioramento. Ogni altra versione non corrisponde alla vera storia di questo progetto.

p. 54

La critica al postmoderno
prima che il postmoderno nascesse

Il Flash Back nacque diversi anni prima del movimento postmoderno e ne costituisce, grazie alla notevole ironia, una forte critica.

p. 55

Esposto anche alla mostra "La Boîte de Nuit" a Villa Noailles, Hyeres, alla mostra "Night Fever" al Vitra Design Museum di Basilea insieme a tutto il progetto, quindi al museo ADAM di Bruxelles, al Centro per l'Arte Contemporanea Luigi Pecci di Prato, al Designmuseum Danmark di Copenhagen e al V&A Museum di Dundee, in Scozia.

p. 57

LA DIREZIONE DI UNA ORCHESTRA
Questo gioco con le costruzioni fu un successo (la scatola di montaggio dell'architettura imperialista)

pp. 60-61

Flash Back il progetto critico
I SIMBOLI DEL POTERE NELLA STORIA
e cioè la traduzione tridimensionale della banalità dei luoghi comuni e contaminazione della storia in un percorso di ambizioni frustrate e voglie represse.

pp. 64-65

IL "PAOLINA B"
Solo Arnaudo seppe trasformare il Flash Back in Paolina B, un altro pianeta più grande e spettacolare.
"Dell'architetto è il fin la meraviglia..."

p. 66

Dato il successo della discoteca Flash Back, qualche tempo dopo il mio cliente mi affidò il progetto di un grande ampliamento della discoteca che, ironizzando sul nome Jackie O' del famoso locale di Roma, avrei chiamato Paolina B, dato il carattere "tremendamente" classico della struttura.

La nuova discoteca aveva tutti gli elementi della nuova tecnologia di luce e di suoni. Per gli appassionati era possibile sentire la musica "in cuffia", mentre formidabili effetti speciali si adeguavano alla tipologia ed a sound della musica pop imperante.

Architettura, musica e pensiero avevano ritrovato, come nel periodo barocco, il momento di unità interdisciplinare.

p. 67

In quegli anni era uscito il libro di Gillo Dorfles *Il Kitsch. Antologia del cattivo gusto.*
Questo progetto racconta il mio pensiero sul kitsch.
Mentre Dorfles condannava senza appello tutto il mondo di questa produzione popolare (o almeno dedicata al popolo), io ero invece affascinato dall'ironia, dalla magia e dalle contraddizioni insite in tanti oggetti stigmatizzati di "cattivo gusto". La "boccia di vetro", che viene venduta a Venezia con la gondola che scorre sotto il naso di un Papa molto popolare con caduta di neve sulla laguna, è una concentrazione di assurdità che andava letta in tutta la sua provocatoria ironia del "non senso". Così pure certi mobili-bar degli anni '50, ricchi di lustrini specchianti fra i quali ballava una danzatrice succinta al suono di un carrillon, costituivano per il consumatore finale una forma di evasione, di trasporto, di sogno.
Nell'oggetto kitsch va colto questo, e cioè l'allegria, l'ironia, l'assurdità, la contraddizione e la "trasgressione", la carica eversiva rispetto all'oggetto "sacrale" prodotto dal freddo e asettico razionalismo.
Così "evasione" è questo interno di piramide, dove la gente si divertiva e rideva proprio per l'assurdità di questo spazio e per continui richiami a quel "mondo" che ho descritto.

p. 69

Mentre il Flash Back era stato realizzato per essere un'esposizione convenzionale, il Paolina B fu un contenitore spettacolare di musica rock, decisamente innovativo. La sua fama raggiunse Montecarlo e il Principe ereditario Alberto volle visitarlo. Fu un evento sensazionale: una bellissima modella vestita di una calzamaglia bianca lucida e con l'acconciatura della famosa opera del Canova accoglieva su una "Paolina" un pubblico entusiasta.

La famosa passerella sospesa di cristallo, "gioia e delizia" di tanti ragazzi, che aspettavano che le "fanciulle" la attraversassero per poterne ammirare... le gambe.

Fu un grave scandalo, per il quale la discoteca fu chiusa e riaperta dopo quasi un mese; venne introdotto un "pudico" tappeto che durò pochissimo e venne presto rimosso, per la felicità di tutti

p. 71

Quarant'anni dopo... al Vitra di Basilea,
al museo ADAM di Bruxelles
al Centro per l'Arte Contemporanea Luigi Pecci di Prato
e poi...

pp. 72-73

---

questa è un'altra storia

p. 74

Pop è stato il mio incontro con Gianni Arnaudo: immediato, empatico, coinvolgente. Pop è accettazione a prima vista, condivisione, appartenenza, riconoscersi in un approccio alla forma e al mondo ironico e distaccato.
Affinità elettiva ma anche percorso comune: il mio Vas-one come citazione, nelle modalità e nel nome stesso, di quel Pratone, realizzato dalla Gufram dove lui operava come Gruppo 65 tanti anni prima, e poi il nostro arrivare, dalla periferia al mondo milanese del design. Ci accomuna quindi un atteggiamento curioso, ammirato, mai succube del centro di questo mondo su cui gravitano da sempre produzione, comunicazione, distribuzione.
Arrivare da fuori permette, a volte, di restare con i piedi per terra, radicati in una realtà che concede poco al protagonismo e che obbliga alla visione e all'esagerazione voluta, per superare i limiti contingenti e banali del quotidiano.
Gianni Arnaudo resta fedele a se stesso, architetto e designer si afferma internazionalmente, citato nelle mostre del MoMA a New York, del Beaubourg a Parigi, ma non partecipa dell'affannoso presenzialismo agli eventi milanesi. Progetta, viaggia, osserva da lontano, con incursioni mirate per intrattenere rapporti umani oltre che professionali.
Il suo sguardo rimane attento ed entusiasta pronto alla provocazione, carattere che ha contraddistinto fin dall'inizio la sua progettazione.
Per chi conosce i luoghi da cui proviene (le colline del cuneese), austeri e poco inclini alla risata aperta, è divertente considerare la carica eversiva dei suoi progetti. Le sue discoteche post-moderne ante litteram, le sue citazioni classiche dissacranti sono realizzate in località improbabili, in "non luoghi" della modernità anonima e sembrano pretendere, a forza, il diritto alla bellezza e al pensiero pur consapevoli di una provvisorietà.
Il contrasto tra capitelli aulici giganti e funzionalità provvisorie, legate all'evasione e alla facile obsolescenza, genera spaesamento.

Forme nobili vengono associate a dimensioni giganti e allestite secondo tecniche scenografiche, quasi televisive, per stupire, creare emozione, scuotere l'attenzione.
C'è critica al sistema, ma anche sincero divertimento, in puro stile pop.
Pop è, infatti, critica e adesione incredula al tempo stesso.
Ci si riconosce nel limite, lo si fa proprio e lo si racconta con ironia, per superarlo. Lo scarto creativo gioca sulla sorpresa, lo spiazzamento, la dimensione fuori scala.
Non ci annoieremo mai del Capitello, della Bocca e di tutti quei favolosi oggetti creati per Gufram, a cavallo degli anni '70, incompresi dal grande pubblico, poi celebrati dalla mostra di New York "Italy: The New Domestic Landscape", oggi diventati icone rappresentative del nostro vissuto.
Come non ricordare le frasi spiazzanti dei manifesti dei prodotti per Gufram, che aggiungono la parola al disegno, e non divertirci con la sua carta da lettera del Gruppo65: Arnaudo e i suoi colleghi che si propongono come dei veri "ricercati" nel campo del design.
C'è il piacere della esagerazione, del colore squillante, del grido da manifesto, ereditato dal '68, della contestazione dell'ordine precostituito, di qualsiasi ordine, proprio attraverso l'ordine classico ridotto a dissacrante poltrona, su cui, alla Fantozzi, ci si abbandona.
C'è, nel tempo, il rifiuto delle liturgie, dello star system, nuovo ordine imperante della comunicazione, per ritornare sempre al progetto vero, costruito, anche e specialmente attraverso l'architettura.
Resta uno sguardo disincantato, ironico ma sempre appassionato che permette di affrontare progetti nuovi, a qualsiasi scala e senza pregiudizi.
Déjeuner sur l'arbre, ancora un gioco recente, è una citazione colta e subito dissacrata, per il piacere del rovesciamento, per la sfida all'ovvio diffuso.
Caro Gianni evviva la tua indipendenza, la distanza e buon lavoro!
Luisa Bocchietto – Presidente ADI

"l'Arca" n. 259, giugno 2010

p. 75

La reinvenzione del concetto di icona: le citazioni dell'arte e dell'architettura classica diventano simboli eversivi per l'uso ironico che ne viene fatto

"Si assiste a tutto un proliferare di un design underground, di 'contestazione'. Che, però, al contrario dei film di un Warhol o di un Pascali, viene reso istituzionale e propagandato da organismi internazionali, e immesso in un circuito di èlite. Attraverso il design e la progettazione del microambiente, le deflagranti contraddizioni delle strutture metropolitane entrano sublimate e sottoposte a una catartica ironia, nell'ambiente della vita privata."
Manfredo Tafuri (*Progetto e Utopia*, Editori Laterza, Bari 1973, p. 130)

p. 76

La COLONNA DI PIATTI
ovvero la ricerca sui "luoghi comuni"
("Passami quella colonna di piatti")

Quando Gianni Arnaudo, ancora studente di architettura nel 1969, volendo sperimentare un materiale nuovo e popolare (rispetto alla più nobile porcellana) chiese in incognito (proprio per eludere l'amicizia del padre Albino Arnaudo con il proprietario della fabbrica Marco Levi) di essere assunto dalla Ceramica Besio come operaio, visto che "disegnava bene" fu subito destinato al reparto della decorazione, ove venivano dipinti i tradizionali "galletti", simbolo della produzione.
Ovviamente la "clandestinità" sarebbe durata solo qualche mese, ma "l'infiltrato" smascherato, a compenso della propria "buona uscita", propose a Marco Levi, banchiere e mecenate, la realizzazione di alcuni suoi disegni, tra i quali quello di un servizio "tête à tête" componibile in ceramica opaca bianca o nera, denominato "Colonna" e di un altro decorato con un disegno pop chiamato "Rha", nonchè di un set da fumo, la "Colonna di fumo".

Marco Levi intelligentemente comprese il valore innovativo delle proposte, anche se esse si ponevano in totale controtendenza rispetto allo standard della produzione della fabbrica, e ne realizzò alcuni prototipi, successivamente esposti nella storica edizione di Eurodomus 4 a Torino.
Siamo nel 1972, e prima ancora della mostra di New York, "Italy: The New Domestic Landscape" al MoMa, un grande estimatore del design italiano, Charles Stending, si recò prima alla Gufram per negoziare l'acquisto e l'esclusiva dei Multipli dello Studio65, e successivamente venne da Arnaudo accompagnato a Mondovì perché conoscesse Marco Levi e potesse vedere il servizio Colonna. Il pezzo piacque a Stending, ma la sua richiesta di una prima fornitura di almeno 10.000 pezzi fece trasecolare Marco Levi, che si rese conto di non poter far fronte a un ordine così grande in un tempo limitato e dovette rinunciare.

p. 77

La Colonna di piatti nasce dalla collaborazione tra l'antica fabbrica Vedova Besio & Figlio e Gianni Arnaudo, che arrivò a Mondovì come collaboratore dell'azienda nel 1969.
Gianni Arnaudo aveva cominciato la collaborazione lavorando nel reparto decorazione, dove sui piatti e sul vasellame prodotti dalla Besio venivano dipinti i tradizionali "galletti".
Essendo io all'epoca responsabile dell'organizzazione aziendale, mi venne presentato dal proprietario della Besio, il dottor Marco Levi, il quale durante una delle quotidiane riunioni programmatiche, mi preannunciò che avrei anche dovuto collaborare con il giovane architetto, che aveva un grande interesse per l'arte ceramica e che proponeva la realizzazione di un progetto così diverso dalla nostra normale produzione da necessitare tutta l'assistenza tecnica di cui io e i miei colleghi disponevamo.
Mi pregò di sollecitare tutti i responsabili dei vari reparti di lavorazione, in particolare il capo foggiatura Arnaldo Bonardo, perché facessero il possibile per assecondarlo e seguirlo nelle varie fasi di realizzazione del progetto, pur senza distogliersi troppo dai normali impegni produttivi.
Effettivamente il progetto del servizio Colonna di piatti, che Gianni Arnaudo sottopose per studiarne la realizzazione, era molto diverso dalla normale nostra produzione, la quale veniva fatta seguendo i dettami tecnici della tradizionale fabbricazione delle stoviglie ceramiche, dicui però Arnaudo, per la sua idea del manufatto da realizzare, rispecchiante l'ironia pop, non teneva quasi conto.
Le maggiori difficoltà tecniche nella realizzazione della Colonna di piatti del progetto Arnaudo consistevano nell'aggregazione di pezzi realizzati con il sistema di' "foggiatura" e altri fatti tramite "colaggio" che in più non avevano spessori uniformi.
Occorre precisare che un articolo in ceramica con difformità di spessori molto accentuata crea un problema nell'essicazione del prodotto crudo (screpolature), e in seguito, dopo la prima cottura (detta "biscottatura"), a causa di un diverso grado di porosità dei manufatti realizzati con tecniche differenti,' il "biscotto" da smaltare avrà un grado di assorbimento dello smalto più o meno accentuato.
Il risultato finale, dopo la seconda cottura, rischiava di essere un prodotto con un grado di colore e finizione non uniforme fra i diversi componenti della Colonna.
Ovviamente Arnaudo non voleva che questa differenza si vedesse e tutti i pezzi dovevano risultare assolutamente uguali.
Le soluzioni tecniche che insieme abbiamo escogitato ci hanno permesso di ottenere ciò che Arnaudo desiderava e cioè che la Colonna, anche se composta da più pezzi diversamente realizzati, risultasse un blocco uniforme.
Per alcuni mesi abbiamo fatto diversi esperimenti che ci hanno permesso di raggiungere un risultato soddisfacente con una finitura in bianco lucido e una in nero opaco.
Abbiamo provato anche a sperimentare il colore blu cobalto, che si è poi deciso di usare per la piccola "colonna" progettata da Arnaudo come set da fumo (portacenere e porta sigarette).
Per fare pubblicità al nuovo prodotto, Arnaudo ci propose di presentare la Colonna di piatti all'Eurodomus previsto nel 1972, per il quale stava lavorando con i suoi colleghi di Studio65, in modo di avere un'occasione di visibilità al pubblico per questo suo progetto e per la fabbrica.
Per l'occasione studiò per la Besio anche un nuovo marchio, con una grafica più moderna, da stampigliare solo sui pezzi della Colonna di piatti per lo stand dell'Eurodomus; un modo per dare un segnale anche grafico dello sforzo innovativo della Ceramica Vedova Besio & Figlio.
Ennio Bonello
Direttore Organizzazione della Fabbrica Ceramiche Besio

p. 78

La colonna di fumo

p. 81

PERCHÉ MANET NON DOVESSE CONTINUARE

a rivoltarsi nella tomba ascoltando i commenti dei molti che dimenticano che il *Déjeuner sur l'herbe* alla sua presentazione al pubblico nel 1863 venne percepito come un'opera talmente eversiva e scandalosa da essere subito collocato nel Salon des Refusés e questo non solo per il nudo femminile della modella Victorine-Louise Meurent, in contrasto con il pittore e l'altro personaggio, entrambi vestiti, ma per l'uso inconsueto dei colori, caldi e freddi contrapposti, e per la composizione e l'attitudine dei personaggi,

nella scena ho inserito...

p. 82

il quinto personaggio

p. 84

e su di lui è stato scritto:

Citazione e cambiamento di scala connotano anche un oggetto recente come Déjeuner sur l'arbre (2005) di Gianni Arnaudo per Gufram; in questo caso l'oggetto appartenente alla quotidianità viene sottratto alla sua funzione originaria, introdotto in una citazione artistica (il quadro di Edouard Manet, *Déjeuner sur l'herbe*, 1863) attraverso una forte immagine che permette un gioco di parole tra il titolo e il nome del prodotto che diventa *Déjeuner sur l'arbre*. Elemento unificante il colore verde, che rimanda a una naturalità ormai artificializzata e reinterpretata in stile pop. In questo caso abbiamo citazione, cambiamento di scala, rapporto ironico tra natura e artificio.
Su questo oggetto si intrecciano i temi di più sezioni: *Il fascino delle lettere*, *Lo sguardo zoom*, *Animalia*. La presenza di caratterizzazioni pop è trasversale secondo questi approcci di lettura individuati per il racconto.
Luisa Bocchietto
Catalogo della mostra "Pop design. Fuori scala, fuori luogo, fuori schema", 2008

La presa di contatto tra produzione industriale e designer, nata per rompere le barriere esistenti tra l'arte e il mondo della strada, diventa un metodo di reinvenzione dell'immagine degli oggetti del quotidiano.

Il prodotto, un simbolo del consumo di massa, diviene allora "luogo dello spirito" con valori evocativi propri tali da farne un soggetto in grado di dialogare con il contesto in cui viene inserito.

Attraverso la Pop Art è stato dimostrato che anche una minestra in scatola o una confezione di detersivo possono essere personaggio, così come Marilyn Monroe o Mao Tse Tung, così come un deodorante per ambienti, l'Arbre Magique. L'Arbre Magique, nato dalla fibra di pino come semplice forma utile per meglio incorporare in carta profumi deodoranti, così riconoscibile da divenire 'luogo evocativo di un immaginario collettivo', viene da Gianni Arnaudo analizzato nelle sue varie componenti, privato della sua originaria funzione e, macrospicizzato, diviene 'Arbre' per un tavolo, richiamando con ironia l'archetipo del tavolo stesso.

Un oggetto del comune quotidiano, di diffusione tale da attraversare le barriere della diversità del linguaggio e delle culture, assume attraverso questa operazione una diversa identità, che si completa e afferma come vero e proprio personaggio, con la sua immagine pubblicitaria, nel quadro *Déjeuner sur l'herbe*.

Se l'ironia e la traslazione in un contesto diverso dell'idea, perché si verifichi una vera e propria rinascita della stessa, sono un connotato d'origine dell'opera di Gianni Arnaudo, con Déjeuner sur l'arbre l'operazione ha una molteplice scala di passaggi e reinvenzioni, incluso il divertito gioco di parole e assonanze con il titolo dell'opera di Manet e il trasparente istinto di riconfermare un'ispirazione irridente delle convenzioni e delle sicurezze dei più.

"l'Arca" n. 259, giugno 2010

"... Qualcuno dice che Gianni Arnaudo ha rovinato il quadro di Manet, ma qualcuno dice invece che l'ha addirittura migliorato..."
Piero Dadone, giornalista, "La Stampa"

p. 85

...per i molteplici piani dell'intervento

che ripropone l'intento eversivo con un colore freddo in contrasto con quelli originali, ora percepiti come caldi e classici,

che rende di nuovo provocatoria una scena che oggi non costituirebbe più nulla di scandaloso,

che gioca ironicamente con il ruolo evocativo delle parole,

che inserisce nell'irreale un oggetto del reale, che irride al mondo borghese e che a propria volta è la trasformazione di un prodotto industriale, così diffuso da essere divenuto nell'immaginario collettivo un luogo comune e, macroscopicizzato, diventa una tavolo non in duro legno, ma in un inatteso morbido poliuretano,

che è una completa sintesi del pensiero pop e ne utilizza in modo trasversale tutto il linguaggio e il metodo, che è quello di scegliere oggetti che la mente conosce già e rielaborarli su altri livelli.

Il Déjeuner sur l'arbre rispecchia il modo pop di intendere cultura ed arte e, come in tutta la produzione della Pop Art, un oggetto di consumo diventa un nuovo mito.

p. 86

Qualcuno dice che il Déjeuner sur l'arbre sia stato acquisito dal Centre Pompidou nella sua collezione permanente non perché pop, ma perché esempio di arte concettuale.
IN REALTÀ È SEMPRE ARTE RADICALE.
È l'ultimo oggetto di design prodotto dalla Gufram che sia stato acquisito da un museo dopo gli anni '70

p. 87

(VICEVERSA)
MUTAZIONE GENETICA

"Agit Pop" era il tema di una sezione di una celebre mostra nel 2001 – "Les années Pop" – del Centre Pompidou, dedicata alle varie creazioni nel campo delle arti plastiche, film, design e architettura degli anni dal 1956 al 1968 nei quali nasce una cultura popolare, che segue l'onda di rinnovamento economico e sociale che cominciava a manifestarsi nel nuovo come nel vecchio continente europeo e preludeva ai movimenti di contestazione degli anni '70. Appartengono a quegli anni le prime opere di Coop Himmelblau, Haus Rucker & Co, Zünd Up, Archizoom, Superstudio, 999, UFO e Utopie in Francia.

In Italia partendo dal Pop alcuni artisti e giovani architetti-designer si evolvono con intenti culturalmente eversivi verso opere dal contenuto critico e politico.

Il "Pop critico", secondo la definizione della mostra parigina, rappresentato dalle opere figurative di Celmins, Vostell, Equipo 57, Monory e Pistoletto, che introduce nel mondo dell'arte un'estetica caratterizzata dall'apparente assenza dell'artista per dare enfasi alle tecniche espressive e alla raffigurazione di oggetti tratti dal mondo del quotidiano e commerciale, è il punto di partenza per il movimento del design e dell'architettura radicale che, a differenza dell'arte Pop, non è legato a un'epoca storica, ma è la continuità dell'idea che la progettazione di un oggetto o di un fabbricato ugualmente siano una mera occasione per sottolineare che l'obbiettivo dell'autore è dare vita a messaggi "critici", leggibili anche su piani diversi e ciò indipendentemente dalla funzione del prodotto creato o dal valore della ricerca tecnologica svolta per produrlo.

Il confine tra arte, design e architettura tende a sfumarsi o, meglio, a unificarsi in un concetto di arte visiva, per l'importanza data al significato dell'opera.
Il concetto di progetto critico nell'opera di Gianni Arnaudo ha una "mutazione genetica", che si afferma come "cambio di prospettiva",come succede per molti artisti anche in altri settori delle arti figurative.
Alba Basile

p. 88

Fizzz®

p. 89

Napulì®
(maniglia scaramantica)
2018

Gli italiani secondo il mondo

p. 90

Aliko®
Barel
2019

Una visione dell'abitare che susciti emozioni: questo è Aliko. Una seduta creata da Gianni Arnaudo per il mondo delle discoteche, celebrato dal Vitra Design Museum di Basilea con una mostra, "Night Fever", che ricrea le atmosfere uniche di luoghi come lo Studio 54 di New York, divenuti mitici per aver attratto personaggi come Andy Warhol, Grace Jones, i Rolling Stones, Carole Bouquet, Keith Haring e molti altri.
Arte, cinema e musica insieme per stimolare la creatività, che nasce sempre da un pensiero rivoluzionario, fuori da canoni imposti.
Il Paolina B, discoteca nata in un luogo di confine italo-francese, era un mondo reso così fantastico da Gianni Arnaudo che anche un giovane Alberto di Monaco volle vedere...
Ora il progetto, le sue foto e Aliko sono esposti nella mostra itinerante del Vitra, celebrata anche dal "Wall Street Journal", perché l'originalità è valore, e lo è nel quotidiano per chiunque.
Con Aliko è evocata la libertà di un pensiero ludico, la leggerezza di un design originale e un frammento d'arte contemporanea.

p. 91

design "soffice"
Tea Time®
(tavolo vagabondo)
Nel frattempo acquisito nella collezione permanente dell'ADAM Museum di Bruxelles.

p. 92

Il vero Pandoro®
Slide
2013

p. 93

(dedicato a tutte le donne)
Sonostufa®
2011

p. 94

FORMA ALTERNATIVA DI COMUNICAZIONE: mettiamoci una toppa!
PAPÌ®
2010

"Il riso non doveva essere cosa cattiva, se poteva farsi veicolo di verità."
Umberto Eco, *Il nome della Rosa*, Bompiani, Milano 1980, p. 134

Le Papì rappresentano l'archetipo, l'idea platonica della classica poltrona italica (presa a pretesto), ironicamente rinnovata con un rivestimento multicolore per richiamare alcuni aspetti emblematici del popolo italiano, il suo profondo desiderio di vitalità e di allegria.

Di fronte a una interminabile crisi, il fatto di "mettere una toppa" colorata a un'Italia in difficoltà, esprime la volontà di sorridere, di ricorrere all' autoironia come via d'uscita, unico stimolo alla creatività.

Papì è tonda e morbida, come le paperette dell'infanzia; oggetto unico perché, oltre a essere personalizzabile nella combinazione dei colori, sulla toppa ognuno potrà scrivere la propria storia, il blasone di famiglia o una frase di contestazione, di poesia o d'amore.

Quello che conta in questa poltrona è la toppa, non la poltrona.

p. 95

UN MESSAGGIO CHE PUÒ DIVENTARE ANCHE PIÙ ESPLICITO...
DEDICATO AI RENITENTI AI SOCIAL NETWORK

p. 96

YouWelcome®
YouWelcome è stata una delle prime opere progettate per Poltrona Frau. Il mio desiderio era di rispettare la classicità dello stile Frau, dandone una lettura contemporanea.
YouWelcome è l'attualizzazione del Barocco e della storia di Poltrona Frau.

p. 97

Sua Eminenza®

p. 98

Mee-Thing®
2019
IN RICORDO DEL CANE THEO

p. 99

Cremino e Prendivoglia®
Slide per Venchi
2018

p. 100

LA "PORTA" NELLA SUA SVOLTA STORICA

p. 101

LA RIVOLUZIONE DEL CONCETTO DI PORTA

1. L'eliminazione di cornice simmetrica
La porta "Boulevard"

2. L'inserimento dello specchio per duplicare lo spazio e introdurre una terza dimensione
La porta "Sezione Aurea"

3. Fine della cornice e chiusura magnetica
La porta "MAG"

p. 102

1 L'illusione di un viale,
la fine di una convenzione

L'idea di porta, nella sua normale e universale definizione, e la sua forma, fatte salve minime varianti di decoro,sono rimaste sostanzialmente immutate nel tempo e cioè un'anta, una cornice, una maniglia, il tutto organizzato secondo una rigida simmetria.

Il valore dell'oggetto è stato sinora attribuito e concentrato nella tecnologia o, più spesso, nella decorazione, che è il tratto distintivo apparente dei vari modelli e delle varie epoche dell'architettura.

Boulevard è la rilettura critica di tutto questo: innanzitutto è "distrutta" la simmetria come valore emblematico di eleganza. È distrutto il "valore" del materiale, che è volutamente un MDF "autentico" (frutto di riciclo, a sua volta riciclabile), rispetto al legno pregiato o a qualche perfetta laccatura.

La cornice asimmetrica è dissacrazione di un canone classico e creazione di uno spazio reale oltre la porta, oltre la realtà...

p. 103

2 L'illusione di uno spazio virtuale

La Boulevard e la Sezione Aurea sono creazioni biplanari: la funzione reale è quella di suggerire una correlazione simbolica tra il tempo e lo spazio prima di aprire la porta e quello che verrà dopo. Nella Boulevard l'intento è attuato attraverso un totale mutamento delle ordinarie proporzioni di una porta, variate in modo funzionale a sottolineare la lettura prospettica del disegno di un viale alberato, che non è decorazione, ma suggerimento di un percorso idealmente infinito.
Nella Sezione Aurea il messaggio è realizzato – a cominciare come sempre dal nome – attraverso il metodo di citazioni facilmente riconoscibili, anche perché riproposte in contesti svariati (film inclusi), e fortemente simboliche.
L'illusione è quella di una porta aperta, realizzata con uno specchio che evidenzia un battente aperto verso uno spazio metafisico: la realtà riflessa si proietta oltre la porta chiusa.
Lo specchio non lega solo questa porta al Pop critico (Pistoletto), e richiama gli affreschi di Paolo Veronese nella Villa Barbaro a Maser, ma ne costituisce un passaggio ulteriore, perché la

funzione questa volta è una componente essenziale per la lettura del messaggio: il passare da un luogo ad un altro può avere una componente irrazionale e criptica, ma la visione autocritica può rendere magico quel cambiamento.
La Sezione Aurea è superamento della porta tradizionale: innanzitutto è "distrutta" la simmetria come valore emblematico e così pure la "cornice". Oggetto di design e opera concettuale nel medesimo tempo. La Sezione Aurea è la ricerca della massima espressione dello spazio proporzionale che è stato inventato in Italia ed ha avuto in Piero della Francesca (1415-1492) la sua prima grande manifestazione.
La linea rossa – tracciata con i led – determina la "sezione aurea" dello spazio.
In quest'ottica la porta è un tema evocativo più di altri, per le sue molteplici interpretazioni documentate dalla storia dell'arte e per gli immediati spunti metafisici sulla lettura dello spazio.

p. 104

3 MAG
(una rivoluzione rispetto alla storia)

MAG ha nuovamente dato vita a una porta che è una rivoluzione nel panorama dei serramenti interni: rivoluzionario è che viene completamente abolita la cornice, elemento da secoli connaturato all'idea di porta.
MAG appare staccata dal muro, risaltando come un quadro o una scultura.
Grazie al nuovo meccanismo magnetico di chiusura può essere anche abolita la maniglia, creando l'effetto di un oggetto d'arte sulla parete, anche tramite i tagli di luce realizzati con un materiale bianco lucido su una superficie di colore bianco opaco assolutamente complanare.
Lucio Fontana con i suoi tagli su tela bianca ha cambiato la visione dell'arte; Gianni Arnaudo quella delle porte.
MAG è magnetica, MAG è magica.

p. 105

Porta XY

p. 106

Una SPA
Castello di Montaldo
2006-2007

Una delle residenze sabaude vicino a Torino è diventata un design hotel con spa.

Il colore della Pink Lady viene studiato con la Gufram come sintesi fra diverse proposte di rossetti utilizzati dalle dive; ne fa fede il rapporto epistolare che testimonia la ricerca di una soluzione eclatante. E così fu.

Il nome Pink Lady venne utilizzato in seguito, traendolo da un catalogo della ditta produttrice di tessuto elastico bidimensionale. Il colore era però riferito a un campione rosa diverso e molto più chiaro.

p. 107

Graal nel Castello

p. 109

massima provocazione
SE ANDY WARHOL FOSSE STATO
UN ARCHITETTO

avrebbe voluto progettare questa cantina così, **un fabbricato come un'installazione d'arte**, una sintesi del linguaggio pop – lo sguardo "zoom" e il fuori scala – e dell'architettura radicale, della quale ha la natura e la funzione di **progetto critico** che si manifesta con un segno architettonico unico e forte.

UN VERO CAMBIO DI PROSPETTIVA

p. 111

"Senza rischio, coraggio e sovversione non c'è creatività, quindi non c'è cultura, industria, progresso."
Oliviero Toscani
(*Dire, fare, baciare*, Rizzoli editore, Milano 2016)

p. 112

CONTRO-ARCHITETTURA come CONTRO-DESIGN,

perché il mio obbiettivo non è provocare o semplicemente scandalizzare, com'è ora di moda.
Il progetto dell'Astemia Pentita – la cui idea è esclusivamente mia, sin dall'origine, e di nessun altro (l'enfasi è dovuta al fatto che qualcuno ha maldestramente cercato di appropriarsene) – nasce dal mio modo di usare l'architettura come strumento visuale per scrivere una frase con un diverso mezzo. Mai ho seguito le mode e per il rivestimento delle due cassette ho scelto, sin dall'inizio, un materiale particolare non per ragioni ecologiste – anche se sono un ambientalista convinto – ma perché di legno sono i contenitori per spedire il vino. Ogni diversa versione su questo punto – e ne ho lette di spassose – denota di non aver capito il progetto.
Il design dell'Astemia Pentita è stato presentato nel 2012 alla Biennale di architettura di Venezia e il 30 maggio 2018 ha vinto il premio nazionale "100 progetti", che vedeva coinvolti altrettanti studi di architettura tra i più importanti d'Italia.
Questa costruzione racchiude tutti gli elementi del pop sotto il profilo formale, lo sguardo "zoom", i riferimenti di pubblicità di un prodotto di consumo, ma è radicale nel pensiero che manifesta, perché è un pensiero critico. Ciò che conta nel progetto non è né la funzione, né la forma o i materiali ma il messaggio eversivo che esprime.
La scelta dei materiali è stata molto importante ed è caduta su un estruso di legno, vale a dire materiale polverizzato e resina. Si tratta dello scarto delle segherie, che verrebbe buttato e che si può riciclare: il cosiddetto Woodn, che permette di mantenere temperatura e umidità costanti.
Ho scelto questo legno perché più resistente e duraturo, mentre per la soluzione degli interni ho pensato a ciò che si trova in una cassetta per il vino, scegliendo quindi un materiale che riproduce il cartone e un nastro rosso luminoso che potesse unire i vari livelli della produzione e della vendita. Tutt'altra cosa è la ricerca di visibiltà con qualunque mezzo, per cui molti sono coloro che si improvvisano cuochi, artisti, progettisti d'interni o pensano che basti comprare un garage per diventare come Steve Jobs.
Gianni Arnaudo

L'idea originale è di concepire l'opera come due scatole sovrapposte, aventi a modello i contenitori in legno da tempo utilizzati per la commercializzazione e vendita delle singole bottiglie di vino, le cui caratteristiche sono rispecchiate in macro nel progetto.
Esso si riconduce a un frammento del linguaggio del mondo del vino; in particolare si riferisce alla parte finale della commercializzazione, e cioè il packaging, che negli anni in cui stiamo vivendo assume un'importanza fondamentale: il contenitore diviene più significativo del contenuto.
Il disegno evidenzia le contraddizioni di un sistema di produzione ove a volte il marketing e l'etichetta sono prevalenti rispetto al vino (per quanto mitico come nel caso del Barolo).
Il significato si amplia a richiami etici, con un'operazione di "zoom" sull'oggetto, per ironizzare, con lo strumento della macroscopicizzazione, sulle forme spesso utilizzate per apparire rispetto ai contenuti dell'essere.

"l'Arca" n. 259, giugno 2010

p. 114

L'Astemia Pentita: chi la reputa troppo moderna per un territorio "classico", chi ritiene che alcune barriere vadano sdoganate. Lei cosa ne pensa?

Ritengo giusto che le "barriere" vadano sdoganate: salvaguardare l'identità di un territorio non deve essere il pretesto per consolidare un processo di "imbalsamazione" ambientale a danno delle attese di una comunità. Nella levata di scudi di Maria Teresa Mascarello (produttrice di Barolo che si era espressa a sfavore, ndr) si legge tutta la logica di chi si affida al ricordo per non guardare al presente che è anche attualità linguistica e creativa, così come il Barolo che, nella dimensione della sua autenticità perché prodotto di uno specifico territorio, trova ampio consenso, nelle nuove generazioni, in contesti internazionali diversissimi tra loro. Certo è che le due macro cassette di legno portabottiglie, incipit immaginativo di una tradizione, hanno dato **fiato al sonno di un territorio**.

Ce ne abbozza una lettura?

La riflessione che ha lanciato sul tavolo del dibattito l'opera dell'architetto Gianni Arnaudo con la cantina "L'Astemia Pentita" va considerata alla luce del ruolo che l'architettura ha oggi o, meglio, della sua **valenza etica.** Quello che meraviglia di Arnaudo è la scelta di concepire i **ridotti volumi esterni** – la parte essenziale della cantina è nascosta sottoterra come l'anima che struttura le qualità organolettiche del Barolo – come qualcosa messa lì temporaneamente, cioè pronta per essere trasportata via, direi "**in transito**", in viaggio dalla terra alle tavole imbandite nelle case o nei ristoranti di tutti i continenti. Ha coniugato aspetti che guardano alle ricadute sul territorio sociale, soprattutto sui giovani che leggono la semplicità di tale linguaggio, perchè vicino al loro essere, con un senso di **attualità.** Anche la **mega scritta**, con caratteri a stampa, richiama scritte o firme proprie della cultura del *writer*: una cultura che è all'opposto di quella celebrata dalla Pop art. Una scritta che interpreta il vivo piacere della "trasgressione", del cedere a "Bacco", all'avventura di ebbrezza dionisiaca che il vino accompagna.

Estratto di un'intervista al professor Massimo Bignardi, docente di Storia dell'Arte Contemporanea e di Arte Ambientale e Architettura del Paesaggio, Università di Siena.

Irene Graziotto, "L'Astemia Pentita: perchè ha 'dato fiato al sonno di un territorio', il Barolo", *I grandi Vini*, marzo 2015.

p. 117

La cosa più difficile è fare un progetto semplice ed esprimere un'idea forte ed evocativa di un prodotto, di una situazione complessa e ricca di più significati.

p. 123

Il nastro che lega oriente e occidente (l'edificio brand)

p. 126

L'architettura deve essere un segno forte e riconoscibile perché, al di là dei valori concettuali, colpisce l'immaginazione del pubblico e induce a vivere l'esperienza diretta di un luogo anomalo.
IL MIO SOGNO DI UNA FABBRICA COME LUOGO DI CULTURA

Ma lo sguardo "zoom" è un modo di trasformare un oggetto in un simbolo, di renderne immediatamente percepibili le valenze evocative.

Un enorme nastro rosso avvolge una fabbrica di panettoni e l'architettura diventa il primo e più vistoso veicolo pubblicitario del prodotto, richiamando con un semplice "segno" tutti i messaggi subliminali della festa.

La funzione della costruzione è un pretesto per riprodurre in macro l'emozione del Natale dell'infanzia, la gioia di aprire i pacchi dei doni e dei dolci e conservarne i nastri per ricordo.

È anche una metafora di quello che per il mondo contemporaneo sono diventate le festività religiose, perché il giocoso nastro rosso avviluppa un polo (eccellente) di produzione industriale.

p. 127

"Ci sono degli edifici la cui impronta è così forte da togliere l'ambiente dall'anonimato."

Uno stesso segno può ricordare mondi e valori diversi se è stato tracciato per riflettere e far riflettere.

p. 129

Il nastro rosso, che sembra svolgersi nell'aria (e che nasconde la scala), moltiplica i messaggi dell'architettura, idealmente accostando il mondo occidentale all'orientale, alla Cina e alle sue usanze per le feste del nuovo anno.

pp. 130-131

Il recupero della storia

p. 132

Architettura contestuale
Recuperare saperi e segni antichi

Il mio pensiero in fatto di ecosostenibilità è stato pubblicato nel libro *Le case del vino*, pubblicato dalla Regione Piemonte (ed. L'Artistica Savigliano, Cuneo 2009) con l'introduzione di Carlo Petrini, Presidente nazionale di Slow Food.
Il metodo progettuale consiste in una attenta analisi del territorio, e in questo caso delle vecchie case contadine, per giungere alla definizione di un "linguaggio" tale da esprimere l'identità di un luogo o di quell'ambiente in cui si creerà una nuova costruzione. Molti di questi elementi costituiscono le frasi di un sapere antico che possono essere utilmente tradotte in una costruzione contemporanea. Come Slow Food ha studiato e catalogato le vecchie vigne e le caratteristiche genetiche di questi vini straordinari del basso Piemonte, anche l'architettura deve essere subordinata a una profonda ricerca: alcuni tratti di un DNA ormai perduto possono rivivere ed essere sorprendentemente utilizzati per una nuova idea progettuale.

Il recupero della tradizione e cioè dei vecchi "tappeti" di mais, che cambiavano d'autunno il colore delle case, ripresi come moderne pareti ventilate, caratterizzano l'involucro del nuovo complesso.

p. 133

Una "parete ventilata"

I contadini delle Langhe usavano dei "graticci" di legno per essiccare al sole le pannocchie di mais. Le diverse qualità dei semi producevano colori diversi, dall'arancio al giallo al nero e costituivano un motivo d'orgoglio per ognuno di essi.

Nacque così una forma arcaica di parete ventilata che avrebbe protetto la casa per tutto l'inverno.

pp. 134-135

Un'unica passerella, un modo di ricordare vecchi percorsi per crearne dei nuovi

p. 136

Interni dello stabilimento Terre da Vino, una passeggiata didattica sulla produzione del vino, ideata come un percorso museale, con un passaggio scenografico su un mare di barriques.

pp. 138-139

IL FANTASMA DEL VIALE DI NAPOLEONE

Questo non è uno dei tanti edifici trasparenti, che connotano l'architettura contemporanea, perché tutto ciò che è costruito per moda ha la propria ragione d'esistere nell'effimero.

È un ghost, è il fantasma del viale sui baluardi napoleonici, che è riuscito a tornare per riproporre una storia quasi dimenticata.

p. 140

NAPOLEONE BONAPARTE

aveva ideato e voluto il piano regolatore di Cuneo del 1802, che costituisce il primo atto urbanistico della città secondo una visione moderna: aveva pensato a un luogo elegante aumentandone le scenografie e rendendolo accattivante con grandi viali e spazi pubblici.

Uno di questi viali che passa davanti al complesso residenziale prevedeva due file di alberi per ombreggiare la passeggiata lungo la traccia delle mura abbattute. Il Comune ne realizza una sola: l'altra sarebbe stata realizzata due secoli dopo in ossequio alla storia.

Ispiratrice di questo progetto è stata una frase di Peggy Guggenheim, che affacciandosi sul Canal Grande pensava che "l'unica immagine in grado di competere con Venezia fosse il suo riflesso nell'acqua."

Lo sguardo di chi arriva a Cuneo da Mondovì e percorre il ponte sul Gesso coglie una sequenza di alberi, memoria della sua storia, alla quale fanno da sfondo le facciate delle case costruite, e l'illusione ottica è che le sagome degli alberi siano integrate in quelle facciate e ne siano parte. Questo effetto si coglie in determinati momenti del giorno, nei quali il sole proietta i rami degli alberi sui muri delle case, creando un rapporto di continuità fra la quinta naturale e quella virtuale.

Da questa idea è nato il progetto, e cioè il disegno di un edificio che si affaccia sul Corso, le cui strutture esterne portanti sono concepite come fossero la proiezione di quegli alberi integrati nella facciata, non come segno grafico fine a se stesso, e quindi semplicemente decorativo, ma come riflesso dell'elemento naturalistico caratterizzante e unificante questa cornice del centro storico.

"l'Arca" n. 259, giugno 2010

p. 141

"...prigionieri del passato si diventa per la perdita e non per il culto della memoria..."
Paolo Portoghesi
(*Dopo l'architettura moderna*, Laterza, Roma-Bari 1980)

L'oblio della Storia

crea il non-luogo, zone "fredde" della città, non frequentate o mal frequentate, in contrapposizione evidente con le zone percepite come "calde", in cui la traccia della storia è stata preservata.
A Cuneo nella zona dell'ex foro boario, come in altre città, questo è evidente e non dipende dalla presenza o meno del verde alberato, ma dalla percezione istintiva di un luogo come privo di un'anima e di un centro di interesse.

Vincitore di un concorso internazionale bandito dalla città di Cuneo è stato il mio sogno per trasformare un "non-luogo" in un'idea che rendesse questa parte degli antichi baluardi un polo culturale, legando il conservatorio musicale alla costruzione di un auditorium, edificato sulla direttrice di uno degli antichi viali napoleonici, il cui ricordo è impresso nella vetrata di ingresso. Innumerevoli esperienze dimostrano che la creazione di occasioni culturali attraverso il riadattamento di luoghi originariamente anche lontanissimi da tale destinazione, come il complesso minerario-industriale di Zollverein nella Ruhr, è un metodo di sicuro successo per dare valore, anche economico, a zone disertate nel quotidiano dalla popolazione.

pp. 142-143

QUESTO ERA IL MIO SOGNO PER LA MIA CITTÀ...
POI È STATO UN CONCORSO VINTO E NON REALIZZATO

p. 145

Île Rousse era un piccolo porto frequentato dai pirati corsi e perciò l'ho battezzato... La Marine Corsaire

p. 146

Con La Marine Corsaire, Gianni Arnaudo realizza in un vuoto periferico un luogo i cui gli abitanti si possono identificare con la propria storia. Île Rousse è un antico borgo di pescatori nella parte nord-ovest della Corsica, dove il segno della storia è visibile nella tipologia urbana del centro storico. Poi c'è un porto, un tempo frequentato da Corsari, e un personaggio, Pasquale Paoli, che nel 1700, con un'intuizione urbanistica moderna, ha concepito l'immagine di quello che è l'attuale tessuto dell'abitato più antico. Quattro strade parallele, un mercato coperto, una piazza ridefinita in periodo napoleonico con il solido impianto di platani secolari ed edifici alti e severi. Infine le scenografie, attraverso strade anguste, concepite per frazionare il vento.

L'intervento di Arnaudo è caratterizzato da un segno semplice e chiaro, dato dal "ribaltamento" dell'asse del nucleo storico di 90°, con la creazione di una grande piazza, che diviene il nuovo centro vitale. Il tessuto, il contorno degli edifici, la dimensione stessa degli spazi sono la riproduzione filologica della pianta urbanistica concepita da Paoli. I caratteri costruttivi delle abitazioni, con la loro severa eleganza e la semplicità delle proporzioni traducono in un linguaggio contemporaneo le antiche convenzioni che definivano le facciate, i vuoti e i pieni, le altezze, le distanze, i passaggi interni e i materiali della tradizione locale.
Gianni Arnaudo

"l'Arca International" n. 116, gennaio-febbraio 2014

Proprio uno specchio ho usato per progettare, perché ho ripreso l'immagine del centro storico di Île-Rousse e ne ho ribaltato l'asse di 90°.

p. 147

Visto che i francesi, ovunque siano, anche sulle rive della Senna a Parigi o in Camargue, uno spazio per giocare alle *pétanque* lo trovano sempre, perché quella è loro anima, ho concepito la piazza della *pétanque* come cardine del mio progetto per lo spazio urbano.

p. 148

Torre Pastor
Gli edifici di Montecarlo hanno la straordinaria capacità di apparire non classificabili da un punto di vista qualitativo, né è possibile, all'interno del Principato, parlare di architettura e confrontare la consistenza culturale del patrimonio edilizio con il dibattito in atto nei vicini Paesi europei o negli ambienti universitari e professionali d'oltreoceano.
Nel piccolo territorio costiero l'ambiente è di totale natura artificiale; l'edilizia e l'assetto infrastrutturale del territorio hanno completamente sostituito ogni riferimento alla conformazione orografica naturale, fino a identificarsi del tutto con essa. Il costruito è il rinnovato elemento naturale per tutti i sudditi del moderno e tollerante Principato e, in quanto tale, è da esso che viene ricavato il sostentamento di ogni attività umana, come accade, in altre circostanze, nei rapporti tra i contadini e la terra, tra i pescatori e l'oceano. In questa estrema condizione di dipendenza, la qualità architettonica è una nozione che assume contorni sfumati: il valore di un manufatto dipende dal tipo di attività che vi viene esercitata e dalla possibilità di rispondere sufficientemente alle aspettative finanziare degli operatori che l'hanno realizzato.
Non può meravigliare, quindi, che vista dall'esterno, senza entrare nella inusuale logica in atto nel Principato, l'architettura realizzata nei suoi confini non abbia lasciato dietro di sé alcun commento; una totale indifferenza all'ambiente costruito ci circonda, riconciliando gli effetti concreti del capitale internazionale con la nostra condizione umana, attraverso il conferimento di una nuova dignità a tutte le attività finanziare legate alle costruzioni.
Tuttavia, ultimamente, in questo mondo ricco di profonde contraddizioni, la volontà di rinnovamento e la necessità di recuperare un'immagine credibile si sono espresse con una serie di riferimenti nuovi, legati ad alcuni grandi progetti, quali l'ampliamento dell'area di Fontvieille, la realizzazione di un nuovo porto turistico e la ristrutturazione urbanistica dell'area della Condamine e del sedime ferroviario che attraversa longitudinalmente il Principato.
In tale contesto, si colloca il progetto dell'edificio polifunzionale di Gianni Arnaudo.
Alcuni suoi precedenti lavori in Montecarlo, quali la ristrutturazione degli uffici della Engeco Pastor e della Lamborghini Chrysler, ne sono stati idealmente la preparazione, o per così dire, la definizione di un programma, di un linguaggio.
Questo nuovo "lavoro ribelle", realizzato a mille chilometri dalle "trasparenze" parigine in un mondo lontano dal dibattito culturale, ha la forza sovversiva di molta nuova architettura grazie a un "alleggerimento" generalizzato del peso di ciascun elemento achitettonico dell'edificio, che dà vita a un'immagine architettonica ridotta ai minimi termini; quanto basta per assolvere efficientemente al programma funzionale, un edificio dal profilo semplice e drammatico, caratterizzato da un'essenzialità impeccabile e organica.
Impossibile evitare il riferimento, nel complesso dei rapporti volumetrici e in particolare nella configurazione della sommità della "guglia" del blocco verticale dei servizi, ad alcune realizzazioni dettate dal segno di quella parte dell'architettura contemporanea più tesa al futuro, di cui il progetto ripropone, in una nuova chiave, l'accostamento insolito e innovativo dei volumi geometrici; la geometria strutturale, nondimeno, sembra derivare da una semplice quanto precisa "memoria" della leggerezza delle vele, o le carene, o le chiglie di antichi velieri, mentre i tiranti d'acciaio e la guglia piramidale richiamano gli alberi degli antichi vascelli dei Principi Grimaldi.
Alessandro Gubitosi

"l'Arca" n. 69, marzo 1993

p. 151

Paglia, legno e pietra del vulcano

pp. 152-153

Capo Verde era uno scalo perfetto per le navi in viaggio tra l'Europa e l'America e per questo per alcuni secoli a partire dalla fine del 1400 divenne un centro importante per il commercio degli schiavi africani.

Perché non venga dimenticata questa parte di storia, la facciata del Museo delle Isole di Capo Verde è concepita come la fiancata di una nave, curva e segnata da strette finestre, come a ricordare sguardi dolenti che seguono lo svanire in lontananza della propria terra.

p. 154

Le Isole di Capo Verde sono tra loro molto differenti sotto il profilo geologico e paesaggistico: vulcaniche come Fogo, o caratterizzate da una flora tropicale come Mindelo.
L'isola di Sal, come si intuisce dal nome, è una salina semidesertica e battuta da venti caldi, e per molti anni è stato l'unico approdo turistico dell'arcipelago, da cui però raramente i viaggiatori si spostavano per visitare le altre isole, anche a causa della relativa difficoltà dei collegamenti.
L'idea del museo è nata per orientare il visitatore alla conoscenza di uno straordinario patrimonio territoriale e di un popolo il cui passato merita di essere conosciuto.
La costruzione si articola su uno spazio di 800 mq. ed è sviluppata secondo l'idea architettonica di un tracciato elicoidale che si snoda attraverso atrio, sale e percorso espositivo a quote diverse, la biblioteca, l'archivio fotografico e informatico, sino a raggiungere una piattaforma superiore dalla quale si potrà vedere il panorama delle saline, in un ambiente quasi metafisico.
Le piccole case sono orientate secondo la disposizione delle isole che rappresentano, e le cui caratteristiche sono illustrate al visitatore in ciascuna costruzione, realizzata rispettando il segno architettonico e i materiali tipici delle abitazioni dell'arcipelago.

pp. 156-157

Lo stabilimento Dromont
Lo hanno chiamato "il Guggenheim" delle Langhe

Con lo sviluppo dell'attività industriale, molti imprenditori illuminati hanno visto nell'architettura dei propri stabilimenti un'occasione importante per creare un valore aggiunto alla propria immagine e alla riconoscibilità del proprio prodotto. Per questo hanno individuato nell'architettura di qualità non soltanto un modo per adeguare alle nuove esigenze i propri sistemi di produzione, ma anche un mezzo per veicolare la comunicazione di una propria rinnovata filosofia aziendale, basata sul concetto di innovazione, di creatività e di sensibilità rispetto alle sollecitazioni esterne del mercato. Come in molti casi, che ormai appartengono alla storia dell'architettura, l'imprenditore ha voluto esprimere con la creazione del proprio luogo di lavoro un forte segno culturale. Questi sono stati gli elementi che hanno connotato gli obiettivi della realtà Dromont di Grinzane Cavour.
Lo stabilimento produce macchinari ad altissima precisione meccanica ed elettronica per il confezionamento di vernici e coloranti industriali, dalle grandi linee di montaggio delle multinazionali del colore ai mixer automatici utilizzati nei colorifici per la produzione delle tinteggiature.
Il progetto consisteva nell'ampliamento e rivisitazione dell'edificio esistente realizzato in tempi relativamente recenti, non più adeguato alle esigenze produttive e connotato da un aspetto estetico piuttosto datato e vagamente postmoderno. La caratterizzazione è stata quella di determinare un segno architettonico molto forte connesso a una "addizione", che sul lato principale dello stabilimento si esprime con una superficie metallica tale da creare un "nastro", un foglio di lamiera abbandonato su un prato verde fra le colline. La facciata curva in metallo è stata realizzata con l'adozione di una pennellatura in "Alucobond", sfruttandone le doti di adattabilità e di flessibilità.
La parte preesistente del complesso è legata alla parte nuova da uno "spiedo" in cristallo che "trafigge" i volumi creando una consequenzialità compositiva.
Questo percorso, realizzato totalmente in vetro strutturale, dà luogo a un ponte sospeso, che consente il percorso degli addetti e delle utilities.
L'idea dominante che ha guidato la progettazione è stata quella di smaterializzare il passato: questa operazione è riuscita grazie alla complicità dell'adozione di grandi superfici vetrate, ottenute con i sistemi costruttivi della Metra e i cristalli della Saint-Gobain.

"l'Arca" n. 259, giugno 2010

pp. 158-159

Un battito d'ali e la sua ombra
L'aeroporto di Cuneo-Levaldigi

p. 160

Centro incontri
Provincia di Cuneo

p. 162

Le colline del Monferrato

Il complesso si riferisce ad una Cantina fra le colline del Monferrato.
L'idea dominante, che ha guidato la progettazione, è stata quella di smaterializzare i volumi ponendoli in contrasto dialettico con un grande spazio espositivo determinato dall'incontro geometrico fra un "foglio" di acciaio curvo e leggero con le parti opache del complesso.
Questo risultato è determinato dalle grandi superfici vetrate e dall'adozione di una struttura in legno lamellare: si è riusciti così a ottenere effetti di leggerezza e trasparenza inaspettati e straordinari.
Uno dei problemi caratterizzanti la progettazione era quello di armonizzare un contenitore industriale con un contesto paesistico significativo, tenendo conto di alcune scelte imposte dalla committenza soprattutto per quanto riguarda la funzionalità e la destinazione degli spazi interni, nonché la definizione di superfici organizzate secondo una logica produttiva, derivata da un ciclo di lavorazione specifico, a cui le forme architettoniche dovevano adeguarsi.
Altro aspetto, date queste premesse, era quello di smaterializzare i "pesi" e i volumi così definiti, mediante una scelta strategica di materiali e di tipologie costruttive.
Si è definita così un'idea attraverso un dialogo tra superfici e volumi, opacità e trasparenze, che caratterizzano la vitalità e al tempo stesso la dialettica delle varie componenti.
Il progetto, in termini sintetici, prevede la definizione di un "nastro" che si pone in continuità con l'andamento delle colline.
La prima parte che si affaccia a un'arteria di grande traffico delinea il volume della zona destinata alla vendita dei prodotti della Cantina; successivamente questa superficie di copertura scompare nel terreno per individuare lo spazio di conservazione del vino, e infine riemerge come parte di produzione.
Tutti questi spazi sono uniti da una passerella: essa nasce nella prima parte del complesso determinando una passeggiata aerea per i visitatori, offrendo ora la possibilità di conoscere le varie fasi della lavorazione del vino, ora, per la parte esterna, il territorio da cui nasce questa nuova ricchezza.
La cantina d'invecchiamento ricorda il ventre di una nave da carico, come quelle che storicamente nel porto di Genova attendevano i carichi del prodotto, che ha reso celebre il Monferrato.

"l'Arca" n. 259, giugno 2010

p. 163

Un edificio produttivo

p. 165

Stabilimento V2

Il complesso realizzato da Gianni Arnaudo per V2 Elettronica, una fabbrica di componenti elettroniche di alta precisione, si trova ai margini dell'abitato della città di Racconigi (Cuneo), collocata a metà della grande pianura che separa Torino dalla cerchia delle Alpi, e dove i Savoia vollero collocare una delle più significative testimonianze del loro segno architettonico in un interessante complesso, castello e parco ora divenuti dominio di tutela dell'UNESCO.

Lo stabilimento si affaccia sul viale secolare che fa da quinta monumentale alla facciata del castello. Uno dei problemi caratterizzanti la progettazione è stato dunque quello di armonizzare un contenitore industriale con un contesto storico e paesistico di notevole rilievo, tenendo conto di alcune scelte imposte dalla committenza quali l'uso di una struttura prefabbricata, la definizione di superfici organizzate secondo una logica produttiva derivata da un ciclo di lavorazione specifico a cui le forme architettoniche dovevano adeguarsi.

Altro aspetto, date queste premesse, era quello di smaterializzare i "pesi" e i volumi così definiti, mediante una scelta strategica dei materiali e delle tipologie costruttive.

È nata così un'idea definita attraverso un dialogo tra superfici e volumi, opacità e trasparenze che ne caratterizzano la vitalità e, allo stesso tempo, la dialettica delle varie componenti.
Con lo sviluppo della propria attività, alcuni imprenditori illuminati hanno colto nella realizzazione di nuovi stabilimenti un'occasione importante per creare e comunicare un ulteriore valore aggiunto alla propria immagine e alla riconoscibilità della propria attività produttiva. Per questo hanno individuato in una architettura di qualità non soltanto una risposta di adeguamento degli spazi alle nuove esigenze e ai nuovi sistemi di produzione, ma anche un modo di veicolare la comunicazione di una propria filosofia aziendale basata sul concetto di creatività, di innovazione, e di sensibilità rispetto alle sollecitazioni esterne del mercato.
Come in molti casi che ormai appartengono alla storia dell'architettura, l'imprenditore ha voluto esprimere con la creazione del proprio luogo di lavoro una forte testimonianza di volontà di trasformazione e al tempo stesso un nuovo segno culturale. Date queste premesse non si poteva che esprimere un "segno forte", testimonianza ed espressione di questi obiettivi.
L'idea dominante che ha guidato la progettazione è stata quella di smaterializzare i volumi, ponendoli in contrasto dialettico con un grande spazio espositivo determinato dall'incontro geometrico fra un "foglio" di acciaio curvo e leggero con la parte opaca del complesso.
Questo risultato è stato ottenuto con grandi superfici vetrate e l'adozione di una struttura in legno lamellare: si è riusciti così a declinare momenti di leggerezza e trasparenza con inaspettati effetti scenografici.

Contributo determinante e finale è stato dato dallo studio dell'illuminazione, che esalta la visione notturna del complesso: così la comunicazione di questa nuova realtà industriale può continuare con uguale forza a trasmetterci ulteriori messaggi. Oltre il crepuscolo l'edificio si trasforma, dando vita a un oggetto che richiama vagamente un'astronave, per comunicare in questo possibile decollo fra LED ed effetti sorprendenti la volontà di conquista di nuovi spazi grazie a quelle capacità imprenditoriali che caratterizzano, anche in momenti di crisi, l'affermarsi della creatività e di un modo diverso di fare impresa.
Gianni Arnaudo

"l'Arca" n. 209, dicembre 2005

p. 166

Villa Vola, Alba

Il nuovo involucro attorno a un piccolo edificio esistente.
Le nuove superfici si disgregano e "volano" verso la pianura.

p. 167

Un progetto per la grande distribuzione

Il primo progetto per la nuova immagine di una grande azienda: Mercatò (Dimar), Fossano (Cuneo)

p. 168

Leggerezza, smaterializzazione e ritorno alla natura
Nuovo stabilimento Bertolotto Porte

p. 170

La nascita di Venere

p. 171

La nascita di Milo

pp. 172-173

Morbida scultura, contrasto tra apparenza e realtà
L'illusione dei sensi

Colpito dalla visione della statua di una kore di marmo del museo di Samos, ho pensato di creare una trasposizione, un gioco basato sulla contrapposizione della materia: freddo marmo e morbido poliuretano.
È sorprendente vedere come chi si siede si attenda una materia fredda e rigida e invece è accogliente e morbida.

Il marmo è una spalla... per portare il tempo (García Lorca)

p. 175

Le mostre e i musei (nonostante tutto)

p. 176

Immortalato il momento "storico" della firma dell'opera

p. 177

La costruzione della mostra "Pop Art Design"

p. 178

E questo è stato il risultato

p. 179

La mostra e il suo format in molti musei...

p. 181

Torino World Design Capital

Nel 2008 Torino è World Design Capital: tra gli eventi ho progettato con Luisa Bocchietto, presidente dell'ADI, anche una mostra al Filatoio di Caraglio: sarà l'embrione della mostra del Vitra Design Museum.

e tutti a chiedersi: Where is Caraglio?

p. 182

Metropolitan, New York

p. 183

Louvre, Parigi
"Le design des années Pop"

p. 184

Centre Pompidou, Parigi

p. 185

Castello di Rivoli
"The Rock Furniture"
Il design della Gufram negli anni del rock

p. 186

Galleria TOT, Padova

Una sera eravamo riuniti in studio e si discuteva della Bocca e del suo meraviglioso modo di essere "barocca".
Proposi immediatamente di utilizzare, per commentarla, i versi di Gian Battista Marino sulla poetica del '600.
L'idea piacque molto e sarebbe stata messa in atto.
La poetica dello Studio65 si arricchiva della parola "stupore".

p. 187

Triennale, Milan
Uomo, ambiente, colore

1972
La Triennale organizza una mostra intitolata "Uomo, ambiente, colore".
Avevamo partecipato, e non ci sembrava vero di essere circondati dalle superstars dell'architettura italiana, da Gae Aulenti ad Albini, a Sottsass, a Zanuso...

Il nostro spazio era dominato da una grande bocca che aveva "divorato" la città con i suoi simboli. All'area destinata all'esposizione si accedeva tramite lo scalone principale, sui cui gradini c'erano le immagini dei protagonisti in scala 1:1, che ti accompagnavano idealmente a visitare i loro pensieri.

p. 188

Fiera, Verona
Cantiere Italia

Nessuno riconoscerebbe in questa immagine il ragazzo vivace e ironico, intrattenitore di Rai Uno la domenica mattina nella trasmissione "Unomattina in famiglia".

p. 189

Palazzo Barolo, Torino
Il design nel quotidiano

p. 190

Palazzo della Ragione, Padova
"La grande svolta anni '60"

p. 191

Ex Ansaldo, Milano
Frammenti di storia

p. 192

Salone del Mobile 2002, Milano

La Poltrona Frau quell'anno aveva scelto tre designers che creassero tre diverse sedute per dimostrare la capacità della Frau di usare la pelle con progetti estremi, del tutto diversi dalla tradizionale produzione dell'azienda.

p. 193

GAM, Torino 2015

p. 194

Triennale 2016, Milano

p. 195

Papì, Fizzz e Déjeuner sur l'arbre da Eataly

Quando Oscar vide la Papì prima dell'inaugurazione della sede di Eataly Ostiense a Roma la volle immediatamente, perché esprimeva bene anche la sua stessa idea dell'Italia: creatività e immediatezza della trasmissione di un messaggio di contagiosa allegria.

pp. 196-197

Il premio Dedalo Minosse 2003 e 2006
premio che viene dato agli EROI delle committenze insieme ai loro architetti.

p. 198

Biennali di Architettura, Venezia

p. 200

A questa Biennale vengono presentati i due progetti di Arnaudo delle cantine a Barolo. Nel Padiglione Italia vengono scelti due soli progetti di cantine, quella di Arnaudo e quella di Arnaldo Pomodoro, come esempi di contaminazione tra arte e architettura su un tema che spesso viene svolto in modo assolutamente tradizionale.

p. 202

Il premio Rēgula, 100 Progetti
Roma 2018

p. 203

La Boîte de Nuit
Hyères, Villa Noailles 2017

p. 204

Compagnia di San Paolo
Dronero, Concorso "99 città" 2005

p. 205

Il Politecnico di Torino
In the great abandoned factory
Binario 18
Torino Mirafiori

p. 206

Lectio Magistralis

p. 207

"Night Fever. Designing Club Culture"
Vitra Design Museum, Basilea
ADAM Design Museum, Bruxelles
Centro Pecci, Prato
Victoria and Albert Museum, Dundee

p. 208

Espressioni d'arte di Torino a Martigny

p. 209

LUCE. Lampade 1968-1973: il nuovo design italiano

p. 210

Frammenti di emozioni

p. 211

Frammenti di grafica

p. 214

era l'esordio dello Slow Food

p. 228

"Quando qualcuno dice: questo lo so fare anch'io, vuole dire che lo sa rifare, altrimenti lo avrebbe già fatto prima."
Bruno Munari

p. 229

Ogni architettura possiede un proprio DNA, una propria ragione d'essere... sta a noi scoprirla. Se non esiste, è una copia, o una mediocre banalità.